LOVE
PEOPLE
USE
THINGS

LOVE
PEOPLE
USE
THINGS

Because the Opposite Never Works

THE MINIMALISTS

Joshua Fields Millburn &
Ryan Nicodemus

CELADON
BOOKS
———
NEW YORK

Day one or one day. You decide.

This book is a work of nonfiction. All people and entities herein are real, and all the events described actually happened, but sometimes the two authors had to make stuff up (specific dialogue, precise dates, the various colors of the sky). A few names and identifying details were changed to avoid pissing off some folks. And it's almost certain that the book's authors misremembered certain incidents, but they did the best they could to accurately represent them as they occurred.

Author contact info: The Minimalists, 7083 Hollywood Boulevard, Los Angeles, CA 90028
minimalists.com | info@themins.com | 1-937-202-4654

The Library of Congress Cataloging-in-Publication Data is available upon request.

ISBN 978-1-250-23651-7 (hardcover)
ISBN 978-1-250-23649-4 (ebook)

Our books may be purchased in bulk for promotional, educational, or business use. Please contact your local bookseller or the Macmillan Corporate and Premium Sales Department at 1-800-221-7945, extension 5442, or by email at MacmillanSpecialMarkets@macmillan.com.

First Edition: 2021

10 9 8 7 6 5 4 3 2 1

For Rebecca and Mariah

You must remember to love people and use things,
rather than to love things and use people.

—Archbishop Fulton J. Sheen, circa 1925

Wish you would learn to love people and use things
and not the other way around.

—Drake, 2013

CONTENTS

PREFACE

Pandemic Preparation

The streets are erumpent with uniformed men wielding titanic assault rifles. Through their megaphones, they command us to lock our doors and stay in our homes. Overhead, military helicopters blare "Stayin' Alive" by the Bee Gees from their intercoms, the soundtrack to our new dystopian future. *Bang! Bang!* Two gunshots in rapid succession. I jolt awake and find my wife in bed next to me and our daughter in her room, both asleep. Walk into the living room. Retract a window shade. Look out at my neighborhood. Los Angeles. Midnight. Empty boulevards. Light rain beneath arc lamps. No sign of martial law. Only a stalled pickup at the bottom of the hill. I let out a deep sigh. Just a nightmare—fortunately. But the world in which I awoke, the so-called real world, is markedly different from the one I'd experienced the first four decades of my life—not necessarily post-apocalyptic, but not normal, either.

Serpentine lines slithering through grocery-store checkout aisles. Boarded windows concealing hollowed-out Rodeo Drive storefronts. Devastating silence blanketing empty movie theaters galvanized by dust and darkness. Crowds, separated at six-foot intervals, being herded into bare-shelved food banks. Anxious families coping with being alone together while "sheltering in place." Hospitals splitting open with overworked nurses and doctors whose apoplectic expressions are hidden only by their own homemade face masks. As I finished writing the final chapter of this book in the spring of 2020, the COVID-19 pandemic was seizing the globe.

Our "new normal" feels grossly abnormal. With the twin terrors of financial and physical uncertainty, an undercurrent of angst continues to pulse through our days. But perhaps there's a way to find calm—and even to prosper—in the middle of the chaos.

I didn't know it at the onset of this project, but while quarantined in my home during the pandemic, I realized Ryan Nicodemus— the other half of The Minimalists—and I had spent the last two years writing not just a relationships book but, in many ways, a pandemic-preparation manual. If only we could have gotten this book into the hands of struggling people *before* the spread of the virus, we would have prevented a great deal of heartache, because intentional living is the best form of preparation. When you step back, it's easy to see that the so-called preppers—the embarrassment of hoarders we see on our TV screens—are the least prepared for a crisis. You can't trade canned corn and ammunition for the support and trust of a loving community. You can survive, however, if you need less—and you can thrive, even in a crisis, if your relationships are thriving.

THE ENEMY ISN'T ONLY CONSUMERISM NOW—IT'S DECADENCE AND DISTRACTION, BOTH MATERIAL AND NOT.

A pandemic has a sneaky way of putting things in perspective. It took a catastrophe for many people to understand that an economy predicated on exponential growth isn't a healthy economy—

it's a vulnerable one. If an economy collapses when people buy only their essentials, then it was never as muscular as we pretended.

The minimalist movement described in this book first gained popularity online in the aftermath of the 2008 crash. People were yearning for a solution to their newly discovered problem of debt and overconsumption. Alas, over the past dozen years, we've once again grown too comfortable. But the enemy isn't only consumerism now—it's decadence and distraction, both material and not.

Amid the panic of the pandemic, I noticed many folks grappling with the question Ryan and I have been attempting to answer for more than a decade: *What is essential?* Of course, the answer is highly individual. Too often, we conflate essential items with both nonessential items and junk.*

In an emergency, not only must we jettison the junk, but many of us are forced to temporarily deprive ourselves of nonessentials—those things that add value to our lives during regular times but aren't necessary during an emergency. If we can do this, we can discover what is truly essential, and then we can eventually reintroduce the nonessentials slowly, in a way that enhances and augments our lives but doesn't clutter them with junk.

To complicate matters, "essential" changes as we change. What was essential five years ago—or even five days ago—may not be essential now, and so we must continually question, adjust, let go. This is especially true during a crisis—where a week feels like a month; a month, a lifetime.

Stuck in their homes, people wrestled with the fact that their material possessions matter less than they originally thought. The truth was all around them. All the things collecting dust—their

---

* We delineate these three categories—essential, nonessential, and junk—with our No Junk Rule in the "Relationship with Stuff" chapter.

high-school baseball trophies, dusty college textbooks, and broken food processors—were never as important as people. The pandemic magnified this reality and demonstrated a crucial lesson: our things tend to get in the way of what's truly essential—our relationships. Human connection is missing from our lives, and it can't be purchased—it can only be cultivated. To do so, we must simplify, which starts with the stuff and then extends to every aspect of our lives. This book was written to help regular people like you and me deal with the external clutter before looking inward and addressing the mental, emotional, psychological, spiritual, financial, creative, technological, and relational clutter that weighs us down and disrupts our connection with others.

If you have followed The Minimalists for any time at all, you will recognize bits and pieces of our story in the "Introduction to Living with Less" chapter—death, divorce, a "Packing Party." But these elements aren't only for new readers. In this book we take a deeper dive into the the struggles, insecurities, substance abuse, addiction, infidelity, zealotry, heartache, and pain that were the catalysts for lasting change in our lives. Then, once those details are on the table, we explore new territory as we navigate the seven essential relationships that make us who we are.

THE BEST TIME TO SIMPLIFY WAS A DECADE AGO; THE SECOND-BEST TIME IS NOW.

This isn't a book written for a pandemic—it's a guidebook for everyday life. The pandemic has simply heightened our everyday problems and rendered them even more urgent. With the most recent financial downturn and a renewed search for meaning, our society will be coping with some critical realities in the not too distant future. Many new norms have been established; others will continue to form as we move forward. Some of us will attempt to cling to the past—to "return to normal"—but that's like struggling to hold a block of ice in our hands: once it melts, it's gone. I've been asked, "When is this going to turn around?" But "turning around" presupposes that we should return to the past, to a "normal" that wasn't working for most people—at least not in any meaningful way. While I don't know what the future holds, I know we can emerge from this uncertainty with a *new* normal, one that is predicated on intentionality and community, rather than "consumer confidence."

To get there, we must simplify again.
We must clear the clutter to find the path forward.
We must find a deeper understanding beyond the horizon.

In the thick of the coronavirus crisis, I had a conversation with one of my personal mentors, a businessman named Karl Weidner, who showed me the characters for the Chinese word for "crisis," *weiji*, which signify "danger" (*wei*) and "opportunity" (*ji*), respectively. While there are arguments among linguists as to whether the character for *ji* actually means "opportunity," the analogy is still apt: a crisis exists at the intersection of danger and opportunity.

In time, there will undoubtedly be more crises. Even now, as I write this, a heightened sense of danger lingers in the atmosphere. But opportunity is also in the air. Surrounded by danger, we have a chance to, as my friend Joshua Becker says, "use these days to reevaluate everything."

Maybe this was our wake-up call. Let us not waste this opportunity to reevaluate everything, to let go, to start anew. The best time to simplify was a decade ago; the second-best time is now.

—*Joshua Fields Millburn*

AN INTRODUCTION
TO LIVING WITH LESS

Our material possessions are a physical manifestation of our internal lives. Take a look around: angst, distress, restlessness—all visible right there in our homes. The average American household contains more than 300,000 items. With all that stuff you'd think we'd be beside ourselves with joy. Yet study after study shows the opposite: we're anxious, overwhelmed, and miserable. Unhappier than ever, we pacify ourselves with even more accumulation, ignoring the real cost of our consumption.

The price tag dangling from each new widget tells only a fraction of the story. The true cost of a thing extends well beyond its price. There's the cost of: Storing the thing. Maintaining the thing. Cleaning the thing. Watering the thing. Charging the thing. Accessorizing the thing. Refueling the thing. Changing the oil in the thing. Replacing the batteries in the thing. Fixing the thing. Repainting the thing. Taking care of the thing. Protecting the thing. And, of course, when it's all said and done, replacing the thing. (Not to mention the emotional and psychological costs of our things, which are even more difficult to quantify.) When you add it all up, the actual cost of owning a thing is immeasurable. So we better choose carefully what things we bring into our lives, because we can't afford every *thing*.

Seriously, we can't afford it—literally and figuratively. But instead of delaying gratification and temporarily going without, we go into debt. The average American carries approximately three credit cards in their wallet. One in ten of us has more than ten active credit cards. And the average credit-card debt is more than $16,000.

MINIMALISM IS THE THING THAT GETS US PAST THE THINGS SO WE CAN MAKE ROOM FOR LIFE'S IMPORTANT THINGS— WHICH AREN'T THINGS AT ALL.

It gets worse. Even before the pandemic of 2020, more than 80 percent of us were in debt, with the total consumer debt in the United States greater than $14 trillion. Now, there are at least a few plausible, albeit regrettable, explanations: We spend more on shoes, jewelry, and watches than on higher education. Our ever-expanding homes, which have more than doubled in size over the last fifty years, contain more televisions than people. Every American, on average, throws away eighty-one pounds of clothing each year, even though 95 percent of it could be reused or recycled. And our communities are peppered with more shopping malls than high schools.

Speaking of high schools, did you know that 93 percent of teens rank shopping as their favorite pastime? Is *shopping* a pastime? It seems so, since we spend $1.2 trillion every year on nonessential goods. Just to be clear, that means we spend over a trillion dollars a year on things we don't need.

Do you know how long it takes to spend a *trillion* dollars? If you went out and spent one dollar every single second—one dollar, two dollars, three dollars—it would take you more than 95,000 years to spend a trillion dollars. In fact, if you spent a million dollars *every single day* since the birth of the Buddha, you still wouldn't have spent a trillion dollars by now.

With all this spending, is it any surprise that roughly half the households in the United States don't save any money at all? As it happens, over 50 percent of us don't have enough money on hand to cover even a month of lost income; 62 percent of us don't have $1,000 in savings; and nearly half of us couldn't scrape together $400 during an emergency. This isn't merely an income problem—it's a spending problem that affects low-income folks as well as six-figure earners: nearly 25 percent of households earning between $100,000 and $150,000 a year say they'd have a difficult time coming up with an extra $2,000 within a month. All this debt is especially frightening because 60 percent of households will experience a "financial shock" event within the next twelve months. This was all true even before the economic downturn of 2020; that crisis simply illuminated how thinly stretched we are.

And yet we keep on spending, consuming, growing. The size of the average new home is rapidly approaching 3,000 square feet. Yet with all that extra space, we still have more than 52,000 storage facilities across the country—that's more than four times the number of Starbucks!

Even with our bigger houses and our storage units teeming with stuff, we still don't have enough room to park our cars in our garages, because those garages are brimming with stuff, too: Unused sporting goods. Exercise equipment. Camping gear. Magazines. DVDs. Compact discs. Old clothes and electronics and furniture. Boxes and bins stretched from floor to ceiling, stuffed with discarded things.

And don't forget about the kids' toys. Despite making up just over 3 percent of the world's population of children, American kids consume 40 percent of the world's toys. Did you know the average child owns more than 200 toys, but plays with only 12 of those toys each day? And yet a recent study has shown what parents already know: children who have too many toys are more easily distracted and don't enjoy quality playtime.

As adults, we have our own toys that distract us, don't we? Unquestionably. If the entire world consumed like Americans, we would need nearly five Earths to sustain our unchecked consumption. The popular maxim "the things we own end up owning us" seems truer now than ever.

But it doesn't have to be this way.

Existential Clutter

There are many things that once brought joy to our lives but no longer serve a purpose in today's world: rotary phones, floppy disks, disposable cameras, cassette tapes, fax machines, LaserDisc players, pagers, PalmPilots, Chia Pets, the Furby. Most of us cling to our artifacts well into their obsolescence, often out of a pious sense of nostalgia. The hallmarks of the past have a strange way of leaving claw marks on the present.

So we hold a death grip on our VHS collections, our unused flip phones, our oversized Bugle Boy jeans—not repairing or recycling these items, but storing them with the rest of our untouched hoard. As our collections grow, our basements, closets, and attics become purgatories of stuff—overflowing with unemployed miscellanea.

So many of our things have fallen into disuse, and maybe this lack of use is the final sign that we need to let go. You see, as our needs, desires, and technologies change, so does the world around us. The objects that add value to our lives today may not add value tomorrow, which means we must be willing to let go of everything, even the tools that serve a purpose today. Because if we let go, we can find temporary new homes for our neglected belongings and allow them to serve a purpose in someone else's life instead of collecting dust in our homegrown mausoleums.

On a long enough timeline, everything becomes obsolete. A hundred years from now the world will be filled with new humans, and they will have long abandoned their USB cables, iPhones, and flat-screen televisions, letting go of the past to make room for the future. This means we must be careful with the new material possessions we bring into our lives today. And we must be equally careful when those things become obsolete, because a willingness to let go is one of life's most mature virtues.

Let's explore how we got here—and how we can let go.

Excessful

How might your life be better with less? The simple life starts with this question. Unfortunately, it took me, Joshua Fields Millburn, thirty years to ask this question.

I was born in Dayton, Ohio, the birthplace of aviation, funk music, and hundred-spoke gold rims. More recently, you may have seen the news that Dayton is the overdose capital of America. It's strange in retrospect, but I didn't realize we were poor when I was growing up. Poverty was sort of like oxygen: It was all around me, but I couldn't see it. It was just—there.

In 1981, when I entered the world at Wright-Patterson Air Force Base, my father, a tall, burly forty-two-year-old man with silver hair and a baby face, was a doctor in the Air Force. My mother, a secretary at the time, was seven years his junior, a petite blond woman with a smoker's rasp, born at the tail end of the Silent Generation, a few months before Nagasaki and Hiroshima.

Given that snapshot, it appeared as though I'd have an idyllic, well-off, midwestern childhood, right? This was the early eighties, and Dayton was still at the tail end of its heyday—before the industrial Midwest became the so-called rust belt, before white flight crippled the city, before Montgomery County's opioid epidemic metastasized to both sides of the Great Miami River. Back then, people called Dayton "Little Detroit," and they meant it as a compliment. Manufacturing was booming, most families had what they needed, and the lion's share of people found meaning in their daily lives.

But shortly after I was born, my father got sick, and everything started to unravel. Dad had serious mental-health issues—schizophrenia and bipolar disorder—which were amplified by excessive drinking. Before I could even walk, my father started to have elaborate conversations—and even full-on relationships—with people who didn't exist in the real world. As his mind spiraled, he grew violent and unpredictable. My very first memory is

of my father extinguishing a cigarette on my mother's bare chest in our home in Dayton's Oregon District. I was three years old.

Mom and I left a year after the abuse started; she began drinking around the same time. We moved twenty miles south to a suburb of Dayton, which sounds nice, doesn't it? The suburbs. But it was the opposite of ideal. We rented a $200-a-month duplex that was literally falling apart. (Today, that same house is boarded up, ready to be torn down.) Stray cats and dogs, liquor stores and churches, drugs and alcohol and homes in disrepair—it wasn't a violent or dangerous neighborhood; it was just poor.

As things deteriorated further, Mom's drinking got worse. For much of my childhood, I thought money came in two colors: green and white. Mom sometimes sold our white bills—I didn't know at the time they were food stamps—for fifty cents on the dollar because she could purchase alcohol with only the green bills. She earned minimum wage whenever she was able to hold a full-time job, but she wasn't able to keep a job for any significant stretch of time; when she drank, she went on benders in which she stayed in our humid one-bedroom apartment for days at a time, not eating, just drinking heavily and chain-smoking on our stained taupe couch. Our home always smelled faintly of urine and empty beer cans and stale cigarette smoke—I can still smell it now.

Cockroaches scattered every time I turned on the kitchen light. They appeared to come from the next-door neighbor's apartment. The neighbor was a kind and lonely man, a World War II veteran in his seventies who seemed to own three or four apartments' worth of stuff and who didn't mind the bugs, maybe because he had seen far worse, or maybe because they kept him company. "Love thy neighbor" was the Matthew 22:39 scripture Mom muttered whenever she killed a roach with her slipper. Although when she drank, it often morphed into "Screw thy neighbor." Throughout most of my childhood, I thought they were two different biblical passages, a sort of Old Testament versus New Testament contradiction.

Mom was a devout Catholic. In fact, she had been a nun in her twenties, before decamping for a life as a stewardess, and then as a secretary, and then, eventually, as a mother in her late thirties. She prayed daily, several times a day, her rosary beads dangling, praying until her right thumb and nicotine-stained forefinger formed calluses, rotating through her string of beads, mouthing the same old Our Fathers and Hail Marys and AA's Serenity Prayer, asking God to please take this from her, to please cure her of her disease, her DIS-EASE, please God please. But prayer after prayer, Serenity was a no-show.

I'd have to remove my shoes to count how many times our electricity got shut off, which happened far more frequently at our apartment than our neighbor's. But it was no problem—we'd just run an extension cord from next door to keep the TV glowing. When the lights went out in winter, and it was too cold to stay home, Mom and I had special "sleepovers" at various men's houses. At home, Mom slept the afternoons away while I played with G.I. Joes. I recall carefully placing each figure back into its plastic bin in an organized and methodical way whenever I was done, controlling the only thing I could control in my disorderly world. I'd separate the good guys into one bin and the bad guys into another bin and their weapons into a third bin. And every so often a few of the men would switch sides from bad to good.

Grocery bags would materialize at our doorstep next to the gap where the three missing wooden planks used to be on our decaying front porch. Mom told me that she had prayed to Saint Anthony and that he had found us food. There were extended periods of time when we subsisted on Saint Anthony's peanut butter and Wonder bread and packaged sugary foods like Pop-Tarts and Fruit Roll-Ups. I fell off that same rotting porch when I was seven. A wood plank gave way under the weight of my pudgy preadolescent body, launching me face-first toward the sidewalk four feet below. There was blood and crying and a strange kind of dual panic: panic about the blood that was flowing from my chin, and panic about Mom, who remained immobile

OUR MEMORIES ARE NOT IN OUR THINGS; OUR MEMORIES ARE INSIDE US.

on the couch when I ran inside the house screaming, arms flailing, unsure of what to do. The lonely walk to the emergency room was just over two miles. You can still see the scars from that fall today.

My first-grade teacher referred to me on more than one occasion as a "latchkey kid." But I didn't know what that meant at the time. Most days after school I'd walk home and open the door and find Mom passed out on the couch, a cigarette still burning in the ashtray, an inch and a half of undisturbed ash burnt down to the filter. It's as if she'd misunderstood the term "stay-at-home mom."

Don't get me wrong. My mother was a kind woman—a sincere woman with a tender heart. She cared about people; she loved me immensely. And I loved her. I still do. I miss her more than anything, so much so that she regularly appears in my dreams. She wasn't a bad person; she had simply lost a sense of meaning in her life, and that loss birthed an unquenchable discontent.

Naturally, as a child, I thought our lack of happiness was caused by a lack of money. If only I could make money—a lot of money—then I'd be happy. I wouldn't end up like Mom. I could own all the stuff that would bring everlasting joy to my life. So, when I turned eighteen, I skipped college, opting instead for an entry-level corporate job, and then I spent the next decade climbing the corporate ladder. Early-morning meetings and late-night sales calls and eighty-hour workweeks, whatever it took to "succeed."

OUR MATERIAL POSSESSIONS ARE A PHYSICAL MANIFESTATION OF OUR INTERNAL LIVES.

By the time I was twenty-eight, I had achieved everything my childhood self had ever dreamed of: a six-figure salary, luxury cars, closets full of designer clothes, a big suburban house with more toilets than people. I was the youngest director in my company's 140-year history, responsible for 150 retail stores across Ohio, Kentucky, and Indiana. And I had all the stuff to fill every corner of my consumer-driven life. From a distance, you would think I was living the American Dream.

But then, out of nowhere, two events forced me to question what had become my life's focus: in the fall of 2009, my mother died and my marriage ended—both in the same month.

As I questioned everything, I realized I was too focused on

so-called success and achievement and especially on the accumulation of stuff. I might have been living the American Dream, but it wasn't my dream. It wasn't a nightmare, either. It was merely unremarkable. In a strange way, it took getting everything I thought I wanted to realize that maybe everything I ever wanted wasn't actually what I wanted at all.

Stuffocated

When I was twenty-seven, Mom moved from Ohio to Florida to finally retire on Social Security. Within a few months, she discovered she had stage 4 lung cancer. I spent a considerable amount of time with her in Florida that year as she struggled through chemotherapy and radiation treatments, watching her grow thinner as the cancer spread and her memory faded until, later that year, she was gone.

When she passed, I needed to make one last visit—this time to deal with her stuff. So I flew from Dayton to St. Petersburg, and when I arrived, I was confronted with three houses' worth of possessions crammed into Mom's tiny one-bedroom apartment.

It's not like Mom was a hoarder. If anything, with her keen eye for aesthetics, she could have been a maximalist interior designer. But she owned an abundance of stuff—sixty-five years' worth of accumulations. Less than 5 percent of Americans are diagnosed compulsive hoarders, but that doesn't mean the other 95 percent don't consume a lot of stuff. We do. And we cling to a lifetime of collected memories. I know my mom certainly did, and I had no idea what to do with any of it.

So I did what any good son would do: I called U-Haul.

Over the phone, I asked for the largest truck they had. I needed one so large I had to wait an extra day until the twenty-six-foot truck was available. As I waited for the U-Haul to arrive, I invited a handful of Mom's friends over to help me sort through her stuff. There was just too much to go at it alone.

Mom's living room was *stuffed* with big antique furniture and old paintings and more doilies than I could count. Her kitchen was *stuffed* with hundreds of plates and cups and bowls and ill-assorted utensils. Her bathroom was *stuffed* with enough hygiene products to start a small beauty-supply business. And it looked like somebody was running a hotel out of her linen closet, which was *stuffed* with stacks of mismatched bath towels and dish towels and beach towels, bed sheets and blankets and quilts. Oh, and don't even get me started on her bedroom. Why did Mom have fourteen winter coats *stuffed* into her bedroom closet? Fourteen! She lived half a mile from the beach! Suffice it to say, Mom owned a lot of stuff. And I still had no idea what to do with any of it.

So I did what any good son would do: I rented a storage locker.

I didn't want to commingle Mom's stuff with my stuff. I already had a big house and a large basement full of stuff. But a storage locker could help me hold on to everything just in case I needed it someday in some nonexistent, hypothetical future.

So there I was, packing what felt like every item Mom had ever owned. When I pulled back the bed skirt and looked under her Queen Anne bed, I found four printer-paper boxes, kind of heavy, decades old, sealed with excessive amounts of packing tape. Pulling them out one by one, I noticed each box was labeled with a number written on the side in thick black marker: 1, 2, 3, 4. I stood there, looking down, wondering what could possibly be inside those boxes. I bent down, closed my eyes, and took a deep breath. Reopened my eyes. Exhaled.

As I opened the boxes, my curiosity ran wild as I uncovered artwork, homework, and report cards from my elementary-school days—grades one through four. At first, I thought to myself, "Why was Mom holding on to all this stupid paperwork?" But then all the memories came rushing back, and it was obvious: Mom had been holding on to a piece of *me*. She had been holding on to all the memories inside those boxes.

"But wait a minute!" I said aloud in that empty bedroom as I became conscious of the fact that Mom hadn't opened those boxes in over two decades. It was clear she hadn't been accessing any of those "memories," which helped me understand something important for the first time: our memories are not in our things; our memories are inside us.

Perhaps this is what the eighteenth-century Scottish philosopher David Hume meant when he wrote, "The mind has a great propensity to spread itself on external objects, and to conjoin with them any internal impressions." Mom didn't need to hold on to those boxes to hold on to a piece of me—I was never inside those boxes. But then I looked around her apartment—looked around at all her stuff—and realized I was getting ready to do the same thing. Except instead of keeping Mom's memories in a box under my bed, I was going to cram it all into a big box with a padlock on it. Just in case.

So I did what any good son would do: I called U-Haul and canceled the truck. Then I canceled the storage locker and spent the next twelve days selling or donating almost everything. It would be an understatement to say I learned some important lessons along the way.

Not only did I learn that our memories aren't in our things, but I learned about value. Real value. If I'm honest with myself, I wanted to selfishly cling to most of Mom's stuff. But I wasn't going to get any real value from those things as they sat locked away in perpetuity. By letting go, however, I could add value to other people's lives. So

I donated most of Mom's things to her friends and local charities, finding the stuff a new home, because one person's junk may be exactly what another person desperately needs. I donated the money from the few items I sold to the two charities that helped Mom through her chemo and radiation. In the fullness of time, I figured out I could contribute beyond myself if I was willing to let go.

When I finally went back to Ohio, I returned with a handful of sentimental items: an old painting, a few photographs, maybe even a doily or two. Which helped me understand that by owning fewer sentimental items, we are actually able to enjoy them. I get far more value from the few items I kept than if I were to water them down with dozens, or even hundreds, of trinkets.

The final lesson I learned was a practical one. While it's true that our memories are not in our things, it is also true that sometimes our things can trigger memories inside us. So before I left Florida, I took photos of many of Mom's possessions, and I returned to Ohio with just a few boxes of her photographs, which I scanned and stored digitally.

Those photographs made it easier for me to let go because I knew I wasn't letting go of any of my memories.

Ultimately, I had to let go of what was weighing me down before I could move on.

A Well-Organized Hoarder

Back at home, it was time to take an inventory of my own life. Turns out, I had an "organized" life. But really I was just a well-organized hoarder. Hoarding, in the clinical sense, resides on the far end of the obsessive-compulsive spectrum. And as a person diagnosed with OCD, I hoarded. But unlike the people we see on television with their superabundance strewn across their floors and counters and every other flat surface, I hid my junk in an ordinal way.

My basement was an advertisement for the Container Store: rows of opaque plastic bins, stacked and labeled, packed with back issues of *GQ* and *Esquire*, pleated khakis and polo shirts, tennis rackets and baseball gloves, never-used tents and various "camping essentials," and who knows what else. My entertainment room was a small-scale Circuit City: alphabetized movies and albums professionally wall-mounted beside an oversized projection TV and a surround-sound stereo system that would violate the city's noise ordinance if turned up halfway. My home office required the Dewey decimal system: floor-to-ceiling shelves lined with nearly 2,000 books, most of which I hadn't read. And my walk-in closets were a scene from *American Psycho*: seventy Brooks Brothers dress shirts, a dozen tailored suits, at least fifty designer neckties, ten pairs of leather-bottomed dress shoes, a hundred different T-shirts, twenty pairs of the same blue jeans, and more socks and underwear and accessories than I could wear in a month—all neatly folded in drawers or displayed on wooden hangers separated at precise intervals. I kept adding to my hoard, but it never felt like enough. And no matter how much I arranged and straightened and cleaned, chaos was always leaking through the surface.

Sure, everything *looked* great, but it was a facade. My life was an organized mess. Smothered by the weight of my accumulations, I knew I needed to make some changes. I wanted to simplify. And that's where this thing called *minimalism* entered the picture.

For me, simplifying started with that one question: *How might your life be better with less?*

I asked this question because I needed to identify the purpose of simplifying. Not just the *how-to*, but the more important *why-to*.

If I simplified my life, I'd have more time for my health, my relationships, my finances, my creativity, and I could contribute beyond myself in a meaningful way. You see, I was able to understand the benefits of simplifying well before I cleaned out my closets.

So when it came time for me to actually declutter, I started small. I asked myself another question: *What if you removed one material possession from your life each day for a month—just one—what would happen?*

Well, let me tell you: I unloaded way more than thirty items in the first thirty days. Like way, way more. Discovering what I could get rid of became a personal challenge. So I searched my rooms and closets, cabinets and hallways, car and office, rummaging for items to part with, retaining only the things that added value to my life. Pondering each artifact in my home—a baseball bat from my childhood, old puzzles with missing pieces, a wedding-gift waffle maker—I'd ask, "Does this thing add value to my life?" The more I asked this question, the more I gained momentum, and simplifying got easier by the day. The more I did it, the freer and happier and lighter I felt—and the more I wanted to throw overboard. A few shirts led to half a closet. A few DVDs led to deep-sixing an entire library of discs. A few decorative items led to junk drawers that shed their adjective. It was a beautiful cycle. The more action I took, the more I wanted to take action.

EVERY POSSESSION I, AS A MINIMALIST, OWN SERVES A PURPOSE OR BRINGS ME JOY. EVERYTHING ELSE IS OUT OF THE WAY.

During the eight months following my mother's death, and through countless trips to the local donation center, I had deliberately jettisoned more than 90 percent of my possessions. The chaos had transmogrified into calm. It was comparatively sparse, but if you visited my home today, more than a decade after minimizing, you wouldn't leap up and proclaim, "This guy's a minimalist!" No, you'd probably say, "He's tidy!" and you'd ask how my family and I keep things so organized. Well, my wife, daughter, and I don't own much these days, but everything we do own adds real value to our lives. Each of our belongings—our kitchenware, our clothes, our car, our furniture—has a function. Every possession I, as a minimalist, own serves a purpose or brings me joy. Everything else is out of the way.

With the clutter cleared, I finally felt compelled to ask deeper questions: *When did I give so much meaning to my material possessions? What is truly essential in my life? Why have I been so discontented? Who is the person I want to become? How will I define my own success?*

These are tough questions with difficult answers, but they've proven to be much more beneficial than simply trashing my excess stuff. If we don't answer these questions carefully, rigorously, then the closets we declutter will be brimming with new purchases in the not-to-distant future.

As I let go, and as I started facing life's tougher questions, my life became simpler. Soon my coworkers noticed something was different, too.

"You seem less stressed."

"You seem so much calmer."

"What's going on with you? You seem so much nicer!"

Then my best friend, a guy named Ryan Nicodemus, whom I've known since we were fat little fifth graders, approached me with a question: "Why the hell are you so happy?"

I laughed and then told him about this thing called minimalism.

"What the hell is minimalism?" he asked.

"Minimalism is the thing that gets us past the things," I said.

"And you know what, Ryan, I think this minimalism thing might work for you, too, because, well . . . because you have a lot of crap."

The Birthplace of a Dream

Ryan Nicodemus was born into a dysfunctional home (before the term "dysfunctional" was in vogue). His story began the way all too many stories begin—with an unpleasant childhood. When he was seven, his parents' marriage ended bitterly. After the split, Ryan lived with his mother, and eventually his stepfather, in a double-wide trailer, and he witnessed a considerable amount of drug and alcohol and physical abuse. And, of course, money problems.

Even though Ryan's mother was living on the dole, her financial woes seemed to be her largest source of discontent. Money was also an issue for Ryan's father, a zealous Jehovah's Witness who owned a small painting business. Despite being a business owner, he struggled to make ends meet, living week to week with no savings and no plan for the future.

As Ryan grew into his teenage years, he spent most of his summers working for his father, painting and hanging wallpaper in comically lavish homes: 10,000-square-foot garages, indoor swimming pools, private bowling alleys. These stately residences weren't anything Ryan aspired to own himself, but they made a lasting impression.

On one sweltering summer day, Ryan and his father began a wallpaper contract at a nice suburban house outside of Cincinnati. It wasn't a multi-million-dollar home, but it was nicer than anything his parents had ever owned. When Ryan met the homeowners, he noticed how happy the couple seemed. The walls in their home were decorated with the smiling faces of family and friends that seemed to affirm the happiness in their lives. The

things in their home—the TVs, the fireplace, the furniture, the accoutrements—filled every nook and cranny. As he worked on the home, Ryan pictured himself living there; he imagined how happy he would be if he owned that house filled with all that stuff. Before the job was finished, he asked his dad, "How much money do I need to earn to live in a house like this?"

"Son," he replied, "if you could make fifty thousand dollars a year, you could probably afford a place like this." (Keep in mind, this was the 1990s. Still, at that time, fifty grand was more money than Ryan's parents had ever earned in a year.) So that became Ryan's benchmark: $50,000.

An Ever-Changing Goalpost

One day, during our senior year of high school, Ryan and I were seated at the lonely lunch table, alone together, discussing our post-graduation plans.

"I don't know what I'm going to do, Millie," Ryan said, using my nickname. "But if I can find a way to make fifty thousand dollars a year, I know I'll be happy."

I didn't have a sound reason to disagree, so that's what we both pursued. A month after we graduated, in 1999, I found myself working as a sales rep for a local telecommunications company. A few years later, after my first promotion to store manager, I asked Ryan, who had been working for his father's business and a local daycare center, to join my team. All I had to do was flash a few commission checks in his face and he was immediately on board.

Within a few months, Ryan became the top salesperson on my team, and he quickly began earning his magical $50,000. But something was wrong—he didn't feel happy. He went back to the drawing board and quickly located the problem: he had forgotten to adjust for inflation. Maybe $65,000 a year was happiness. Maybe $90,000. Maybe six figures. Or maybe owning a bunch of stuff—maybe that was happiness. Whatever happiness was, Ryan knew that once he got there, he'd finally feel free. So as he earned more money, he spent more money—all in the pursuit of happiness. But as each new purchase brought him closer to the American Dream, he moved further away from freedom.

By 2008, less than a decade after high school, Ryan had everything he was "supposed" to have. He held an impressive job title at a respectable corporation, a successful six-figure career managing hundreds of employees. He bought a shiny new car every couple years. He owned a three-bedroom, three-bathroom home with two living rooms (one for him and one for his cat). Everyone said Ryan Nicodemus was successful.

True, he owned the trinkets of success, but he also possessed an assortment of things that were hard to see from the outside. Even though he earned a lot of money, he had heaps of debt. But chasing happiness cost Ryan much more than money. His life was filled with stress and dread and discontent. Sure, he may have looked successful, but he felt miserable, and he didn't know what was important anymore.

But one thing was clear: there was a gaping void in his life. So he attempted to fill that void the same way many people do—with stuff. Lots of stuff. He bought new cars and electronics and clothes and furniture and home decorations. And when he didn't have enough cash in the bank, he paid for high-priced meals and rounds of drinks and vacations with credit cards, financing a lifestyle he couldn't afford, using money he didn't have to buy things he didn't need.

He thought he'd find happiness eventually. It had to be somewhere just around the corner, right? But the stuff didn't fill the void—it widened it. And because Ryan didn't know what was important, he continued to fill the void with stuff, going further into debt, working hard to buy things that weren't increasing his happiness or joy or freedom. This went on for years, a vicious cycle. Lather, rinse, repeat.

The Downward Spiral

As the sun was setting on Ryan's twenties, his life was perfect on the outside. But inside, after constructing an existence he was anything but proud of, he was a mess. In time, alcohol began to play a major role in his life. Before the end of each workday, he was thinking about who he was going to meet for happy hour. Soon, he was drinking every night—half a case of beer, half a dozen shots. Sometimes more.

Ryan would often drive home from bars and corporate events fully intoxicated. (It was a good night if he could find his wallet and phone the next morning.) He did this so often, in fact, that he crashed his new truck at least three times on his drunken drives home. There may have even been a fourth time, but it's all a blur. In truth, every new car he owned was wrecked within the first few months of buying it. Somehow, though, he never got a DUI, and thankfully he didn't hurt anyone except himself.

On one of his lowest nights, he recalls vomiting everywhere, more than once, ruining a coworker's living room rug, a friend's birthday cake, his $1,000 suede jacket, and his reputation. All in one night. It was like a scene from a bad sitcom. Except this was real life, *his* life, spiraling out of control one drink at a time.

But it wasn't just the drinking. The decline was accelerated by drugs. After another drunken night, a few weeks after crashing his car again, Ryan woke with a broken thumb. No problem, he thought; it could have been worse. The urgent-care doctor prescribed Percocet to help with the pain. Within a couple months, Ryan was hooked. When he couldn't get another refill from a doctor, he bought pills illegally. Percocet, Vicodin, OxyContin—whatever opioids he could get his hands on. A broken thumb, combined with an intense feeling of despair, quickly turned into a habit of twenty—sometimes as many as forty—pain pills a day. With all the booze and drugs, he was spending upwards of $5,000 a month to numb the pain—just to tolerate the life he had created.

Then came the overdose. Overwhelmed with hopelessness—*my relationships suck, my job sucks, my house sucks, my car sucks, my debt sucks, my stuff sucks, my entire life sucks*—Ryan downed an entire bottle of pills. He didn't want to kill himself; he just wanted it to stop. Although he survived the incident, he wound up in a mental institution for a week, sobering up under the oppressive glow of the hospital's fluorescent lights. His stay led to a new clump of medical debt he couldn't afford, so he soon turned back to alcohol and pills, trying to hide from life itself.

HOW MIGHT YOUR LIFE BE BETTER WITH LESS?

And of course his relationships suffered because of his behavior. He didn't realize it at the time, but he was a classic victimizer. After his divorce, he cheated on almost every girlfriend. He lied habitually—to everyone, about everything. Wanting to hide his secrets, he withdrew from his closest relationships because he was ashamed of the person he'd become. Instead of spending time with family and friends, he hung out with people just because they enjoyed the same drugs.

His mother lived nearby, but he hardly saw her, claiming he was busy with work, which was partially true, so she seemed to understand, but really he was busier with the drugs and alcohol and the life of lies he'd created.

The facade was nice, but the structure behind it was crumbling. Even with the oversized home, the new cars, and the "right" material things, Ryan couldn't find meaning in any of it; his life lacked purpose and passion, values and direction, contentment and love. Falling apart—slowly at first, and then rapidly—he didn't recognize himself anymore. The teenager who had once imagined a $50,000 happy life was not the man staring back at him in the bathroom mirror each morning.

Ryan continued to work sixty or seventy—sometimes eighty— hours a week, forsaking the foremost aspects of life. He barely considered his health, relationships, or creativity. Worst of all, he felt stagnant: he wasn't growing, and he wasn't contributing beyond himself.

On yet another Monday at the office, Ryan and I stood in a windowless hallway after yet another vapid marketing meeting, and I asked him what he was passionate about. Hungover from the night before, he looked at me like a deer in headlights. "I have no idea." He wasn't just living paycheck to paycheck, he was living *for* a paycheck. Living for stuff. Living for a career he didn't enjoy. Living for drugs and alcohol and harmful habits. But he wasn't really *living* at all. He didn't know it then, but he was depressed. He was a shell of his potential self.

A Different Kind of Party

In many ways, Ryan's life was not unlike that of an abandoned shopping mall. Years of overindulgent consumption, years of chasing ephemeral pleasures and putting people on the back burner, years of grasping for more, more, more left him feeling hollow inside. Everyone gone. Everything meaningful removed. An empty carapace.

Then, as he approached age thirty, he noticed something different about the man who had been his best friend for twenty years: me. He told me that I seemed happy for the first time in years. But he didn't understand why. We had worked side by side at the same corporation throughout our twenties, both climbing the ranks, and I *had* been just as miserable as him. To boot, I had gone through two of the most difficult events of my life—my mother died and my marriage ended—so I wasn't supposed to be happy. And, come to think of it, I definitely wasn't supposed to be happier than *him*!

So, Ryan bought me lunch at a fine-dining establishment (Subway), and as we ate our sandwiches, he asked me that question: "Why the hell are you so happy?"

I spent the next twenty minutes talking about my minimalist voyage. I explained how I'd spent the last few months simplifying my life, getting rid of the clutter so I could make room for what was truly important.

Being the overcompensating problem solver that he is, Ryan decided to become a minimalist right there on the spot. He looked up at me over our half-eaten meals and excitedly announced, "Okay, I'm in!" He paused for a moment when he saw a confused grimace on my face, a look that said "Huh?"

"I'm going to be a minimalist!" he exclaimed.

"Umm. Okay," I said.

"Now what?" he asked.

I didn't know. I wasn't trying to convert him—or anyone—to minimalism, so I didn't know what to do. I told him about my eight months of paring down, but that was too slow for Ryan. He wanted faster results.

A moment later, I had a wild idea: "When is the one time you're forced to confront all of your stuff?"

"When?" he asked.

"When you move," I said, having moved less than a year earlier myself. "So, what if we *pretend* you're moving?"

And that's what we did. Right there at Subway, we decided to pack all of Ryan's belongings as if he were moving, and then he would unpack only the items he needed over the next three weeks. We called it a Packing Party (because if you add "party" to anything, Ryan will show up).

That Sunday, I drove to Ryan's home and helped him box up everything: clothes, kitchenware, towels, electronics, televisions, framed photos, artwork, toiletries. Everything. We even covered his furniture with sheets to render it useless. After nine hours— and a couple pizza deliveries—everything was packed, and his entire home smelled like cardboard. There we were, sitting in his second living room, feeling exhausted, staring at boxes stacked halfway to his twelve-foot ceiling.

Everything Ryan owned—every single thing he had worked for over the past decade—was in that room. Boxes stacked on top of boxes stacked on top of boxes. Each box was labeled so he would know where to go when he needed a particular item: "junk drawer," "living room 1," "kitchen utensils," "bedroom closet," "junk drawer 7," so forth and so on.

CONSUMPTION IS NOT THE PROBLEM— THOUGHTLESS CONSUMPTION IS.

He spent the next twenty-one days unpacking only the items he needed: a toothbrush, bedsheets, clothes for work, the furniture he actually used, pots and pans, a tool set. Just the things that added value to his life. After three weeks, 80 percent of his stuff was still in those boxes. Just sitting there. Unaccessed. When he looked at the boxes, he couldn't even remember what was in most of them. All those things that were supposed to make him happy weren't doing their job. So that's when he decided to let go—to sell or donate everything stored in that cardboard jungle.

At the end of his multi-week "party," Ryan commented that he felt free for the first time in his adult life—he felt free once he got everything out of the way so he could make room for everything that remains. Getting rid of the excess didn't change his life; it created the space for the changes that would happen in the weeks and months that followed.

As Ryan recalibrated his life—clearing the remnants and prioritizing new, empowering habits, which we will highlight throughout this book—it was like he was reclaiming that metaphorical abandoned shopping mall as a community space, restoring his life to its initial intent. In the months after he simplified, life was difficult, but more meaningful. For the first time in a long time—maybe ever—he looked beyond himself. He started focusing on community, not consumerism; giving, not taking; people, not stuff. This is often what happens as the gluttony fades; solipsism dissipates, too, making room for others. Although it wasn't his intended outcome, Ryan was beginning to understand that he isn't the center of the universe.

The Minimalists

A month after Ryan let go, amid the habit changes he was incorporating into his life, his entire perspective had shifted, and he realized that some people might find value in his newfound contentment, if only he could find an effective way to share his story. He knew I had been passionate about writing for a while, so he and I did what any two thirty-year-old dudes in 2010 might do: we started a blog. We called it *TheMinimalists.com*.

After going live on December 14, something remarkable happened: fifty-two people visited our website in the first month! I realize that might sound unimpressive, but Ryan and I were excited because it meant that at least a few dozen people found value in our tales of living with less.

Soon, other remarkable things happened: 52 readers turned into 500, 500 became 5,000, and now we have the privilege of sharing minimalism with millions of people every year. It turns out that when you add value to people's lives, they're eager to share your story with their friends and family—to add value to their lives. Adding value is a basic human instinct.

Now, a decade after simplifying our lives, Ryan and I, known collectively as The Minimalists, help more than 20 million people live meaningful lives with less stuff—all because people find value in a simple message: it's important to let go so we can make room for what's important.

What Is Minimalism?

Minimalism starts with the stuff, but that's just the beginning. Sure, at first glance, it's easy to think the point of minimalism is only to get rid of material possessions. Decluttering. Simplifying. Eliminating. Jettisoning. Detaching. Paring down. Letting go.

If that were the case, then everyone could rent a dumpster and throw all their junk in it and immediately experience perpetual bliss. But, of course, you could toss everything and still be miserable. It is possible to come home to an empty house and feel worse because you've removed your pacifiers.

Eliminating the excess is an essential part of the recipe—but it's only one ingredient. And if we're concerned solely with the stuff, then we're missing the larger point. Getting rid of the clutter is not the end result—it is merely the first step. Sure, you'll feel a weight lifted, but you won't experience lasting contentment by pitching all your possessions.

That's because consumption is not the problem—thoughtless consumption is. And we can change that by being more deliberate with the decisions we make every day. True, we all need some stuff; the key is to own the appropriate amount of stuff—and to let go of the rest. That's where minimalism enters the picture.

Minimalists don't focus on having less, less, less; they focus on making room for more: more time, more passion, more creativity, more experiences, more contribution, more contentment, more freedom. Clearing the clutter creates room for the intangibles that make life rewarding.

Sometimes people avoid minimalism because the word itself sounds extreme, radical, subversive. Afraid of stepping outside cultural boundaries, these people sidestep simplifying their lives because they don't want the label "minimalist."

So if minimalism seems too austere, you can relabel your flavor of simplification—just pick your-*ism*: intentionalism, enoughism, selectivism, essentialism, curationism, practicalism, living-within-your-means-ism. No matter what you call it, minimalism is the thing that gets us past the things so we can make room for life's important things—which aren't things at all.

What, then, are these so-called important things? That's what we will soon uncover.

This book isn't just a guide to decluttering your house. There are plenty of those out there. While we will present some practical tips for letting go of excess stuff, what we really want to do is take you past the easy part, past that first step of decluttering. This book is your guide to navigating the world of possibilities that decluttering opens up—to the difficult next stage of learning to live deliberately. That starts with the stuff, and then once you have *less*, we want to show you how to make room for the right kind of *more*.

Love People, Use Things

This book's title was inspired by two unlikely muses. It was the venerable Fulton J. Sheen, circa 1925, who first said, "You must remember to love people and use things, rather than to love things and use people." I encountered this epigram almost daily as a child, every time I walked past my Catholic mother's bedroom and saw it, artfully framed and mounted, on the wall above her bed. Nearly a century later, pop-rap superstar Drake echoed Sheen's line when he sang, "Wish you would learn to love people and use things and not the other way around." The Minimalists reworked this sentiment to create the catchphrase that has come to define our message: "Love people and use things because the opposite never works," which ends every episode of our podcast. When Ryan and I close our live events with this line, the crowd often echoes the phrase in unison. A few brave souls have even tattooed the phrase on their bodies as a permanent daily reminder.

> **MINIMALISTS DON'T FOCUS ON HAVING LESS, LESS, LESS; THEY FOCUS ON MAKING ROOM FOR MORE.**

Minimalism itself is not a new idea: the concept dates back to the Stoics, to every major religion, and, more recently, to Emerson and Thoreau and Tyler Durden. What's new is the problem: never before have people been more seduced by materialism, and never before have people been so willing to forsake loved ones to acquire heaps of meaningless stuff.

With this book, we will shine a new light on minimalism's time-tested wisdom, one lesson at a time. The book's aim isn't to remove you from the modern world, but rather to show you how to better live within it.

How do we learn to live confidently without the material things we've convinced ourselves we need? How do we live a more intentional and rewarding life? How do we learn to reset our priorities? How do we transform the way we look at ourselves? How do we get what we want out of life?

Ryan and I explore these questions by examining the seven essential relationships that make us who we are: stuff, truth, self, values, money, creativity, and people. These relationships crisscross our lives in unexpected ways, providing destructive patterns that

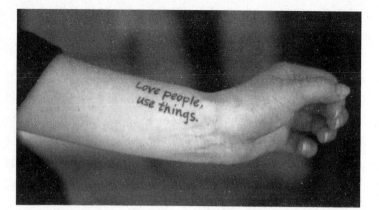

frequently repeat themselves, too often left unexamined because we have buried them beneath materialistic clutter. This book offers the tools to help in the fight against consumerism, clearing the slate to make room for a meaningful life.

Ryan and I believe that by highlighting our flaws and working through our issues publicly, we can help people deal with their own issues and the shame that surrounds the decisions of the past. It just so happens that this book is the best medium for us to pour our guts onto the page. Throughout these pages, we'll also use expert insights and case studies to peel back the facade covering the hidden truths of everyday people who've been hiding their shame, like we once did, under a mountain of useless objects.

How to Make This Book Work

At its core, every good book is attempting to do two things: communicate and express. A book wants to *communicate* something valuable to the reader and *express* something profound about the world. Often nonfiction books do only the former. While Ryan and I want to communicate what we've learned over the years, we want to cement it by way of expressive stories that make our lessons both actionable and memorable.

The author Derek Sivers says, "A good book changes your mind; a great book changes your actions." I believe we have written a good book, one that has the potential to change your mind, but it's up to you to make it great. So, as you read through these chapters, highlight and underline useful passages. Write notes in the margins. Buy a fresh notebook (or perhaps finally put to use one of the many that have accumulated around the house) and complete the exercises at the end of each chapter. And most important, once you understand the benefits of living with less, take action.

According to the American educator Edgar Dale's learning pyramid:

We remember

10 percent of what we read,

20 percent of what we hear,

30 percent of what we see,

50 percent of what we see and hear,

70 percent of what we discuss with others,

80 percent of what we personally experience,

95 percent of what we teach others.

If you read this book but do nothing with what you've learned, then you're missing the point. It's fine to absorb the information to start, but it is *action* that will change your life. And if you really want the info in this book to stick, discuss it with—and even consider teaching what you've learned to—other people.

To help you retain as many lessons as possible, Ryan, the

mentorly half of The Minimalists, will complete each chapter with a coda that includes five questions to answer once you've finished the chapter. Those questions will be accompanied by a list of five dos and five don'ts related to that chapter's theme—specific action items you can immediately incorporate into your daily life. Take your time answering these questions and then take action on the dos and don'ts before moving on—they will help crystallize what you've read.

As you read on, it will soon become clear that *Love People, Use Things* is not just a *how-to* book—it's also a *why-to* book. We want you to walk away from every chapter with practical advice for *how* to change your life, and the compelling stories you've read will give you the leverage you need to remember *why* change is necessary. When you combine the *how* and the *why*, you will have a recipe for lasting transformation.

RELATIONSHIP 1 | STUFF

I first met Jason and Jennifer Kirkendoll in the post-show hug line at one of The Minimalists' live events. They told me that when they married, at age twenty-four, they were both filled with hope for their future. Before they knew it, they were living the American Dream: four kids, two dogs, a cat, and a home just outside Minneapolis. Jason worked for a large insurance company; Jennifer was a stay-at-home mom.

In time, however, their dream slowly devolved into a nightmare.

The house that was once their dream home no longer fit their ever-expanding lifestyle. So they found a bigger home in a distant suburb, taking on the burden of a larger thirty-year mortgage and a longer commute.

The expansion didn't stop with their home. To keep up appearances, they bought new cars every few years and outfitted their walk-in closets with designer clothes. To alleviate their anxiety, they shopped at the Mall of America on the weekends. They ate too much junk food, watched too much junk TV, and distracted themselves with too much junk on the Internet, exchanging a meaningful life for ephemera.

And yet *too much* wasn't enough.

Before they were thirty-five, Jason and Jennifer were drowning in problems. Most serious were their money troubles. Even with overtime pay, Jason's fifty-hour workweeks no longer kept them afloat, so Jennifer sought a part-time job to help keep the bill collectors at bay: credit cards, car payments, college loans, private-school tuition, house payments.

But the money problems were only the top layer covering a labyrinth of deeper issues.

Their sex life was nonexistent.

Their careers were unfulfilling.

They hid purchases from one another.

They lied to each other about their spending.

They ignored their creative desires.

They took each other for granted.

They grew petty and resentful.

They were ashamed of who they'd become.

A decade after their nuptials, they were anxious, overwhelmed, and stressed because they'd lost sight of their ideal vision. They'd squandered their most precious resources—time, energy, and attention—on fruitless miscellanea. The exuberant, hopeful twenty-four-year-olds who'd exchanged vows were so far in the rearview they were completely out of view.

Well.

The only way to mask their discontent was to hop back on the hedonic treadmill—spending money they didn't have to buy things they didn't need to impress people they didn't like. They worshipped at the altar of consumerism, and stuff had become their new God.

Then, on Christmas morning, in 2016, they discovered a fresh perspective. With the carpet under their Christmas tree bare from the morning's unwrapping, Jennifer switched on Netflix, like she had hundreds of times before, and stumbled across a movie called *Minimalism: A Documentary About the Important Things*. Throughout the Matt D'Avella–directed film about Ryan's and my journey,* she found herself contrasting the simple lives on the screen with the heaps of wrapping paper, empty boxes, and untouched gifts strewn across her living room floor. Not even four hours had gone by, and her kids were already bored by half their new toys. And the obligatory gift Jason had purchased for her—with *their* credit card—was back in its box, already tucked away in their closet, uninteresting and unused, like most of the things they owned.

Jennifer thought back to her college days.

Her life was so simple then.

When did everything get so complex?

The Latin root of the word "complex" is *complect*, which means "to interweave two or more things together." Jason and Jennifer had interwoven so many unnecessary possessions, distractions, and obligations into their daily lives that they were no longer able to distinguish the junk from the essentials.

The opposite of complexity is simplicity. The word "simple" shares a Latin root with the word *simplex*, which means "having only one part." So when we talk about simplifying, what we're really talking about is un-complecting our lives—removing that which is no longer serving the complex structures we've created—because anything that's too complex gets tangled.

---

* If you aren't already a Matt D'Avella fan, do yourself a favor and subscribe to his YouTube channel, YouTube.com/mattdavella. He'll quickly become your favorite minimalist filmmaker.

Jennifer knew that if they were going to be happy again—if their family was going to reconnect with what was important—a change was critical. They needed to simplify. But she was unsure where to start, so she turned to the online world.

The Internet exposed Jennifer to a plethora of people who had simplified their lives with minimalism. Colin Wright, a twenty-something entrepreneur from Missouri, left behind his 100-hour workweeks to travel the globe with only fifty-two items in his back-pack. Courtney Carver, a wife and mother to a teenage daughter in Salt Lake City, jettisoned 80 percent of her material possessions and was able to fully focus on treating her multiple sclerosis. Joshua and Kim Becker, parents in the suburbs of Phoenix, let go of most of their excess and founded a nonprofit that builds orphanages on the U.S.-Mexico border. Leo Babauta, a husband and father of six in Guam, quit smoking, lost eighty pounds, moved his family to California, and finally pursued his dream of being a full-time writer.

ENOUGH IS ENOUGH WHEN YOU DECIDE IT'S ENOUGH.

Jennifer found dozens of inspiring stories like these scattered across the web. Although each of these people led considerably different lives—married parents, childless singles, men and women, young and old, rich and poor—she noticed they all shared at least two things in common. First, they were living deliberate, meaningful lives—they were passionate and purpose-driven, and they seemed much richer than any of the so-called rich people she'd encountered. Second, they all attributed their meaningful lives to this thing called *minimalism*.

And then, of course, there was The Minimalists' story, which Jennifer had seen in our documentary. At the time, Ryan and I were two seemingly normal thirty-five-year-olds (like Jason and Jennifer) from the Midwest (ditto) who had achieved the American Dream (double ditto) and then walked away from our overindulgent lifestyles to pursue a more meaningful life.

After falling down the rabbit hole, Jennifer was excited to clear the clutter. Jason, on the other hand, was skeptical, but the evidence was overwhelming, and deep down he knew they had to do something to get back on track.

Fueled by the excitement—and fear—of letting go, they rented a dumpster and placed it next to their overstuffed house. During the New Year's weekend, they began chucking everything they hadn't used in the last year: clothes, cosmetics, toys, books, DVDs, CDs, electronics, utensils, plates, cups, mugs, pet accessories, tools, furniture, exercise equipment—even a Ping-Pong table. Anything that wasn't bolted down was subject to dismissal.

They let go aggressively.
Within a week, their house felt different.
The physical mess was dissipating.
The visual clutter was reduced.
The echo in their home was new.
Was that the sound of simplicity?

As January 2017 came to a close, Jason and Jennifer were nearly finished excising their home of its excess. Within a week, the dumpster would be gone, and years of unintentional hoarding would be removed from their lives forever.

They were making significant progress. Their closets and basement and garage were organized. Their remaining furniture had a function. Their things were in order. They could breathe better. They laughed more. They were more agreeable. They worked together as a family. Everything they owned served a purpose, and everything else was out of the way. Their house was a home again. A rush of calm overtook them as they recognized their priorities were finally at the forefront of their lives.

Then—the unexpected.

The day before its scheduled retrieval, their dumpster caught fire. No one knows exactly how it happened, but while Jason and Jennifer were at work that Tuesday, something ignited the contents of the now-overflowing dumpster, and by the time they returned from work, their house had burned to the ground, including everything they wanted to keep.

Fortunately, their kids had been at school during the conflagration, and all three pets had escaped through the doggie door at the back of the house. But everything else was gone. Everything. Every. Thing.

With tears in their eyes, Jason and Jennifer held their children and stared blankly at the smoldering rubble. How could this happen? After years of hard work, achieving, and accumulation, they had nothing to show for it. Nothing. No. Thing.

It was terrifying.
It was depressing.
It was . . .
Freeing?

The past month had been an exercise in letting go, and at this moment they realized they were capable of letting go of anything. Any. Thing.

Their kids were safe. Their family was intact. And their relationship was considerably better than it was a month ago. Their future was whatever they wanted to make it. For the first time in their adult lives, they weren't tethered to the lifestyle and possessions and expectations that had constrained them until now. They had un-*complected* their weave. As their complexities went up in smoke—literally—they were thrust into the simple life by way of a dumpster fire.

A month before, Jason and Jennifer would have been devastated by this setback. But with their new perspective, they didn't see it as a setback—it was an inconvenient push forward. Now, with everything out of the way, their only question was "What are we going to do with our newfound freedom?"

Freedom from Impulse

It's shocking how many people have the same story as Jason and Jennifer—minus the dumpster fire, obviously. Most Westerners have chased happiness through impulse purchases, ephemeral pleasures, and the trophies of ostensible success. Really, all of our detrimental decisions—and, ironically, our discontent—can be traced back to our desire to be happy. That's because we often conflate happiness with instant gratification.

"Happiness" is such a slippery term. Different people mean different things when they use the word. Some people mean pleasure. Others mean fulfillment. Some mean contentment. Others, satisfaction. A few erudite thinkers mean well-being.

I would posit, however, that people aren't searching for happiness—they're searching for *freedom*. And true happiness—that is, enduring well-being—is a by-product of that freedom.

Freedom. The word itself conjures myriad images: a flag popping crisply in the wind, a war hero returning home, an eagle soaring high above a canyon. But real freedom moves beyond the imagery and involves something more abstract.

When you think about freedom, you often think of doing whatever you want, whenever you want.

Whatever.
Whenever.

Dig deeper, however, and you quickly realize that's not freedom—it's self-inflicted tyranny.

Left to her own devices, my six-year-old daughter, Ella, will happily do "whatever she wants": throw her toys across the room, binge-watch YouTube videos, gorge on chocolate cake, refuse to brush her teeth, play in traffic.

These decisions feel good in the moment, but as our poor decisions compound, we reap the rotting fruits of our indiscretions. In time, thoughtless decisions lead to thoughtless habits that damage our relationships, until, eventually, we've distanced ourselves from the very thing we sought—freedom.

We occasionally deploy euphemisms to describe our lack of freedom.

Tethered.
Chained.
Anchored.
Trapped.
Stuck.

What we mean, though, is that we've lost control, and we no longer possess the discipline necessary to walk away from that which holds us back: we're tethered to the past, chained to a career, anchored by a relationship, trapped by debt, stuck in this two-bit town.

Worse, some possessions and achievements actually ape the form of freedom—the glimmering sports cars, the mammoth suburban houses, the corner-office promotions—although they often accomplish the obverse of freedom: faux freedom. The average American stands on their manicured lawn, imprisoned by the picket fence of their American Dream.

> THE AVERAGE AMERICAN STANDS ON THEIR MANICURED LAWN, IMPRISONED BY THE PICKET FENCE OF THEIR AMERICAN DREAM.

This is, of course, a little dramatic, but it illustrates an important point. Real freedom stands beyond the accoutrements and decor of faux freedom. And to get there we must travel outside the deceptively beautiful fences we've constructed.

You see, real freedom involves much more than material possessions and wealth and traditional success. Real freedom can't be tracked on a spreadsheet—it is an abstraction. But unlike distance and time, we don't have units of measurement for freedom. That's why it's so difficult to grasp. So we settle instead for what can be counted: dollars, trinkets, and social-media clout, all of which lack the meaning and rigor and payoff of real freedom.

And the more we pursue faux freedom, the further we travel from actual freedom. And when this happens, we feel threatened by the freedom of others. So we protect our hoard, we question anyone who approaches life differently, and we cling tightly to the status quo because we're scared that someone else's nontraditional lifestyle is an affront to our own. If that person is free, then we are not.

But we forget that freedom is not a zero-sum game. The rising tide of freedom—real freedom—lifts all boats, large or small, while faux freedom only beaches them.

Sure, faux freedom is comfortable, not unlike a child's security blanket, but it is not the blanket that keeps a child secure. Security resides in our ability to move on, to walk away from what's holding us back, and to walk toward that which is worthwhile.

Minimalist Rules for Living with Less

Rules can be arbitrary, restrictive, stodgy—and they often get in the way of meaningful change. Sometimes, however, a few loosely held rules can keep us on track, but only if we possess a deep understanding of the problems we want to address.

Whenever we attempt to simplify, we often get stuck before we even get started. When faced with a hoard of possessions—some useful, others not—it is difficult to determine what adds value and what doesn't, which makes letting go extremely difficult.

I wish I could hand you a list of the 100 items you're supposed to own. But minimalism doesn't work like that. What brings value to my life could very well clutter yours. Further, the things that once added value may not continue to add value, so we must constantly question not only the things we acquire, but the things we hold on to.

Because minimalism is not an antidote to desire, and because, like most people, Ryan and I still act on impulse, we've created a collection of Minimalist Rules for Living with Less, which we use to resist the tug of consumerism and get organized. You'll find these rules—the Just in Case Rule, the Seasonality Rule, and more than a dozen others—sprinkled throughout the pages of this book (just look for the gray boxes like the one on the next page).

It's worth noting that these "rules" aren't really rules in the traditional sense. Meaning, they are not prescriptive or dogmatic. Nor are they one-size-fits-all—because what works for Ryan or me may not work for you. These are our recipe for simple living, and like any recipe, you may need to adjust for taste. If the 30/30 Rule is too strict, or the 20/20 Rule is too inflexible, or the 90/90 Rule is too restrictive, then consider setting your own parameters based on your desired outcome and current comfort level.

It's crucial to get a little uncomfortable, though, because a bit of discomfort is required to build your letting-go muscles. As time goes by and your muscles grow, you can continue to adjust the rules to challenge you. Before you know it, you might be more of a minimalist than The Minimalists. We've seen it happen dozens of times.

MINIMALIST RULE FOR LIVING WITH LESS

No Junk Rule

Everything you own can be placed in three piles: *essential, nonessential, junk.* Since most of our *needs* are universal, only a few things belong in the *essential* pile: food, shelter, clothing, transportation, vocation, education. In an ideal world, the majority of your stuff would fit in the *nonessential* pile; strictly speaking, you don't need a couch or a dining table, but they're worth owning if they enhance your life. But sadly, almost all of the things you own fit in the *junk* pile, the artifacts you *like*—or, more accurately, *think* you like. While this junk often masquerades as indispensable, it actually gets in the way. The key is to get rid of the junk to make room for everything else.

Consumerism Tantalizes

Because our material possessions are a reflection of our internal well-being, it is helpful to first get a grip on our external clutter before we can repair our other essential relationships.

Changing our relationship with stuff isn't easy. Even I, one of the titular Minimalists, still struggle with the siren song of consumerism. I wish I could tell you that Ryan and I let go of our excess possessions, simplified our lives, and never felt the desire to buy any more material goods going forward.

Yeah, I wish.

But that jacket sure looks nice in that banner ad.

So do those shoes in that marketing email.

If you pay attention, it's everywhere you look.

The pair of skinny jeans on the highway billboard.

The shampoo in the television commercial.

The makeup on the drugstore window banner.

The miracle diet pill on the radio advertisement.

The mattress they shill on your favorite podcast.

The big-screen television in the newspaper insert.

The kitchen backsplash on the direct mailer.

The vacation home on that fixer-upper show.

The Mercedes-Benz in your Instagram feed.

The Rolex on the back cover of the magazine.

Yet a Rolex won't buy you more time. A Mercedes won't get you there any faster. And a vacation home won't earn you more vacation days. In fact, the opposite is true in most cases. We are attempting to purchase that which is priceless: time. You might have to work hundreds of hours to buy an expensive watch, years to pay off a luxury car, and a lifetime to afford a vacation home. Which means we're willing to give up our time to purchase the illusion of time.

Now, I'm sure Rolex and Mercedes make high-quality, well-crafted products, and there's nothing inherently wrong with the items themselves. The real problem is feeling as though these material items will make your life better, meaningful, or complete. But your stuff won't make you a more whole person. At best, the things we bring into our lives are tools that can help us be more comfortable or productive—they can augment a meaningful life, but they cannot bring meaning into our lives.

> **THE EASIEST WAY TO DECLUTTER YOUR STUFF IS TO AVOID BRINGING IT HOME IN THE FIRST PLACE.**

A Brief History of Modern Advertising

The industrial advertising complex tells us that if we acquire all the right things—the perfect cars and clothes and cosmetics—they will make us happy. And they tell us this over and over. According to *Forbes*, Americans are exposed to around 4,000 to 10,000 advertisements each day. As it happens, I was just hit with a few dozen ads while researching that stat.

That's not to say that all advertising is innately evil, because not all advertisements are created equal—they run the gamut from informative to downright destructive.

In Latin, *advertere* means "to turn toward," and that's the exact aim of today's ad agencies: they pay heaps of money to turn your eyes toward their products and services. And if the demand for a product isn't as high as the supply, no problem! Advertising can create a false demand if the budget is high enough.

In recent years, worldwide spending on advertising has topped half a trillion dollars a year. Even writing the full number—500,000,000,000, commas and all—doesn't come close to truly understanding its depth.

But that's not so bad, is it? After all, it's just money being spent on informing people about useful stuff, right?

Sort of.

Before the twentieth century, advertising largely connected the producers of goods with consumers who genuinely needed those goods. But then, as Stuart Ewen describes in his book *Captains of Consciousness*, "Advertising increased dramatically in the United States as industrialization expanded the supply of manufactured products. In order to profit from this higher rate of production, industry needed to recruit workers as consumers of factory products. It did so through the invention of [advertising] designed to influence the population's economic behavior on a larger scale."

THERE ARE NO REFUNDS ON MISSPENT ATTENTION.

By the Roaring Twenties, thanks to Edward Bernays, who is sometimes referred to as the founder of modern advertising and public relations, advertisers in the United States adopted the doctrine that human instincts could be "targeted and harnessed." Bernays, a nephew of Sigmund Freud, realized that appealing to the rational minds of customers, which had been the mainstream method advertisers used to sell products, was far less effective than selling products based on the unconscious desires he felt were the "true motivators of human action." Since then, we've witnessed ten decades of advertising agencies reaching—and overreaching—into the depths of the human psyche.

Advertisers have gotten so skilled that they can even sell us trash and tell us it's good for us. Literally. Just look at the ubiquity of junk food.

Curing Problems That Don't Exist

Fast-forward to the present day. One of the most obvious examples of advertisers' rapacious (over)reach in recent years is the drug sildenafil, which was created as a treatment for hypertension. When clinical trials revealed the drug wasn't effective, that should have been the end of its life cycle.

But then advertisers stepped in.

After discovering several male test subjects experienced prolonged erections during clinical trials, the makers of sildenafil had a solution that desperately needed a problem. So they hired an ad agency that coined the term "erectile dysfunction," and Viagra was born. This campaign took a relatively flaccid problem and created a raging $3 billion–per–year market for a blue pill.

Of course, Viagra is a rather anodyne example. There are many pharmaceuticals whose side effects are so expansive that their commercials are forced to use gratuitous green pastures, yearbook smiles, and hand-holding actors to conceal the terror of "rectal bleeding," "amnesia," and "suicidal ideation."

In a sane world, the marketing of potentially harmful prescription drugs might be considered a criminal act. In fact, it's illegal in every country in the world—except the United States and New Zealand—to advertise drugs to consumers.

But we let the almighty dollar get in the way.

In 1976, Henry Gadsden, then CEO of Merck & Co., told *Fortune* magazine that he'd rather sell drugs to healthy people because they had the most money. We've been sold new "cures" ever since.

Please don't mistake this for an anti-boner-pill diatribe.

According to the research, Viagra seems to be a relatively benign drug. Thereby, there's little wrong with the pill itself. It's the paid advertisements that are troublesome.

Many ad agencies employ writers, demographers, statisticians, analysts, and even psychologists in an effort to divorce us from the money in our checking accounts. With the help of a fine-tuned agency, even the "disclaimer" is part of the sales pitch: "Consult your doctor if your erection lasts longer than four hours." I don't know about you, but I'd rather consult my significant other.

Viagra isn't the only product pushed beyond its initial conception. Did you know that Listerine was previously used as a floor cleaner, Coca-Cola was invented as an alternative to morphine, and the graham cracker was created to prevent young boys from masturbating?

MINIMALIST RULE FOR LIVING WITH LESS

Just in Case Rule

Are you holding on to anything "just in case" you might need it someday? You don't need to. Enter: the Just in Case Rule, aka the 20/20 Rule. Here's how it works. Any JIC item you get rid of that you truly need later, you can replace for less than $20 in less than 20 minutes from your current location. At first, this sounds like a rule of privilege. Who can afford to spend $20 every time they replace something? Wouldn't that cost thousands of dollars every year? Actually, no. It turns out that you rarely have to replace the items you've donated because most of them are useless.

Selling Scarcity

Why does it seem like the advertisements we experience are always taking place in a state of perpetual emergency?

Act now!
Limited time only!
While supplies last!

These advertiser-induced artificial limits are almost always imaginary. The truth is that if you "miss out" on a so-called sale, you'll be just fine because corporations are always looking for a new opportunity to sell you something today. I mean, what's the alternative? "Sorry, Ms. Customer, you waited an extra day to make your decision, and now we no longer want your money!" Yeah right.

Why, then, does almost every company inject urgency into their ads? Because, as Bernays recognized a century ago, this tactic takes advantage of our primal nature: humans make quick—often rash—decisions in times of perceived scarcity.

This made sense when our number one concern was starvation; it makes much less sense when we think we'll never be able to own that sofa, video-game console, or clutch purse unless we get in on this weekend's doorbuster bonanza. An item might be deeply "discounted" today, but it's 100 percent off if you don't buy it. Not buying something is your future self letting go of that thing in advance.

A World with Fewer Ads

While I was driving from Burlington to Boston a few years ago, something felt off. The rolling emerald landscape was unsullied, not unlike a tranquil screensaver, and I felt an unnameable calm as the mile markers ticked away.

Then I crossed the Massachusetts state line, and it became obvious: the trip's serenity was produced largely by its lack of billboards, which are illegal in the state of Vermont. Currently, four states—Alaska, Hawaii, Maine, and Vermont—prohibit billboards. And more than 1,500 cities and towns have banned them throughout the world, including one of the largest cities on Earth—São Paulo, Brazil.

When São Paulo introduced its "Clean City Law" in 2007, more than 15,000 billboards were taken down. To boot, an additional 300,000 intrusive signs—pylons, posters, bus and taxi ads—had to go.

The strangest result of ridding the world's third-largest city of these advertisements? In a poll done after the removal, a majority of *paulistanos* actually preferred the change. What a novel idea: ask people what they like instead of letting profitability dictate the city view.

Unfortunately, we've accepted ads as part of our everyday life; we've been conditioned to think they are a regular slice of "content delivery." After all, advertisements are how we get all those TV shows, radio programs, online articles, and podcasts for free, right?

But there's no free lunch. Every hour of network television is peppered with nearly twenty minutes of interruptions, and the same is true for most other media, which one could argue is more costly than the "free" price tag because we are forswearing our two most precious resources—our time and attention—to receive the product.

If we don't want ads storming our attention (or our children's attention), then we must be willing to pay for the things we associate with "free."

Netflix, Apple Music, and similar services are able to side-step the traditional advertising model by providing a service people value. Other businesses and individuals—Wikipedia and Bret Easton Ellis come to mind—follow a variation of this ad-free model, frequently called a "freemium" model, where creators provide content for free, and a portion of their audience supports their work monetarily. (By the way, this model keeps *The Minimalists Podcast* advertisement-free.)

> A ROLEX WON'T BUY YOU MORE TIME. A MERCEDES WON'T GET YOU THERE ANY FASTER. AND A VACATION HOME WON'T EARN YOU MORE VACATION DAYS.

No matter your feelings about these particular companies and individuals, their approach undoubtedly improves their creations by making them interruption-free, and it increases trust since their audience knows these creators aren't beholden to the desires of advertisers, which allows them to communicate directly with their audience in a way that strengthens the relationship because the customers are in control, not the ad buyers.

Moreover, as consumers, our willingness to exchange money for creations forces us to be more deliberate about what we consume. If we're paying for it, we want to make sure we're getting our money's worth. It's a mystery why we don't do the same for so-called free programming, where we pay no money but rarely get our attention's worth.

Whether your time is worth $10, $100, or $1,000 per hour, you likely spend tens of thousands of dollars every year consuming messages from advertisers. Think about that: in a real way, you're paying to be advertised to. And there are no refunds on misspent attention.

You Don't Need That

Ryan and I moved to Los Angeles in 2017 to establish a film and podcast studio for The Minimalists. As soon as we arrived in the city, I noticed I was drawn to what everyone else already had: granite countertops, Teslas, limited-edition Air Jordan sneakers. Perhaps the American neo-conceptual artist Jenny Holzer was onto something when she painted "the unattainable is invariably attractive" on the side of a BMW "art car" at the Porsche museum in Germany. Even as a minimalist, I found that the overwhelming pull of consumerism made it difficult not to think I *needed* everything I saw. Luckily, I'd unknowingly been preparing for the land of Lamborghinis, Melrose Place, and triple-decker strip malls for nearly a decade.

If there is a core message within minimalism, it's this: you probably don't need that. Yet we trick ourselves into believing that we do need that couch, that cookware, that eyeliner, that skirt, that statuette. Perhaps that's because we've evolved to dupe ourselves. "The prime directive of the mind is to deceive itself," claims the analytic philosopher Bernardo Kastrup, author of *More Than Allegory*. "Our reality is created by an extraordinarily subtle process of self-deception."

When you extend Kastrup's claim to the material world, it instantly seems obvious. If the average household contains hundreds of thousands of items, most of which get in the way and don't increase our tranquility, then why do we hold on to all that junk? The answer is simple: because of the stories we tell ourselves. What disempowering stories do you tell yourself about your stuff? What new empowering stories could you create to change the narrative?

I often hear members of the media say that the American Dream is more out of reach than ever. But that's not true. In terms of access, it's easier than ever to reach the American Dream. The problem is we're reaching for things that increase our discontentment.

Once upon a time, the American Dream was modest: if you worked hard at your modest job, you could afford to build a modest house on a modest piece of land and live a modest life. You would have *enough*. Today, however, we want it all, and we want it now: a bigger house and a bigger car and a bigger life; shopping sprees and lavish dinners and Instagram-worthy moments. Because we're addicted to the dopamine rush of each new purchase, it's never enough to simply have enough.

How much is enough?
Without asking this question, we blindly pursue excess.
We drink from the fire hose of consumption.
Acquire, consume, indulge. More, more, more.

How much is enough?
Without an answer, we don't know how to proceed.
Because we don't know when to stop.
Mindless desire takes us by the hand.

Naturally, "enough" is different for each of us.
Enough changes as our needs and circumstances change.

Your enough may include a sofa, coffee table, and TV.
A dining table that seats six.
A three-bedroom home.
A two-car garage.
A backyard trampoline.
Or that might be too much.

Enough changes over time.
Yesterday's enough may be too much today.

How much is enough?
Less than enough is depriving.
More than enough is indulging.

Enough is the sweet spot in the middle, the place where intentionality intersects with contentment, where lust doesn't get in the way of creating something meaningful.

Sure, you could pursue more.
But "could" is not a reason to do anything.
Enough is enough when you decide it's enough.

Six Questions to Ask Before Buying

Every time you part with a dollar, you part with a tiny piece of your freedom. If you earn $20 an hour, then that $4 cup of coffee just cost you twelve minutes, that $800 iPad cost you a week, and that $40,000 new car cost you an entire year of freedom.

At the end of your life, do you think you'd rather have an automobile or one more year? That's not to say we must eschew coffee or electronics or cars. I personally own all three. The issue is that we don't question the things we bring into our lives. And if we're not willing to question everything, we'll fall for anything.

Before you commit to a new purchase—before bringing yet another possession into your life—it's worth asking yourself the following six questions in anticipation of the cash register consuming your hard-earned money.

1. Who am I buying this for?

The things we own don't tell the world who we are, but, sadly, they often communicate who we want to be. When this happens, we mistakenly let our possessions shape our identity. We showcase our favorite brands in a futile effort to signify our individuality: *See this shiny new thing? This is who I am!* Our logos make us feel unique, just like everybody else.

The brands themselves aren't the problem, though. We all need some stuff. So we rely on companies to create the things we need. The problem arises when we feel external pressure to acquire, as if new trinkets were a shortcut to a more complete life.

That external pressure needn't be a sign to consume. If anything, it's a sign to pause and ask, *Who am I buying this for?* Is that new thing for you? Or are you buying it to project an image for others? If it's truly for you—and it makes sense to purchase—then, by all means, go ahead, get it. Let's not deprive ourselves of the things that enhance our lives. But if you're buying things just to signal a sort of consumerist equanimity, then you're getting in the way of the freedom you're attempting to purchase.

2. Will this add value to my life?

I don't own many things, but everything I own adds value to my life. Meaning, each of my belongings—from my car and clothes to my furniture and electronics—functions either as a tool or adds aesthetic value to my life. In other words: Does it serve a function or increase my well-being in a meaningful way? If not, it's not worth buying.

3. Can I afford it?

If you have to charge a new purchase to a credit card, you can't afford it. If you have to finance it, you can't afford it. And if you're in debt, you can't afford it. Just because you *can* buy something today, that doesn't mean you can actually afford it. If you can't, it's better left on the shelf.

But what about a buying house, or going to college—surely, those are exceptions, right? While they might be *different* debts—and they're better than, say, credit-card debt—they're still debt. It's been said for thousands of years that the borrower is slave to the lender, and so it makes sense to pay off any debt as quickly as possible. I know this point of view isn't normal, but "normal" is what thrust us into our current $14 trillion mess. We'll address many misconceptions about debt in the "Relationship with Money" chapter.

4. Is this the best use of this money?

In other words, how else can you use this money? What are the alternatives? The songwriter Andy Davis sings a line in his song "Good Life" that succinctly captures our culture's misappropriation of finances: "We struggle to pay rent / 'cause jeans are expensive." Sure, you might be able to afford those pricey jeans, but would the money serve you better elsewhere? Say, in a retirement savings account or on a family vacation (or rent)? If so, why not avoid the purchase and allocate the dollars to the most effective place?

5. What's the actual cost?

As we discussed in the introduction, the true cost of a thing goes well beyond its price tag. In business, they call this full-cost accounting. But let's call it what it really is: these are the actual costs of owning all the things we think we need.

When it comes to the items we own, we must consider the storage costs, maintenance costs, and psychological costs. When we add it all up, we're able to understand the true cost, and we often realize we can't afford it, even if we can afford the up-front cost.

6. Would the best version of me buy this?

A few years ago, my friend Leslie stood in her local grocer's checkout line, fumbling with her wallet's zipper, preparing to make an impulse purchase. But then, suspended in the queue, she was given time to question the thing in her hand. She pondered the item carefully and asked herself a question: *What would Joshua do?* That is, if I were in her shoes, would I make this purchase? *No,* she thought, and promptly returned the item to the shelf.

When she told me about her experience, she joked that she wanted to buy one of those WWJD? bracelets to help her avoid compulsive consumption going forward. I laughed, but then realized that I, too, could benefit from making more frequent use of this question—and so could others.

To be clear, I don't want you to walk around asking yourself, *What would Joshua do?* Please don't. Rather, it's a rhetorical question: *What would the best version of you do in this situation?* If he or she wouldn't buy it, then you know what to do.

Pausing to consider each new purchase with these six questions seems like a hassle at first. But in time, it's a habit that will reward you—and your family—with less clutter around the house and more money to spend on what's important. After all, the easiest way to declutter your stuff is to avoid bringing it home in the first place.*

---

* If you'd like a smartphone or desktop wallpaper with a streamlined version of these questions, visit minimalists.com/wallpapers to download it for free. It's a nice reminder to pause and consider each purchase, whether you're in line at the mall or getting ready to click the "checkout" button online.

MINIMALIST RULE FOR LIVING WITH LESS

Emergency Items Rule

There are a handful of just-in-case items it's best to keep: emergency items. This category might include a first-aid kit, jumper cables, and a few gallons of water. If you live in a cold climate, tire chains, road flares, and an emergency blanket could be on your list. While you hope you'll never need them, a basic level of emergency preparation can give you peace of mind. Be careful, though, it's easy to justify just about anything. But remember: most emergencies aren't. Besides, no matter how much we prep, we can't prepare for everything.

Unpacking a New Life

Nearly a decade after Ryan's Packing Party experiment, The Minimalists decided to formalize a case study to see what a similar analysis would reveal in other people's lives.

After touring for ten years—speaking about minimalism and talking to thousands of people in hundreds of cities—we've collected countless stories of letting go. We've learned firsthand that Ryan's and my stories are not unique, and consumerism is indeed affecting the lives of many people around the globe. We hadn't, however, been able to quantify the secrets, emotions, and pain that were hiding under the veneer of stuff.

Face-to-face, people told us how they had simplified their lives using the methods we discuss on our blog, and a few courageous readers had even embarked on modified versions of Ryan's Packing Party. Yet we hadn't collected these stories in a formal way.

While each anecdote affirmed our belief that people could live meaningful lives with less, we needed more data if we were going to write about it in an informed way.

Enter: the Packing Party Case Study.

In March 2019, The Minimalists enlisted forty-seven participants—a select group of individuals and families from our online audience—to spend a chunk of the next month eradicating their hoards by way of a Packing Party. Because packing up an entire house wasn't ideal for everyone participating, we gave these "partyers" three options.

Option 1: Whole-House Packing Party. "Just like Nicodemus, you'll pack everything as if you're moving. Then, you'll unpack only the items that add value to your life over the next three weeks."

Option 2: One-Room Packing Party. "You needn't be as drastic as Nicodemus. Often a twenty-one-day Packing Party in just one room jump-starts the decluttering process."

Option 3: Multi-Room Packing Party. "Maybe you don't want to pack everything in your home, but you want to have a Packing Party in your office, garage, and bathroom? Or maybe your kitchen, bedroom, and living room? You decide!"

A party is a party only when people party together, so we asked all forty-seven participants to party at the same time: April 2019. Because April 1 fell on a Monday, we guided partyers through packing their belongings the weekend before the start of the month. On March 30 and 31, everyone procured enough used cardboard to box up their possessions, and then they spent the weekend pretending they were moving. Then, each day, beginning April 1, and continuing through April 21, each partner began unpacking anything that would serve a purpose or bring them joy. Partners were also able to interact with each other via a private community board to share their experiences, struggles, and photos with their fellow participants.

IF THERE IS A CORE MESSAGE WITHIN MINIMALISM, IT'S THIS: YOU PROBABLY DON'T NEED THAT.

Along the way, Ryan and I observed their progress. After the first day, we asked each participant to describe their process. We were shocked to see the variety of strategies, many of which were considerably different from Ryan's.

Natalie Pedersen, a whole-house partner from Deerfield, Wisconsin, wrote, "We started with the kitchen and then worked our way through the rest of the house. It took longer than we anticipated but was so satisfying when we were all packed up!"

Abigail Dawson, a multi-room partner from Fairfax, Virginia, said, "I share a one-bedroom apartment with my husband, who is not a minimalist, and together we packed up everything in our kitchen and the bedroom—except his clothes!"

Ellie Dobson, a whole-house partner from Roswell, Georgia, claimed, "I've been a minimalist for a few years now, so it took only an hour or two. After the things were all packed away, I felt a little like, 'Okay, what now?'"

Fair question.

Now what?

Once everyone's possessions were residing in their new cardboard homes, partners cataloged the items they unpacked on that important first day. Because they were the first things unpacked, these urgent first items would be the things that add the most value to their lives, right?

Many families found the most value in items of utility.

Holly Auch, a multi-room partyer from Brunswick, Maryland, unpacked "essentials: toothbrushes, toothpaste, hairbrush, outfits for me and two toddlers, diapers, wipes. Utensils for preparing and serving food, plates, bowls, forks, spoons, knives, Ziploc bags, can opener, measuring spoon, Magic Eraser, Motrin, bath toys, shampoo, washcloths, bath towels, calendars, pens, ruler, wineglass (!), phone charger, pillows, blankets, white-noise machines, coffee maker and coffee supplies, vitamins, sippy cups, toilet paper, and flushable wipes."

Ian Carter, a multi-room partyer from Fleet, Hampshire, England, unpacked his "computer, some financial records, a single pen, a scanner, and a bass guitar." He also had dinner guests that evening, which caused him to unbox "several plates, a kettle, tea, coffee, glasses, and cutlery." The experiment gave Ian and his guests plenty to talk about that evening.

Other partyers unboxed only a few items that first day: Autumn Duffy, a one-room partyer from Toano, Virginia, unpacked "a dress, a sweater, all my daily hygiene products." While Ellie Dobson unpacked "all my backpacking gear because I'm going camping today. Except, when I pulled it all out, I realized I didn't even need to bring most of it."

Once the party was over, participants had the opportunity to determine the next step for their excess: sell, donate, recycle, or keep. Many partyers chose to let go; some retained things for the future. We'll continue to unpack their stories throughout this book.

MINIMALIST RULE FOR LIVING WITH LESS

Just for When Rule

So far, we've established that you want to let go of the junk you're clinging to "just in case," and we've determined when it's appropriate to keep a small stock of emergency items, but what about the things you *know* you'll need in the future? We call these "just for when" items, and they're totally fine, within reason. These are usually consumables, and although they seem similar, they are different from those sneaky JIC items—because you're *certain* you'll use them. Nobody purchases their toilet paper one square at a time, their soap one droplet at a time, their toothpaste one nurdle at a time. You buy a small supply of each *just for when* you need them. The key to letting go, then, is to be honest about the trinkets you're saving just in case you *might* need them, and the goods you acquire just for when you *will* need them.

Coda: Stuff

Howdy! Ryan Nicodemus here. I'll be here at these end-chapter sections throughout the book to help you reflect on what you've read and to consider how you can implement the lessons learned from each chapter.

To get the most out of each of these sections, consider two things:

1. Purchase a companion notebook for the exercises in these sections, as well as for notes and reflections. Date

your entries as you go so you can periodically review your progress.

2. Find an accountability partner to join you on your journey. You can do many of the exercises together, or you can schedule a regular time each week to meet for coffee and discuss the answers and reflections recorded in your notebooks.

The companion notebook and an accountability partner will help you be more engaged with these codas, and the more engaged you are in this process, the more growth you'll realize as a result. Take action to take control!

Now that Joshua has had the opportunity to wholly explore how our relationship with stuff affects our lives, I'd like to take some time to consider how that relationship specifically affects *you*. To do that, I've got a few questions and exercises I'd like to share.

QUESTIONS ABOUT STUFF

First, answer the following questions. Be honest. Be considerate. Be rigorous. Your future self will appreciate your hard work, contemplation, and candor.

1. How much is *enough* for you and your household? Be specific: amount of bedrooms, televisions, coats in the closet. Think closely about the things that actually add value to your life.
2. What are you afraid to let go of? Why?
3. What is your freedom worth? What are you willing to give up to be free?
4. What is the real cost (beyond the financial cost) of holding on to your possessions? Stress? Anxiety? Discontent?

5. How will shedding the excess make room for a more meaningful and enjoyable life? Be specific. The clearer your vision, the more leverage you'll have while decluttering.

THE DOS OF STUFF

Next, what did you learn about your relationship with your material possessions in this chapter? What will stick? What lessons will
encourage you to let go of the excess and live more deliberately?
Here are five immediate actions you can take today:

- **Understand your benefits.** Make a list of all the benefits you'll
  experience with less clutter.
- **Establish your rules.** Using the Minimalist Rules for Living with
  Less introduced in this chapter, identify the rules you will start
  using today. If a particular rule doesn't fit your situation, feel free
  to modify it or create your own.
- **Create your "stuff budget."** To help regulate your things, create a
  stuff budget by following these steps:
  - Choose a room you want to declutter.
  - Open your journal to a fresh page, and at the top of the
    page write the three different categories: Essential, Nones-
    sential, and Junk (No Junk Rule).
  - List every item in that room under its appropriate
    category.
  - Ask yourself whether everything in the Essential category
    honestly fits there. If not, recast it as Nonessential or even
    Junk. Repeat with the remaining categories.
- **Relinquish your stuff.** At this point, you will have leftover junk that
  needs to be donated or recycled. It'll be easy to get caught up in
  emotional attachments. So, if you're attached to a particular item

but you know it must go, think of how you would feel if it spontaneously combusted. Or imagine how it could add far greater value
to someone else's life. If you are afraid that one day you will forget
the memory associated with the item, take a picture to help trigger
the memory in the future.

- **Find your support.** Today, find at least one person who will support you in your journey: a friend, family member, neighbor,
colleague. Or you can find online communities of open-minded
people willing to help (Minimalist.org is one such resource).
Also, there's always the option of hiring a professional organizer
in your local area; they understand that the best way to organize
is to let go.

THE DON'TS OF STUFF

Finally, let's consider the stumbling blocks of material possessions.
Here are five things you'll want to avoid, beginning today, if you
want to steer clear of re-cluttering your life:

- Don't expect to get rid of everything at once. It took time to acquire those possessions, and it will take time to let go.
- Don't let others' expectations dictate your decisions regarding
your possessions. The only standards you must live up to are your
own.
- Don't assume you'll be miserable without an item. The truth
is that if you aren't happy with yourself, no *thing* will make you
happy.
- Don't hold on to possessions just in case you might need them
someday in some nonexistent future.
- Don't just organize your things—minimize them! Organizing
often turns into well-organized hoarding.

RELATIONSHIP 2 | TRUTH

I received a panicked voicemail from Mom two days before Christmas. The year was 2008, and she had just moved to Florida a few months earlier to avoid the midwestern winters that had plagued her first sixty-three years. When I returned her call that evening, after a busy workday, she spoke through sobs as she told me about the stage 4 lung cancer that was eating away at her body. "This can't be true!" I thought aloud. Unable to find the words to comfort her, I stared at the phone in denial, paralyzed by helplessness.

After learning about Mom's illness, I spent much of 2009 in St. Pete, shuttling her from doctor to doctor, trying in vain to keep her cancer from metastasizing. As she grew weaker, I worked hard to repair our tenuous relationship. Her alcoholism had made for a less-than-ideal childhood. She became sober during my high school years, but the damage of the previous decade—the drinking, the uncertainty, the lies—had strained our connection. I moved out the day I turned eighteen, and within a few years, she had returned to the bottle.

I remember visiting Mom in the county jail on my twenty-first birthday. A month earlier, she had been arrested for her second DUI and was sentenced to sixty days. Somehow she had charmed the guards into turning the visitation area into a make-shift birthday-party room. I wish I had pictures from that surreal day: Mom standing proudly, all four feet and eleven inches of her, dressed in her orange Warren Correctional Institution jumper, presenting a bouquet of multicolored balloons in front of a back-drop of mental-hospital-white walls and burly corrections officers; me, at six foot two, towering over Mom, embracing the small woman and then eating store-bought vanilla birthday cake with her and a hand-ful of inmates.

> AS WE BEGIN TO SORT THROUGH OUR EXCESS POSSESSIONS, WE ARE OFTEN CONFRONTED BY A CASCADE OF PROFOUND AND UNEXPECTED TRUTHS.

In the years that followed, she seemed to wean herself off the booze again, though I remained cautious, avoiding the source of the pain, not unlike a child who might avoid a stovetop burner after being scorched throughout his childhood. But my avoidance was detrimental to our relationship. There was a war being fought inside me, between my mind and my heart. My mind encouraged me to keep my distance, but my heart never stopped loving Chloe Millburn.

It was easy to love her, after all. Mom was kind and caring and loving. Each year on Thanksgiving, regardless of her own finan-cial problems and personal demons, she organized a Thanksgiv-ing feast for the people who were (shockingly) less fortunate than us. A local church offered up their kitchen and gymnasium. A Boy Scouts troop came through with tables and chairs. Two local grocery stores donated the turkeys and hams, the boxed stuffing and dehydrated mashed potatoes, the canned cranberries and gravy and soda pop. A local seamstress supplied the tablecloths and napkins. And members of Mom's church provided a mosaic of plates and cutlery. Each year, Mom set aside her own problems and fed more than 200 people in that cobbled-together cafeteria. Her benevolence wasn't limited to the holiday season, though—it constantly emanated through the cracks, like a thousand-watt lightbulb trapped in a black box—all she needed was a reason to shine.

A Crisis of Belonging

As we begin to sort through our excess possessions, we are often confronted by a cascade of profound and unexpected truths. Truth is simple, but *simple* isn't *easy*. It's *easy* to hide behind our deficiencies, excuses, programming, habits, and possessions, but this prevents us from living a life that's congruent with the truth. Yet we hide because the alternative—facing the truth that our culture has handed us expectations that have broken us—is overwhelming. So we create a facade, built on lies and exaggerations, that doesn't comport with reality. The more we complicate our lives with these untruths, the more anxious and depressed we feel—and the more we would benefit from simplifying, because simplicity exposes the truth that's buried beneath the lies of complexity.

THERE ARE NO SHORTCUTS; THERE ARE ONLY DIRECT PATHS.

When I spoke with the journalist Johann Hari about his book *Lost Connections: Uncovering the Real Causes of Depression—and the Unexpected Solutions*, he explained that we don't have a problem with depression and anxiety as much as we have a crisis of meaning. Hari's book highlights the nine main causes of depression, two of which involve human biology, but the major factors that have rapidly increased depression in the Western world throughout the last century involve disconnection from a meaningful life.

This was certainly the case with my mother. Her fall into depression and substance abuse didn't occur until she'd lost her connection with worthwhile work, other people, and meaningful values (three of Hari's nine causes), which led to a loss of hope (another cause). Yet there were times when she willingly walked away from alcohol, but each time it wasn't as though she was running away from the beer or wine—it was because she had something meaningful to run toward. "The opposite of addiction is *not* sobriety," Hari said. "The opposite of addiction is connection."

I spoke with Mayor Pete Buttigieg of South Bend, Indiana, about this topic during his 2020 presidential campaign. Like me, he hails from an industrial midwestern city that has fallen on hard times since the deindustrialization of the so-called rust belt, which presented a bevy of problems for the residents of his city. What Buttigieg realized, after interacting with thousands of citizens, is that the thing that undergirds problems from increased crime and drug abuse to unemployment and blight is what he refers to as a "crisis of belonging." You see, when everything seemed hunky-dory in South Bend, people felt like they *belonged* to something greater than themselves: they belonged to a workforce and a community that gave them hope for their future. It was only when they lost that hope that despair crept in. And when despair takes over, we create a false truth about the world around us—a self-fulfilling narrative that says, "Nothing is worthwhile and this can't get better, so I might as well give up."

That's what happened to my mother. Instead of facing the truth that living is accompanied by some degree of difficulty, she developed a nihilism that saturated everything: "Because we're poor, because times are hard, because we don't have what we want," she thought, "alcohol is the off-ramp from the misery." We all fall victim to this line of thinking at some point. We look for the easy way out because attending to the truth is messy.

Jason Segedy, an urban planner for the city of Akron, Ohio, another rust belt city that has faced its own unique set of challenges since the 1970s, talks incisively about why this problem isn't merely economic in nature: "There are plenty of people, and there is plenty of economic activity, in most of these regions. There's even a lot of wealth, and there are many highly educated residents. Despite what some academics who don't live here think, Dayton [or South Bend or Akron] won't be disappearing. The issue isn't that there is no wealth or economic activity in these places. It's not that there are no jobs, or that there is no opportunity. The issue is the extreme geographic disparity between the urban core neighborhoods and those in the suburbs. Those disparities are worse in the rust belt than anywhere else in the country." In other words, for a multitude of reasons, we've grown disconnected— literally (*geographically*) and figuratively (*interpersonally*).

Obviously, this lack of connection is not limited to the industrial Midwest. We see the same disconnection throughout the rest of our society—not just in the poor and disenfranchised neighborhoods like the one in which I grew up. The environmentalist Bill McKibben, author of *Deep Economy: The Wealth of Communities and the Durable Future*, has found that as a person's floor space increases, the number of close friends he or she can depend on decreases. Meaning that as we obtain larger homes and more status and greater wealth, we often grow disconnected from the very things that make us feel alive: community, cooperation, communication, participation, problem solving, and enriching experiences.

Ex-Rated Truth

It was clear that, notwithstanding her troubles, my mother was a loving woman, and the characteristic that most defined her was a rollicking sense of humor. With the cunning wit of a politically incorrect standup comic, her jokes seemed incongruous with her aging-church-lady-wearing-a-thick-brimmed-hat appearance.

In her final years, as Mom reflected on her life, she often said she wanted to write a memoir titled *Ex-Rated: The Explicit Life of an Ex-Nun, Ex-Stewardess, Ex-Secretary, Ex-Wife, and Ex-Alcoholic*. She never got around to it, but I fondly remember the highlights because they shaped my childhood.

Growing up, nothing brought Mom more joy than telling raunchy jokes to me and my brother, Jerome, and the band of neighborhood kids who kept our screen door working overtime.

We lived in an almost all-black neighborhood. I say "almost" because there were two exceptions: Mom and me, the only white folks. Even my brother, Jerome, was black (he still is, last time I checked). It would not have occurred to me to mention this detail if it weren't for Mom's irreverent sense of humor.

A few weeks before I turned thirteen, Mom decided that Jerome and I, and a handful of pubescent friends from the neighborhood, needed to celebrate the beginning of summer with a barbecue, so she ushered us to Pleasant Park, located on Pleasant Street, a thin plastic sack full of charcoal, hot dogs, buns, and condiments in tow. In retrospect, the park's name, and the name of the street on which it resided, seems mordant considering the amount of dilapidation in our neighborhood. There's a thin line between aspiration and irony.

As my friends and I dribbled up and down the disintegrating asphalt, sinking mid-range jumpers into a couple rusty rims,

Mom cooked the wieners on the park's tiny iron grill until they were sufficiently burnt. Soon, the paper plates came out and the preservative-laden buns were split open and lunch was served. We were slathering ketchup and mustard onto our dogs when my friend, a diminutive, curious kid named Judton, looked at his plate, and then at my mom, and asked, "Where do hot dogs come from?"

A mischievous smile broke across Mom's face.

She looked at my brother, and then at me, and then at Judton and said, "Depends on the type."

"The type?" Judton asked.

"Regular hot dogs come from pigs," she paused for effect. "But foot-long hot dogs come from black pigs."

The park erupted in laughter. "How could this little old white lady be this cool?" they asked each other.

Look, I know this joke plays into a particular stereotype, but it was never Mom's intention to sully anyone. It was always the opposite: she loved people with her quips and witticisms. And the fact of the matter is the neighborhood kids loved Mom effusively, not despite her off-color jokes, but because of them.

I think it was Kafka who said, "Life's most difficult issues can be discussed only through jokes." Or maybe I made that up. I'm not entirely sure. I swear I remember reading it in my twenties, but I've never been able to locate the exact quote again. Either way, it certainly rings true. Society's truth tellers aren't our staid politicians or corporate executives; the real truth tellers are comedians like Dave Chappelle, Jerrod Carmichael, and, without a doubt, my mother.

Of course, as a kid, I took for granted Mom's inappropriate rejoinders. Yet because she was so comfortable with illicit topics, at ease in her own body and willing to discuss any subject without judgment or shame, I've had the privilege of never feeling restrained or embarrassed by sexuality or intimacy or sensitive subjects. Her prurient stories shed a light on the bliss and the burdens of post-pubescent life years before I shaved a single hair on my face.

After an "excruciatingly boring" five-year term being "married to Jesus," which is how she described her time living in a convent, Mom moved to Chicago with her best friend, my godmother, Robyn, to become a stewardess, which allowed her to explore the world, or at least the parts of the world within Delta's reach. Not only is that how she met her first husband, Brian, a rich playboy who owned a chain of grocery stores in Bermuda and who cheated on her openly and frequently, but it was also her introduction to the "free love" movement that shaped much of her post-vestal life.

Because Mom was blond and pretty and petite and confident and kind, she received endless attention from men, especially the famous ones who boarded her aircraft. And because Mom herself was independent and unencumbered by taboo, she didn't have a

problem showing men a good time during her off-hours as they came through O'Hare International. According to Mom, one of those men was Jim Brown, the famous running back for the Cleveland Browns, who she joked was "sweet and funny and big in more ways than one." She even knew a young Laurence Tureaud, more than a decade before he was the famous Mr. T. At the time, he was simply a gold-chain-draped nightclub bouncer who worked for the bar at the bottom of Mom's high-rise apartment building. She never shared the particulars with me, though I could read between the lines.

But even during the best times, it wasn't all ponies and rainbows. For every ten Jim Browns there was one deplorable, like Father David, the charming priest who impregnated Mom and then forced her to have an abortion. Although Mom survived this type of abuse more than once, she felt it was important not to be defined by her victimhood. She didn't repress it—she talked about it and expressed the weight of the experiences she carried—but she didn't let it shackle her to the past. "The truth will set you free, but not until it is finished with you" is my favorite line from *Infinite*

Jest, David Foster Wallace's novel about addiction and loneliness, because it appends a common platitude with reality. Yes, talking about the truth, no matter how dark, was difficult for Mom, but once the difficulty was finished, it set her free. And that freedom created a sense of humor that illuminated even the darkest of times.

On my nineteenth birthday, Mom presented me with a gift that was covered with extravagant wrapping paper and an assortment of ornate bows and ribbons and streamers. I pulled back the paper and accoutrements to reveal a pair of Groucho glasses. You know the ones: those silly nose-eyebrow-and-mustache spectacles you can buy at a lowbrow trinket store at the mall. Except on this pair, instead of a nose resting beneath the glasses, there was a large, semi-erect penis.

Mom and I spent the better part of the next decade regifting those glasses to each other. I'd FedEx them to her secretarial job. A few months later, she'd pay a courier to interrupt a corporate meeting to hand deliver them to me. The cycle continued even when she was dying of cancer: I sent them to Florida with a "get well soon" card. In turn, the next time I visited, I walked into her hospital room to see her fifteen pounds lighter, her hair thinning from chemotherapy, reclined in her adjustable bed, wearing thick glasses and a giant penis on her face. Indeed, life's most difficult situations require levity. Otherwise we will choke on our own sorrow.

Keep in mind, this was a woman who was an alcoholic for the majority of the second half of her life. But she was also a woman who fed the homeless and donated countless hours to charities and attended Catholic mass every week, sober or not. It's almost like I'm writing about two different people. But aren't we all two different people? We are saintly sinners, loving jerks, and authentic frauds. We are each a duality—three-dimensional beings living in a world of two-dimensional expectations.

Because of our tangled lives, it is possible to be exceedingly loving and still inflict pain. Truly, we tend to cause the most pain to the people we love the most. We're careless with what we love, and if we're careless with anything for long enough, it breaks.

Comfort Is a Liar

My marriage was over years before it was over. At first, I didn't know it was ending. Eventually, though, as the years passed and the dissatisfaction mounted, I simply didn't have the courage to end it. Nor did I have the courage to tell the truth. So I lied. I pretended everything was okay and it would magically get better—that's the lie I told myself.

Needless to say, ignoring the problem is not the solution. While you don't want to overreact, it's also a bad idea to underreact. If a crowded theater is on fire, you don't want to panic and trample others on your way to the exit. But you don't want to keep watching the movie, either, no matter how comfortable your seat is.

I was comfortable in my marriage. If you would have ranked my comfort level at age twenty-seven, it was a solid six out of ten—just enough to avoid change. But I wasn't happy, content, or joyous; I was merely comfortable enough to do nothing. Because if I changed, I'd experience discomfort. And who wants that? But when you look at every great success throughout history, you'll find that discomfort—and even suffering—is the place from which great people grow. Discomfort is where the truth sits—it exposes the flaws, the inaccuracies, the incongruities—and comfort is a liar.

Keri and I met in high school, but we didn't start dating until I was nineteen or twenty. I'm uncertain of the exact time because it was a slow-burning courtship. But before I knew it, we were living together, and within a few short years, as our relationship snowball accumulated mass, we were engaged, and then married, and then building our first house and amassing consumer debt and living a life that felt unintentional. We were following predetermined steps instead of living a thoughtful and deliberate life.

AS WE OBTAIN LARGER HOMES AND MORE STATUS AND GREATER WEALTH, WE OFTEN GROW DISCONNECTED FROM THE VERY THINGS THAT MAKE US FEEL ALIVE.

It's a cliché to say "We loved each other, but we weren't *in* love." But most clichés are grounded in profound truth. According to Christopher Ryan, PhD, author of *Sex at Dawn* and *Civilized to Death*, intimate relationships contain three essential elements: chemistry, compatibility, and love. Humans tend to enter into relationships based on one—sometimes two—of these factors. Maybe there's an initial sexual attraction (chemistry), maybe there are shared interests (compatibility), or maybe there's a deep connection that propels the relationship forward (love). Over time, however, the absence of any of these elements creates thoroughgoing dissatisfaction and, eventually, pain.

This is true even if one or two of the elements are strong. You can have great sex (chemistry), and still have an unfulfilling relationship. You can agree about finances and lifestyle (compatibility), and still have an unsatisfying relationship. You can care deeply about each other (love), and still not want to be in a relationship together. That last one was the case for me: I loved and respected Keri immensely. But love isn't enough. We need all three elements to thrive. Keri and I had a spark of chemistry early on, but it never turned into a flame. And, more important, we weren't compatible in myriad ways: our desires, interests, goals, beliefs, and values did not align. Hence, the slow-mounting frustration that followed our wedding vows.

I was too afraid to face the truth of our relationship, the truth that what we had wasn't working. Instead of simply sitting down with Keri at some point and entering into a difficult discussion about our relationship and its deficiencies, my own cowardice eventually led me to step outside the marriage in an attempt to find the elements that were missing. This is why many people cheat more than once. As soon as the pleasure is gone, the relational deficit is once again exposed. And the cycle of lies continues.

The One Lie

In my favorite relationship book, *Some Thoughts About Relationships*, Colin Wright outlines a series of "relationship policies" upon which all meaningful relationships—intimate or otherwise—are built. Among these policies are the Argument Policy, the Jealousy Policy, and the Cheating Policy. But my favorite might be something called The One Policy:

> From a very young age, many of us are told stories about The One: a mystical person who is placed on this planet for us and us alone. It's our "hero's journey" to find this individual, wherever they may be. If pop culture is to be believed, there will be a series of comedic situations and dramatic adventures that lead up to our finding them.
>
> In real life, however, The One is a concept that isn't

just irrational, it's potentially harmful. The idea that there's someone out there who is customized to make you whole implies that you're not capable of being complete on your own. It also implies that everyone other than The One is just a stepping-stone toward grand fulfillment, which is a horrible way to approach relationships.

Wright goes on to explain that we're capable of loving more than one person throughout our lives. Or even concurrently. You can love your daughter, your husband, and your mother at the same time. Thus, there isn't a magical *one*. "*You* are The One," Wright says. "You are the only person in the world who can complete and fulfill you, and ensure your happiness. Everyone else is a potential (hopefully) wonderful addition to that fated situation. You are born complete, you die complete, and you decide whom you spend your time with in between."

From the onset of our relationship, Keri and I were so focused on finding someone who "completed" us—hoping to mold the other person to fit each of our belief systems—that we didn't realize we were already complete on our own. And instead of the relationship multiplying our collective qualities, it stifled them because we weren't honest about our compatibility. We had diametrically opposed views on consequential matters: kids, communities, and finances were among the areas upon which we could not agree. The resentment from these grievances eventually spilled into the rest of our lives, creating an overflow of unspoken discontent.

Neither of us was "wrong"; we just wanted different outcomes. If you like rock music and I like jazz, neither of us is in error, though we might not enjoy going to the same concert together.

Certainly, Keri and I would have benefited from communicating better before we tied the knot:

Do our values align?
What does your ideal partner look like?
How do you deal with challenges?
What are your nonnegotiables?

"You want to kill Godzilla when he's a baby," the famous motivational speaker Tony Robbins once remarked. "Don't wait until he's taking over the city." Had Keri and I done that—had we asked the relevant questions up front—we probably wouldn't have gotten married in the first place. But we did get married, and then I ignored all the exit signs—all the opportunities to end the relationship without increasing the pain. Eight years in, Godzilla was a full-blown monster lurking on the outskirts of our marriage, ready to burn it all down. We were lying to ourselves.

SINCERE PEOPLE DON'T CARE WHAT KIND OF CAR YOU DRIVE, WHERE YOU LIVE, OR THE BRAND OF THE CLOTHES YOU WEAR.

When two people hold values that have them traveling in different directions, one of two things is bound to happen: either one person conforms and is unhappy, or the other person gets dragged and is unhappy. Either way, heartbreak is around the bend. And if you pretend nothing's askew, the pain only gets worse.

Another cliché seems appropriate here: "It's not you, it's me." Although that wasn't entirely true for my marriage. "It wasn't her, nor was it me—it was *us*" seems more apropos, albeit less pithy. Keri was a great friend, and although I had good intentions when I entered the relationship, I transformed into a bad husband over the course of our marriage because I wasn't able to experience happiness traveling in her direction, and I wasn't willing to let go of the relationship.

The irony is that we both kept the relationship going because we didn't want to hurt the other person's feelings. We believed that honesty would destroy our marriage, as though the truth was mean or malicious and the only way forward was to hide reality from the world. But truth is the only thing that can preserve a relationship. Even when it's uncomfortable or difficult or painful, truth is the glue that strengthens a bond.

Mistakes and Dumb Decisions

I cheated on my wife the day after my mother died. I'd like to tell you that it was a mistake, but it wasn't. It was worse than that. Adultery is a despicable act, the deepest betrayal, a type of murder. But even after the victimizer kills the relationship, the victim continues to suffer. And it's never the result of just one "mistake"; even a single instance of infidelity is spawned from a series of untold destructive decisions.

A politician commits a white-collar crime, gets caught, and says he "made a big mistake." A businesswoman omits a chunk of revenue on her taxes and says something similar to the IRS. A teenager joyrides in his mother's car without permission and later fesses up to his "mistake."

But these aren't mistakes—they're dumb decisions.

Selecting the incorrect answer on a test is a mistake; not studying for that test is a dumb decision. The mistake was something you did without intention; the negligent decision was made intentionally—often without regard for the consequences.

It's easy to dismiss regrettable decisions by reclassifying them as mistakes. It takes the edge off, softens the blow. But it's also disingen-uous. Recasting a careless decision as a mistake removes your role in the indiscretion. And it's much easier to live with your decisions if they aren't your fault. Consequently, you're more likely to make the same thoughtless decision repeatedly if you simply consider it a mistake.

We all make mistakes. We all make poor decisions. They are part of the human experience. We can celebrate our mistakes and learn from our reckless decisions, but let's not confuse one with the other. If we admit when we mess up, and take ownership of our decisions, we'll find the most noble path forward—the truth. Yes, owning up is more difficult than obfuscating, but the truth is difficult precisely because it's the only thing worth pursuing. Everything else is a lie.

The Cost of Lies

A fairy tale well told isn't more true. Sadly, one of humanity's de-fining characteristics is our ability to lie.

"People lie so that others will form beliefs that are not true," says the neuroscientist Sam Harris, author of *Lying*, a book that ar-gues that lying—even the tiniest white lie—is *never* appropriate,* and that, fundamentally, we lie because we want to pretend to be someone we're not.

What's surprising, though, is that we're most likely to lie to our closest friends and family members. In a study titled "Everyday Lies in Close and Casual Relationships," Bella M. DePaulo and Deborah A. Kashy found that 10 percent of communication be-tween spouses is deceptive. This finding seems counterintuitive at first. You would think we'd be most honest with the people

---

* Unless it's a lie told in self-defense to avoid physical violence.

we love, wouldn't you? But according to "Deceptive Behavior in Social Relationships," a study in the *Journal of Psychology*, "People tell lies when their behavior violates other people's expectations for them. Because close relationship partners have more expectations for each other, the likelihood that expectations will be violated and lies will be told is greater in close relationships than in casual ones." We simply take for granted those closest to us.

No matter how you slice it, human beings have a complicated relationship with truth telling. Somewhere around age four, we discover the power of deceit. We begin with "white lies" that test the boundaries of truth, and as those boundaries expand, we learn how to mislead and cheat and manipulate others with falsehoods. We don't, however, immediately understand the cost of our lies. Nor do we grasp the miraculous power of the truth.

Lying is tempting the same way overeating is tempting—it's easy, and it provides us with instant gratification. A lie allows us to shift blame, skirt responsibility, and deflect from our own deficiencies in the moment; it creates a shortcut toward short-term reward. In reality, though, there are no shortcuts; there are only direct paths. And truth is the most direct path. But telling the truth is difficult the same way planting a garden is difficult—we'd rather eat a Twinkie today than put in the work to reap the benefits of a healthy garden next year.

The classic HBO docudrama *Chernobyl* begins with a simple question: "What is the cost of lies?" What we soon discover, over the course of five beautifully crafted episodes, is that our lies cost us *everything*. Lies strip us of our integrity, honor, rectitude, virtue, and trust. Lies cost us friendships and love, meaningful experiences and worthwhile interactions, respect and freedom. And in extreme cases like *Chernobyl*, lies can cost people their lives.

The cost of the truth, on the other hand, is drudgery and diligence and delayed gratification, but the reward is a peace of mind so great that the labor is *always* worth the price.

"Honesty is a gift we can give to others," Harris writes in his book about lying. "It is also a source of power and an engine of simplicity. Knowing that we will attempt to tell the truth, whatever the circumstances, leaves us with little to prepare for. We can simply be ourselves."

Honesty is an engine of simplicity. Just consider that for a moment. If that's true, then why do we have such a difficult time telling the truth? Well, because simplicity isn't easy.

More Than One Kind of Truth

It's difficult to talk about "the truth" because truth means different things to different people. It might be true that chocolate is your favorite flavor of ice cream, and it's also true that two plus two equals four. That's because some "truths" are subjective opinions, while others are objective facts.

You might refer to subjective truths—such as religion or food preferences—as beliefs or personal truths (as in the overused phrase "You have to live *your* truth!"). It's impossible for these types of truths to be "false" because of their perspectival nature. After all, you wouldn't tell someone their preference for vanilla ice cream was false.

Objective truths—like gravity or arithmetic—are what you might call principles, rules, or laws. They apply to everyone all the time because facts don't require your belief; they are universally true irrespective of your beliefs. No matter what you think the answer is, two dollars plus two dollars will always equal four dollars.

Regardless of whether a truth is subjective or objective, one thing is clear: the more difficult the truth, the harder it is to admit—especially the truths that have been covered up with lies.

Some truths are expressed publicly; others we try to keep inside. Much of what you read in the introduction to this book—Ryan's and my travails with consumerism, discontentment, and childhood dysfunction—are of the first kind: hard truths we've nevertheless been willing to share with the world over the last decade, not all at once, but slowly, expanding the bounds of our comfort zones one freshly disclosed truth at a time.

Other truths have been harder for Ryan and me to discuss, even as time has passed. Not until this year has Ryan gone into detail about his opioid addiction—the $5,000-a-month habit that fueled his downward spiral. We're going to expand our comfort zones even further throughout this book by writing about these truths: the truths we've kept bottled up until now, many of which we've been ashamed to admit.

MINIMALIST RULE FOR LIVING WITH LESS

Spontaneous Combustion Rule

Your material possessions cause more stress than you realize. As you grow more and more burdened by past purchases, the discontent heats up. But you needn't wait until the temperature is scorching. This is why we invented the Spontaneous Combustion Rule, which starts with a simple question: If this item spontaneously combusted, would I feel relieved? If so, give yourself permission to let it go!

Shame and Insignificance

We need to talk about shame for a moment. Which means we must also talk about guilt. Although these two terms are frequently used interchangeably, they are fundamentally different. Guilt tells us something about our *actions*: we broke a rule, hurt someone's feelings, or acted incongruously with our ideal self, and now we feel awful about it. But shame says something about *who we are*—about our identity.

"Shame informs you of an internal state of inadequacy, dishonor, or regret," according to Mary C. Lamia, writing in *Psychology Today*. That's why our hidden truths are so difficult to discuss. We think that if we let them out, our incompetence or powerlessness will be revealed, leaving us vulnerable or helpless.

But letting the truth out is how we become free. It might be uncomfortable, but it's better to feel discomfort than shame, because discomfort evanesces with time, but shame persists and builds upon itself.

While we can get over our guilt by fessing up to our mistakes and poor decisions—"I admit I screwed up, now let's move on"— shame can linger after a confession because now the world knows the truth: "I'm not who I pretended to be." And if everyone hears this truth, we believe we instantly become less exceptional than the perfect persona we projected. To make matters worse, this fall from grace destroys our sense of significance, which is a fundamental human need.

Recently, my daughter, Ella, scored her soccer team's only two goals. Immediately after the game, her mother and I praised her for her *skill*; we were careful, however, not to compliment her for her innate *talent*. "You played a great game" is more powerful than "You're so good!" The former praises her actions; the latter comments on her aptitude. Because a healthy sense of significance is elevated by specificity, we elaborated on what made Ella's playing "great," citing specific examples of what she did, when and how she did it, and why we were proud of her actions. *Earned* significance strengthens over time because our self-worth increases as we gain a sense of competence, accomplishment, and purpose from our endeavors. A year from now, Ella will be better at soccer, and she'll earn a robust sense of self-worth along the way.

> DISCOMFORT IS WHERE THE TRUTH SITS— IT EXPOSES THE FLAWS, THE INACCURACIES, THE INCONGRU- ITIES—AND COM- FORT IS A LIAR.

The opposite path—*unearned* significance—is paved with instant gratification. This type of significance is fleeting, which causes us to resort to toxic behaviors in order to maintain a modicum of attention: "Hey, look at me!"—as if yelling loud enough will somehow make us more important. Then, when shouting no longer works, we resort to silly stunts: the drunken Facebook posts, the attention-seeking tweets, the shirt-off-in-the-mirror Instagram photos. None of which serve the greater good. Finally, when innocuous attention seeking stops working, we push further toward the obscene. Stepping over ethical and moral boundaries, we resort to insults, self-harm, and even violence. These are surefire ways to feel important in the moment, but these brief bursts of significance disappear shortly after each offense. That's because instant gratification isn't actually gratifying—not in the long term.

Sure, attention-seeking behavior might attract scads of attention, much like a car crash—people can't help but slow down and eye the wreckage—but the onlookers don't stick around to admire the post-accident cleanup, which leaves the attention seeker feeling empty and alone, further fueling the feeling of insignificance that instigated their behavior in the first place. Naturally, this only amplifies the shame they sought to avoid.

That said, shame isn't always a "bad" thing. It is helpful insofar as it encourages you to do your best. There are times when it's perfectly appropriate to feel shameful—namely, when you continually act against the interests of your future self. If you wish to become a writer but you never write, if you aspire to get in shape but you avoid exercise, if you hope for a promotion but you're unwilling to do the work, shame is a natural response. It is an emotional punishment for continually doing the "wrong" thing.

Unfortunately, all too often the natural response to shame isn't to correct one's actions, but rather to retreat, withdraw, ruminate, and deny the problem even exists. Done consistently, this defeatist cycle leads to regret about past (in)actions—and despair about what the future holds.

The key to eradicating shame, then, is this: find significance *not* in the persona you portray, or the person you were, but in the best version of yourself. Then align your actions with that best self. You do this by starting with an admission of past indiscretions, which will resolve the ever-present guilt. But then you go further. You refuse to hide. You show up every day in tiny, unexciting ways. You drudge through the drudgery, even when it isn't fun or sexy or stimulating. You behave in a way that will make your future self proud. Not someone else's future self—*your* future self—because living up to other people's ideals is what created the shame in the first place.

Like everyone else you have ever met, you have told myriad lies. You have made mistakes and disappointing decisions. But, going forward, you don't need to be a liar. You are better than that. You have the capacity to be honest—with yourself and others—and the ability to care about the truth. Because if you don't care about the truth, you don't care about anything.

Yes, I have personally made shameful decisions in my life. I have acted lazily. I have lied. I even cheated on my first wife. But the past does not equal the future, and I don't have to be the same person I was. I can learn from him, and be grateful for—not proud of, but grateful for—his errors without needing to repeat them.

Some questions worth considering before we move on: Are you ashamed of changing careers because of what someone else might think about your decision, or are you running away from something? Are you ashamed of your body because of someone else's idea of beauty, or are you not as fit as you'd like to be? Are you ashamed of your creative output because the next person is more "productive," or do you realize you could do better? Are you ashamed you're not married because society has set an expectation, or are you searching for a partner with whom you can share your life?

These are personal questions that don't have universal answers. And thus, only you have the right answer for *you* because what's abnormal to you may be perfectly normal for me. And vice versa. Allowing others' expectations to shape our desires and behavior and, ultimately, our lives will always lead to guilt and shame because we'll never be able to live up to everyone else's conflicting values. As long as you're not harming anyone, you need only live congruent to your own standards—everything else leads to discontent. Put plainly: when you live a congruent life, you're never worried about clearing your browser history.

A Truth More Valuable Than Silence

Not all truths are equally necessary. We often mistake radical transparency and openness with truth. While all three are forms of truth telling, they are different in important ways, and we do ourselves a disservice when we conflate them.

We hear politicians talk about "having a transparent administration," but we don't actually want a truly transparent government because some things—nuclear codes, for example—must be kept secret to protect us from bad actors. What we want is an honest and responsible government. The same goes for our personal lives. If I were fully transparent, I'd happily write my home address, Social Security number, and mother's maiden name here on these pages. But that level of absorptive detail isn't just unnecessary—it's harmful.

There are times that openness can go too far, too. If I were to walk around the coworking space I'm renting to write this book and tell every man, woman, and puppy what I think about their outfits and meal choices, I'd be obnoxiously "open." I'd also be a jerk. Most things are better left unsaid, either because they are unnecessarily hurtful, or because the cost is too high, or because they don't serve the greater good (or often all three).

INSTANT GRATIFICATION ISN'T ACTUALLY GRATIFYING—NOT IN THE LONG TERM.

That doesn't mean that you should lie if someone approaches you and asks, "What do you think of my new shirt?" Even then, you can be honest without battering them with openness. We needn't be mean to be truthful.

There are also some truths that are not worth stating publicly because the cost is too high. If I were to tell you I'm a Republican, then half the Americans reading this would tune out; ditto if I said I'm a Democrat (I'm actually a registered Independent, but even that carries a small cost). But my political thoughts have little or nothing to do with the message I'm trying to communicate in this book, which means they would actually get in the way of a greater truth: I'm not trying to express a political ideology; I'm attempting to communicate a set of ideas—to show readers how to live a more meaningful life, regardless of their politics.

Or what if I told you I dislike onions and beaches and children? Even if that were true (I plead the Fifth), how would admitting it here, on this page, serve anyone? Some truths are better left unsaid because they add to the noise and get in the way of that which is meaningful. My friend the writer Nate Green once told me, "Speak only when your words are more valuable than silence." If we were to live by that motto, we would all be better listeners, and each of our words would carry more gravitas every time we spoke.

Yet there are times when silence is not the answer. Some truths must be confronted aloud if we want to live a fulfilling life. What are some truths in your own life that you've been afraid to admit publicly but that would ultimately make your life better if you did? It feels callous or even selfish to confess these truths at first—and it's uncomfortable to admit you've been living a life that doesn't comport with the person you want to be—but it's the only way to become the best version of yourself.

Unpacking Truth

Let's check in with some of our Packing Party Case Study partici-pants. At the end of the first day of their experiment, we confronted each partyer about how this experience had elucidated their relation-ship with the truth in the first twenty-four hours. Not surprisingly, since they'd been dealing with physical stuff intensely throughout the day, these initial truths centered on material possessions.

Mae Frankeberger, a one-room partyer from Brooklyn, New York, said, "I try to be conscious of what I have and what I bring into my life, but sometimes I don't scrutinize everything as much as I should. Being truthful about what and who is important in my life is a large part of what I need to work on."

Christin Hewitt, a whole-house partner from Atlanta, Georgia, admitted that "even as a self-proclaimed minimalist, I've been in denial about the amount of things I've accumulated just in the last twelve months! As I sorted, I recognized I didn't need many of these items."

Kaitlin Mobley, a multi-room partner from Savannah, Georgia, confessed that her "relationship with the truth is changing because even though I'm pretty conscious about what I bring into my life, I still cave to the societal pressure of what I 'should' have in my home."

As the weeks unraveled, and as our partners continued to unpack their hoards, more truths were revealed. Ryan and I checked in at the end of each week, prodding each participant to move beyond the possessions and talk about how the experiment had exposed previously unconscious truths in their lives.

After the first week of unpacking, Ellie Dobson found a broader truth about her and her partner's life: "We have an evasive relationship," she said. "We say we know each other, but we avoid actually looking at each other."

After two weeks, Luke Wenger, a whole-house partner from Lenexa, Kansas, peered at his remaining stacks of cardboard and said, "Whatever the 'truth' is, I doubt it's in one of these boxes."

At the end of the full three weeks, many folks had come to terms with the fact they needed far fewer things than they thought, and along the way, they had unpacked some unexpected struggles. One partner realized she struggles with "finding balance" in her life, while another admitted, "I still have trouble deciding what the actual 'truth' is versus what I've been taught to believe."

MINIMALIST RULE FOR LIVING WITH LESS

Ten Most Expensive Possessions Rule

Take a moment to write down your ten most expensive material purchases from the last decade: car, house, jewelry, furniture, purses. Next to that list, make another list with the ten things that add the most value to your life: experiences like catching a sunset with a loved one, watching your kids play baseball, making love with your spouse, eating dinner with your parents. Compare the two lists and discover they share very few things in common. And it's possible there's no overlap at all.

Trapped by Fear

Holly Auch, a Packing Party Case Study participant to whom we were introduced in the previous chapter, learned a striking truth about her relationship with material possessions on the first day of her unpacking experiment. "I rely on stuff to fill a void that I'm afraid of exploring," she said.

Fear is a common theme with people who are starting to confront their stuff. We're afraid to pull back the curtain because we're afraid not of the stuff itself, but of the work that must be done to live a more rewarding life after getting rid of it. Yet if we don't take the first step—if we don't address the clutter that is in the way—how will we make room for the truth?

How, then, do we get past the fear?

Like Holly, we start by acknowledging it. We start by telling the truth. We're all afraid of something. Some of our fears are obvious: spiders, heights, death. Other fears are less concrete, like the fear of loss. Loss of things. Loss of acceptance. Loss of friends. Loss of status. Loss of love.

Fear traps us. It stops us from growing. It prevents us from contributing to other people. It blocks us from living happy, satisfied, fulfilled lives. Fear is the antithesis of freedom; it is, by definition, constricting.

Holly isn't the only person we encountered with a fear of letting go. Many others expressed similar fear-based responses, including Leslie Rogers, a multi-room partyer from Athens, Georgia, who said, "I tie memories and emotions to many of my things. However, because I was not adequately processing my emotions, I was not taking care of these possessions. As they were sitting in boxes or on the floor, some items had gotten broken or soiled by my cats. I was forced to let go of several sentimental items—and it surprisingly felt good! I had procrastinated only out of fear."

Like Leslie, we often hold on to things because we are afraid to get rid of them: we fear losing the things we think we *might* need. We don't just fear the loss of these things, though; we fear the loss of what these things might mean to us in the future. Consequently, we keep holding on to that which we don't even have.

When you express your fears out loud, they commonly sound absurd. Try it. Say, "I'm afraid to get rid of this shirt, book, or phone charger because it would have a serious effect on my life."

Ridiculous, right?

So there's an obvious question we must ask ourselves when we're holding on to something and need to get to the truth: *What am I afraid of?*

Give it a try.

I can't say *no* to that person. What am I afraid of?

I can't write the novel I've always dreamed of writing. What am I afraid of?

I can't learn to play that instrument I've always wanted to play. What am I afraid of?

I can't exercise and eat healthy foods. What am I afraid of?

I can't quit the job I hate to pursue my passion. What am I afraid of?

I can't let go of my coin collection. What am I afraid of?

I can't [fill in the blank]. What am I afraid of?

The answer to this question is almost always illogical:

I'm afraid people won't like me.

They won't respect me anymore.

The people I love won't love me back.

Really? People won't like you if your shirt doesn't have the appropriate logo? People won't respect you if you jettison your mascara? People won't love you if you drive a cheaper car? If that's the case, you're hanging out with some toxic people. But, more likely, you've manufactured these false fears, and it is these manufactured fears that keep you from doing what you want to do with your life.

Sincere people don't care what kind of car you drive, where you live, or the brand of the clothes you wear.

I have good news, though: fears can be overcome. Humans developed their fear response to protect ourselves from imminent danger, but these days it seems we fear almost everything: a slight downturn in the stock market, a negative comment on social media, the mere thought of letting go of a material possession. We choose to be afraid, which means we can also choose to live without fear. When something stands in your way, ask yourself, *What am I afraid of?*

Countless people have chosen to get rid of their fears and move on with a more fulfilling life. But don't take my word for it—try it out for yourself.

Do something you wouldn't normally do.

Donate your favorite shirt.

Get rid of your television.

Recycle your old electronics.

Trash your box of old letters.

Live your life, a better life.

What are you afraid of?

Isn't it time to step away from whatever is preventing you from being free—starting with the excess stuff in your life?

The Night After the Crash

The atmosphere inside the hospice was so thick it was hard to breathe. The overhead lights glowed soft and placid. My chair sat bumped against Mom's bed, her small living quarters decorated with miscellanea, niceties strategically placed to make her feel at home: picture frames, artwork, rosary beads. Next to us, a complex machine with a pixelated LED screen was set up to monitor Mom's vitals. It was switched off. I found myself crying for the first time in my adult life.

As the tears burned my cheeks, and the October sunset shot through the blinds in long, repetitive slats, I apologized to Mom's lifeless body. Peace radiated from her benevolent face, though it felt too cold to touch. Not icy cold, but it lacked life—the temperature of an object, not a person. My sobs spilled out uncontrollably. I didn't even notice them until they were already there, a natural reaction, like tectonic plates shifting inside me, a tremor of emotion.

She looked tiny lying there, fragile and small, as if her gigantic personality never extended to the size of her body. I wanted to hug her, to lift her frail, wilted body and hold her, to somehow shake her back to life, back to this world, and tell her I love her, tell her I'm sorry that I didn't know what to do and that I wasn't the grown-up man I pretended to be, wasn't as strong as she assumed I was. I wanted to tell her I would have done things differently. I wanted to yell this at her—at everyone. Sometimes we don't know how to love the ones we love until they disappear from our lives.

"I'm sorry," I said through the sobs, my shirt wet with my emotions. The room was inhabited by only me and what was left of my mother—her flesh, but not her. She wasn't missing; she just wasn't there anymore. "I'm sorry. I'm sorry. I'm sorry," I repeated, rocking back and forth in my chair with a mental patient's sway.

The tears were a strange catharsis, a release of every spasm of guilt and rage and regret. But they were also a departure for me, those tears, a turning of a page I didn't know needed to be turned.

Eventually it was time to leave when I ran out of tears; there was nothing left for me to say or do. Before hailing a cab back to Mom's apartment, her nurse, Shelly, stopped me in the hallway. She must have seen the wreckage on my features. A fluorescent light flickered overhead as she embraced me with a long hug. A day later we were lying in bed together, Shelly and me. It was the one and only time I've ever cheated on anyone. But when it comes to infidelity, anything greater than zero is an affront to the truth.

A man doesn't cheat on his wife without a serious surplus of self-hatred. Sure, there are other reasons—despair, frustration, desperation, compulsion, lust—but the ceaseless tug of self-hatred is stronger than them all. That's what made me step outside my marriage. I didn't realize it at the time, but I intensely disliked the person

I'd become. And I had been lying to myself for years. I wanted it to stop. Unconsciously, I wanted to shatter the whole thing.

I had avoided the truth for so long, and it finally caught up to me. It didn't hurt only me; it hurt everyone around me. My marriage suffered because I refused to face the truth that we were incompatible, so we both got dragged in a direction we didn't want to go. My relationship with my mother suffered because I was too busy being "successful," and I'll never get that time back with her. My friendships and community suffered because I was focused on myself, but my achievements were hollow and fleeting. My creativity suffered because I was more concerned with consuming than creating, which opened a void in my soul that can't be filled with trinkets.

I spent my twenties pursuing status and success and materialism. But each promotion, each achievement, each new purchase moved me one step further from the truth. I wish I would have known that buying a luxury vehicle wasn't going to make me a better person. I wish I would have questioned what was essential instead of letting outside expectations dictate how I spent my time, money, and attention. I wish I would have realized that alone in an empty room, each of us is already a whole person, and the role of everything else is only to augment, enhance, or amplify our lives, not get in the way.

Coda: Truth

Hey there! Ryan again. After Joshua shared some hard truths throughout this chapter, it's clear that the truth isn't neat and tidy. It's raw. It can be ugly. It's often not "like"-able. But the truth is the truth, and that's what we want to explore today—how your relationship with the truth affects *you*. To do that, I've prepared a few exercises below. Please take your time with each. Really consider what they're asking of you. If you do that, you'll find the truth within the chaos of everyday life.

And remember—record the responses in your journal (and date the entries so you can reflect on your progress). Once you're finished, schedule time with your accountability partner to share what you've learned.

QUESTIONS ABOUT TRUTH

1. What is one essential truth you are hiding right now?
2. How has hiding the truth caused discontent or hurt relationships?
3. What is the worst thing that will happen if you tell the truth? What is the best that will happen?
4. What difficult conversations must you conduct in order to avoid making more regrettable decisions?
5. How will the truth help you grow? How will the lies prevent you from growing?

THE DOS OF TRUTH

Next, what did you learn about truth in this chapter? What will stick? What lessons will encourage you to be more honest in your daily life? Here are five immediate actions you can take today:

- **Acknowledge.** Write down the lies you want to get out in the open.
- **Get uncomfortable.** Out of the lies you wrote down, which one makes you feel the most uncomfortable? How will you confront that lie?

- **Eliminate.** Today, choose one lie that you are willing to stop carrying on. What actions will you take to eliminate this lie?
- **Apologize.** Whom have you hurt by lying? Reach out to them and apologize. How will the experience affect the relationship moving forward?
- **Heal.** Ask for forgiveness from those who have been affected by your lies. Understand you are not entitled to forgiveness, and it may take some time to be forgiven, but now true healing can begin.

THE DON'TS OF TRUTH

Finally, let's discuss the perils of dishonesty. Here are five things you'll want to avoid, beginning today, if you want to be a more honest person:

- Don't assume things are okay and will magically get better on their own.
- Don't convince yourself that hiding the truth makes the situation or your relationships better.
- Don't isolate yourself from others to avoid telling the truth.
- Don't tell more lies to cover up the ones you have already told.
- Don't assume it's impossible to recover others' trust—it takes time and a repeated pattern of honesty to reestablish trust.

RELATIONSHIP 3 | SELF

I never struggled with depression. Until I did. Before that dark cloud arrived in 2019, culminating in what I now call the New Great Depression, I had always considered myself a blind optimist. For years, I was *the* happy person in the room, someone able to find the silver lining in all of life's clouds. Sure, I'd experience sadness and melancholy and mourning, like everyone else, but, even in the darkest of times, my sorrow didn't spiral into depression. I'd always been able to traverse the valley as quickly as possible—to go through it but not sit in it—and then return to the nearby peaks: smile at myself in the mirror when I was down, exercise when I was emotionally tired, and change my language when I was in a psychological rut.

Even in my chaotic twenties, amid the drudgery of the corporate world, I found ways to be elated by the most mundane encounters. Around five each morning, before riding the immense elevator to the eleventh floor, before navigating the fluorescent hallways and cubicle farms on the way to my office, before firing up my desktop computer and BlackBerry and hopping between spreadsheets and emails and instant messages, I'd walk into the coffee shop in my building's atrium and be greeted by a sleepy, obligatory, "How's it going?"

Every day, I'd respond with a smile, a pause, and the same emphatic answer: "Outstanding! How are you?"

Admittedly, this response caught people off guard—especially at first. They expected a standard "Good" or "I'm fine, thanks," but they were met instead with an enthusiasm that's incongruent with the early-morning crowd. The comedian George Carlin said that when people ask you how you're doing, you should always respond with "Great!" because it makes your friends happy and your enemies angry. While I appreciate the sentiment, that's not what I was attempting with my response, which was never disingenuous. I was, in fact, outstanding, because I was paying attention, making an effort to *notice* the extraordinary bits inside life's banal experiences.

> BY REMOVING THE PHYSICAL DISTRACTIONS AROUND US, WE'RE ABLE TO LOOK INSIDE OURSELVES AND BEGIN THE PROCESS OF MENTAL, EMOTIONAL, PSYCHOLOGICAL, AND SPIRITUAL DECLUTTERING.

Years before minimalism entered my life, I discovered my *routine* needn't be defined by its dictionary definition: regular, commonplace, ordinary. Even though the life I lived was relatively unremarkable, something as simple as purchasing a cup of coffee could be a remarkable experience, a chance to live in the moment, no matter how brief.

Some baristas found my enthusiasm jarring—even off-putting—but, in time, nearly everyone warmed to my gusto. "Outstanding?" they'd ask, as if the word itself was a riddle. Soon, a smile would break. "Outstanding. Yeah, I kinda like that!"

"You're welcome to borrow it," I'd say. "It's free and transferable." In time, the staff stopped writing "Joshua" on my coffee cup, opting instead for "Mr. O."

The Art of Noticing

I didn't want people to simply *perceive* me as happy. A miserable person with a smile is still a miserable person. Rather, I responded with verve because I know that, like most people, I'm terrible at being present. But by using language, volume, tone, inflection, physical gestures, and facial expressions, we're able to change our internal state to help us notice and appreciate the present moment, even with its naked imperfections. This is where minimalism is particularly helpful. By removing the physical distractions around us, we're able to look inside ourselves and begin the process of mental, emotional, psychological, and spiritual decluttering.

It's hard to *notice*, to *appreciate*, particularly when we're bombarded by the material world. Noticing requires precious resources—attention, energy, focus. Appreciation requires all of that, and more—the recognition of the exceptional qualities in everything, especially the unexceptional. And both require physical and mental presence, which is increasingly fleeting in today's fire-hose world.

There's only so much we can process at once, and we tend to get wrapped up in our own heads, our own stories, our own lives, as if everyone else is an unpaid extra in our story, as if they don't have the same struggles happening between their ears. And so we stumble through life, forsaking the present moment. I know I have. I've abandoned so many moments, living in the past or the future. But life is merely a collection of present moments. And if we forsake the moment, we are forsaking life itself.

Browsing.
Scrolling.
Emailing.

Texting.

Posting.

Tweeting.

Updating.

Replying.

Replaying.

Responding.

These are just a small fraction of the ways we dispense with the moment in our modern world. Of course, these activities alone aren't a problem. Unless they get in the way of a more meaningful experience. Most of us ignore the natural beauty all around us, searching for synthetic beauty inside a tiny glowing screen.*

Not to mention the countless pre-tech ways of avoiding the moment:

Ruminating.

Worrying.

Fretting.

Brooding.

Analyzing.

Stressing.

Agonizing.

You see, this problem isn't new. Ever since we grunted out a few syllables in caves, we've found ways to divert our attention from the now. It's just that today we have more ways than ever to distract ourselves.

---

* More on tech distractions in our "Relationship with Creativity" chapter.

Back to the Now

Today, more than a decade after Mr. Outstanding left that coffee shop, I still struggle with living in the moment, with awareness, with noticing that which is right in front of me. Like everyone, I wrestle with distraction, pacification, and boredom. But because we're "bad" at something doesn't mean we must surrender to it; being "bad" is precisely the reason we must make a concerted effort to live in the here and now. Mercifully, there are a few techniques that bring me back to the now—whenever I veer off course. And I veer a lot.

When it comes to being present, two of my greatest influences are individuals with polar-opposite beliefs: the Christian pastor Rob Bell and renowned atheist Sam Harris. Although both have appeared on *The Minimalists Podcast*, I first discovered their work as a fan of their writings.

To avoid atrophying, it's crucial to seek out opposing points of view—to challenge and strengthen our own. When it comes to spiritual viewpoints, these two public intellectuals reside on opposite ends of the spectrum. Bell, a former megachurch pastor from Grand Rapids, is best known for his controversial book *Love Wins*; Harris, a neuroscientist and meditation teacher, is known for his critiques of religion (as well as his public scuffle with Ben Affleck on *Real Time with Bill Maher*).

In his first book, *Velvet Elvis: Repainting the Christian Faith*, Bell recounts a story in which God instructs Moses to climb to the top of a mountain. Moses obliges, and when he finally reaches the summit, God commands him to "be on the mountain."

I imagine Moses was a bit annoyed at first. "I heard you the first time! 'Go to the top of the mountain!' Here I am, just as you asked. Now what?"

Equally annoyed, God likely responded, "Just be on the mountain."

Puzzled by the redundancy of God's request, Moses might've furrowed his brow because he didn't understand that God didn't want him to simply travel to the peak and then immediately contemplate his next move. God didn't want him preoccupied, standing up there worrying about how he was going to get down, or what bills needed to be paid, or whether he turned off the lights before leaving the house. God wanted Moses to *be* on the mountain—to enjoy the moment. Which is impossible when we're stuck in a state of perpetual planning. Or perpetual worry. Or perpetual whatever.

You needn't hold the same beliefs as Rob Bell (or Sam Harris) to find value in this modernized parable. This story simply reminds us that humans have been struggling with the same thing for thousands of years. Before televisions, before the Internet, before smartphones and YouTube and Instagram, we were still distracted. It's part of the human condition. What Bell illustrates, though, is that when we pause for a moment, we can appreciate *that* moment. It takes tremendous effort to reach a mountaintop, so why not stop to enjoy it, even if only for a little while? The pause is just as essential as the action. Without it, we're simply barreling through a to-do list.

If we want to enjoy life, we must be on the mountain. That doesn't mean we shouldn't plan—but let's enjoy the planning process. And it doesn't mean we shouldn't work hard, either—but we can enjoy the work when it is executed from a place of total awareness.

Without dwelling on the past.

Without worrying about the future.

Be on the mountain.

Just. Be.

The Enemies of Being Here

In his tenth book, *How to Be Here: A Guide to Creating a Life Worth Living*, Bell explores the joy of living in the moment. Moreover, he addresses the three enemies of "being here"—boredom, cynicism, and despair:

Boredom is lethal. Boredom says, *There's nothing interesting to make here.* Boredom reveals what we believe about the kind of world we're living in. Boredom is lethal because it reflects a static, fixed view of the world—a world that is finished.

Cynicism is slightly different from boredom, but just as lethal. Cynicism says, *There's nothing new to make here.* Often, cynicism presents itself as wisdom, but it usually comes from a wound. . . . Often, this is because the cynic did try something new at some point and it went belly up, he was booed off the stage, and that pain causes him to critique and ridicule because there aren't any risks in doing that. If you hold something at a distance and make fun of it, then it can't hurt you.

And then there's despair. While boredom can be fairly subtle and cynicism can appear quite intelligent and even funny, despair is like a dull thud in the heart. Despair says, *Nothing that we make matters.* Despair reflects a pervasive dread that it's all pointless and that we are, in the end, simply wasting our time.

If I were to append to Bell's thoughts, I'd add:

If you're bored, you're boring.
If you're being cynical, you're being lazy.
If you're wallowing in despair, you're not here.

But, of course, when I write "you," I'm really talking about myself:

If I'm bored, I'm boring.
If I'm being cynical, I'm being lazy.
If I'm wallowing in despair, I'm not here.

According to Bell, these "spiritual diseases" of boredom, cynicism, and despair "disconnect us from the most primal truth—that we are here." They distance us from living in the moment; they prevent the necessary pause that's required to appreciate the beauty of the now.

It Is Always Now

Sam Harris, on the other hand, considers the preciousness of the moment by reflecting on the inevitable: death. In his popular talk *It Is Always Now*, Harris grapples with mortality and priorities. Harris notes that people generally try to avoid discussing death, but that we are all just "a phone call away" from a reminder of our impermanence:

The one thing people tend to realize at moments like these is they wasted a lot of time when life was normal. It's not just what they did with their time. It's not just that they spent too much time working or compulsively checking email. It's that they cared about the "wrong" things. They regret what they cared about. Their attention was bound up in petty concerns year after year when life was normal.

Which brings me back to that corporate coffee shop more than a decade ago. Occasionally, a skeptic would ask, "What makes you so *outstanding*, anyway?" as if there was a grand explanation—maybe I'd gotten a pay raise or won the lottery—but the honest answer was "Because I'm above ground." When you're paying attention, even the most banal experiences appear extraordinary.

To your average cynic, a sunny demeanor might seem obnoxious or out of sync with the "real" world, but, for me, it was—and still is—the way to be attentive, to pause, to find crumbs of joy in the present moment. Our ability to find satisfaction in rote activities is a kind of superpower.

Lately, however, I've struggled finding Mr. Outstanding in my day-to-day interactions. It's as if he abandoned me—no note, no forwarding address—and left a deep depression in his wake.

The Cost of Poor Decisions

A short while ago, I stumbled across a meme that accurately encapsulates my recent tribulations: a rock star on a concert stage shouts, "How's everybody doing tonight?" The crowd responds with a zealous "Woo!" while one guy toward the back of the venue says, "Actually, it's been a rough few months."

Indeed.

The year after signing the contract to write this book has been the most difficult year of my life. There isn't even a close second. Strangely, it started on a high note.

The months after I turned thirty-seven, in the summer of 2018,

were idyllic. Often, I didn't even need to *try* to be in the moment—it felt easy. My creative life was in a flow state. My personal and professional relationships were thriving. My ability to contribute to worthwhile causes was greater than ever. And after several years of minor health struggles, I had reached peak health again: I was sleeping well and was filled with energy and focus and a calm that blanketed my productive and enjoyable days. Without hyperbole, that was the best I'd felt in my adult life.

How did I get to this apex? The answer isn't sexy. It took a decade of incremental steps, changed habits, and repeated failures. It took letting go of myriad material possessions to make room for living. It took walking away from a life that was fueled by others' expectations. It took aligning my actions with the person I wanted to become, focusing on my values rather than my impulses.* To live a meaningful life, I had to live congruently.

But it wasn't always this way.

I treated my body poorly most of my life. As a child, my weight doubled from ages six to seven, around the time my mother's alcoholism grew untenable. As chaos filled the space around me, food was the one thing I could control. Frosted Flakes, Twinkies,

---

* More on this in our "Relationship with Values" chapter.

PB&Js, cheeseburgers, French fries—these were my certainty. My weight ballooned as a result. Within a few years, I was morbidly obese, literally the fattest kid in my elementary school.

In my teens it became evident that most girls don't like overweight boys as much as their lean counterparts. So I lost the weight in an unhealthy way: I didn't eat. This, too, gave me control, which gave me certainty. But my lack of nutrition, coupled with the onset of puberty, was a recipe for illness. I was constantly sick. But at least I was losing the fat, I told myself.

At six foot two and 139 pounds, I entered high school rail thin, a hundred pounds lighter than a year earlier. Other students didn't recognize me. (At least one classmate asked whether I was related to Josh Millburn.) It felt as if I had a new identity. I could be anyone.

Because I lost the weight quickly—without a change in understanding, education, or mindset—I gradually gained it back after high school. One pound at a time, I was once again overweight in my early twenties, all gut and chin and muffin top. The stress of the corporate world didn't help. I picked up habits that didn't serve me: snacking on vending-machine food throughout the day, omitting exercise and physical activity from my routine, and sleeping as little as I could get away with. Who had time to focus on health amid the busyness of business? Climbing the corporate ladder required all of me, so I let the rest of me go.

Along the way, I accepted every pharmacological solution any doctor would give me. Modern medicine seemed to have a quick fix for everything. Skin issues from a poor diet? Here, take a pill. Oh, that last drug didn't work? Take *this* pill. Side effects from the last prescription? Don't worry, we've got a pill for that, too.

The consequences of every shortcut are greater than its

temporary benefit. Each pill came with a list of side effects that seemed worse than the ailment it was treating: dry skin, itching, rash, dry mouth, peeling skin, inflammation of the whites of the eyes, joint pain, back pain, dizziness, drowsiness, nervousness, changes in fingernails and toenails, depression (these were the advertised side effects of just one of the drugs I took).

Not once did any doctor ever mention changing my diet; I would eventually have to figure that out on my own. Until then, I listened blindly to my doctors' orders, taking whatever pill, cream, inhaler, or potion they prescribed. Compliance was easier than questioning their solutions. And their solutions were much easier than taking ownership of my own life.

I didn't think my habits were unhealthy. Not really. I mean, I didn't smoke or drink or take recreational drugs or have un-protected sex—all the standard questions doctors ask during a checkup. But they weren't healthy, either. I didn't really know what *healthy* was. I had been taught the food pyramid, but not about processed foods, food sourcing, or the downsides of prescription-drug overuse. Hell, at age twenty-one, I thought if I ate enough French fries, I was getting an adequate amount of veggies in my diet.

A Minimalist Diet

Even now, in the twenty-first century, it's hard for experts to agree on what's healthy. One reputable website might recommend a Pa-leo diet, the next a plant-based diet, and another a low-carb diet. After falling down the rabbit hole of contradictory advice, we slam our laptops shut and return to our deep-fried Oreos (which are totally vegan, by the way).

On an episode of *The Minimalists Podcast*—episode 184, "Minimalist Diets"—we hosted a discussion between a vegan athlete, Rich Roll, who eats nothing but plants; a carnivore doctor, Paul Saladino, MD, who eats nothing but animals (that's not a typo); and an omnivore doctor, Thomas Wood, MD, who, like 99 percent of the world, eats both plants and animals. Although all three experts were shining examples of health, they held radically different views.

Instead of playing host to a "debate," I was more interested in what these professionals agreed upon. Despite their different approaches, everyone agreed that processed foods are not ideal for a healthy life. Nor is sugar, gluten, chemicals, refined oils, or factory farming. They also agreed that every human being is genetically unique; therefore, two people might experience completely different results on the same diet.

No wonder health is so complicated. What works for you might not work for me? That's exhausting. If I've learned anything from my conversations with experts, as well as my own dietary changes, it's that it's best to focus on universal principles instead of prescribing a one-size-fits-all lifestyle. Thus, this is the framework for a healthy minimalist diet:

Eat real food.

Don't over- or undereat.

Avoid inflammatory foods.

Keep away from refined oils.*

Steer clear of processed foods.

Don't eat foods that make you feel crummy.

---

* Stay away from canola oil, vegetable oil, soybean oil, safflower oil, corn oils, margarine, and the like, because these oils are refined by using chemicals that are harmful to us. Opt instead for healthy organic alternatives like extra-virgin olive oil, avocado oil, coconut oil, and grass-fed butter or tallow.

Focus on the problem, not the symptom.

Eat organic plants and grass-fed meats.

Buy local whenever possible.

Results may vary, but a sturdy framework allows us to build the house that best suits our needs and desires.

By my mid-twenties—after doing my own research, no longer waiting for someone to show up with a pill to fix my problems—I had changed my diet to remove the causes of my obesity. For me, that meant eliminating sugar, bread, and processed foods; it also meant eating whole foods, avoiding snacks, and consuming only two meals a day.

Stewardship of the Self

Although my weight was under control by my mid-twenties, I continued to listen to my doctor's pharmacological advice without questioning it, without looking for a second opinion, without listening to my own body. For facial acne, I was prescribed several rounds of Accutane, a drug that is now off the market in the United States; it was so potent, I had to get my blood tested monthly to make sure my liver wasn't failing. I didn't know it at the time, but that acne was mostly caused by a dairy sensitivity; when I removed milk, cheese, and yogurt from my diet, it dissipated.

Then, I was prescribed Bactrim, a supposedly "benign" antibiotic, to treat nodular acne on my scalp. Again, though I didn't know it at the time, that acne was actually caused by a soy allergy; when I removed tofu, edamame, and other soy products from my diet, it went away. At age twenty-seven, after having taken this antibiotic every day for years, a catalog of symptoms I'd never experienced began to surface: seasonal allergies, multiple chemical sensitivities, food allergies, digestive issues, chronic fatigue. A few years later, the overuse of antibiotics led to a dangerous *Clostridium difficile* bacterial overgrowth in my gut (a bacterium that kills upwards of 15,000 Americans every year).

Little did I know that many—if not most—of my health issues had stemmed from a dysbiotic gut microbiome and the resulting inflammation. According to Chris Kresser, author of *Unconventional Medicine*, your microbiome "influences everything about your health," including but not limited to allergies, autoimmunity, bone health, brain health, cancer, cardiovascular disease, diabetes, gastrointestinal health, immunity, obesity, skin health, and thyroid disorders. There's also extensive evidence that gut dysbiosis is responsible for increased inflammation in the human body, according to *Nutrients* and other peer-reviewed journals.

LETTING GO IS A TYPE OF FREE MEDICINE.

Kresser claims there are eight factors that disrupt the microbiome, all of which have something to do with our modern quick-fix worldview: antibiotics, certain pharmaceutical drugs, cesarean-section births, the standard American diet, genetically modified foods, sleep and circadian-rhythm disruptions, chronic stress, and existing chronic infections. It's no surprise I was unhealthy, even after dropping the weight: by my early thirties, I fit all eight of these criteria.*

At this point, you may be wondering what any of this has to do with minimalism. In a word: everything. Minimalism is a practice of intentional living. While it starts with the stuff, it's ultimately a stewardship program for one's life. If I could go back in time and

---

* If you want to learn more about gut health, *Healthy Gut, Healthy You* by Dr. Michael Ruscio is a digestible foray into the subject.

impart wisdom to my childhood self, I'd focus on that one word: stewardship.

From a young age, I was reckless with my body, acting as if it were simultaneously indestructible and disposable. I was not a good steward of my vessel. I exhibited the behaviors of a man who didn't own his own flesh—like there was some sort of "me" that existed separately from my body. I didn't know any better.

Sadly, as I grew older, I still didn't know any better, so the behaviors continued. Even when I thought I was being healthy, I made repeatedly unhealthy decisions—a diet jam-packed with packaged foods, sugars, refined oils, and chemicals; overuse of antibiotics and other pharmaceutical drugs; very little exercise and sleep; and obscene amounts of stress from work and relationships and a life I wasn't proud of—for which I would eventually pay the toll. Just like the excess stuff in our lives, our health problems don't go away when ignored—the clutter and the disease mount with each year that passes.

MINIMALIST RULE FOR LIVING WITH LESS

Gift-Giving Rule

We've programmed ourselves to give gifts on birthdays and holidays to communicate our love. But gift giving is not a "love language" any more than Pig Latin is a Romance language. What people actually mean is "contribution is a love language." And if a gift is the best way to contribute, then don't let minimalism stand in your way. Enter: the Gift-Giving Rule, which says you can avoid physical gifts and still participate. Since presence is the best present, what if you gifted only experiences this year? How much more memorable would that be? Consider these gifts: concert tickets, a home-cooked meal, breakfast in bed, a massage, a parade, a car trip somewhere without a plan, an evening with no distractions, a festival of lights, sledding, dancing, a vacation together, a sunrise. And if you must present an experience in a physical manner, print it in full color and wrap it in an ornate box. Or if you feel the need to give material goods, gift consumables—a bottle of wine, a bar of gourmet chocolate, a bag of coffee from a local roaster—instead of another unwanted widget.

Letting Go as Medicine

Marta Ortiz, one of our Packing Party Case Study participants, from Mexico City, suffered from significant health issues before she began simplifying her life a few years ago. "I was ignoring the clear signals my body was sending me," Ortiz said during the first week of her unpacking experiment. She had embraced some of the tenets of minimalism over the last three years—donating many of the things that no longer added value to her life—but now dealing with all her possessions at once was bringing to light many new revelations about herself and her health: excess stress, a poor diet, a lack of sleep and exercise, and serious digestive issues, to name a few.

Even after her first stint with minimalism, Ortiz was still "overcommitting, overworking, overconsuming, overeating." She realized this while sorting through her boxes, trying to unpack what was important to her. "I was still overdoing every aspect of my life, and I was paying the price physically and mentally. I had pushed myself to the edge." She claims that had she not continued simplifying, she would have "gone over that edge," the implications of which seemed both obvious and ominous.

"Eliminating the noise from my life helped me hear what was truly important—my well-being," Ortiz said. Today, as she continues to let go, she takes it one day at a time. While confronting her excess during her "party," she has committed to herself to "establish clear boundaries, eat more healthfully, shop more intentionally, and pay attention to what my mind and body are telling me."

This change in mindset, Ortiz acknowledges, didn't happen just because she recently boxed up the stuff in her home. Nor did it happen because she donated some old clothes a few years ago. Rather, it occurred because removing the things that absorbed most of her *attention* made room for *intention*. This allowed her to focus on improving her own well-being instead of adorning her life with material distractions. This small shift has had a significant effect on her overall health without her spending a dime in the process. In a way, letting go is a type of free medicine.

Food as Medicine

According to Dr. Thomas Wood, a research assistant professor in the Department of Pediatrics at the University of Washington and chief scientific officer at Nourish Balance Thrive, an online-based company that uses advanced biochemical testing to optimize performance in athletes, "The best medicines are free: diet, exercise, sleep, sunlight."

Let's discuss these "medicines" one at a time, starting with the foundation of health: food.

Many athletes, doctors, and researchers will tell you that to regain control of your health, you must first take control of your diet because what you put into your body fuels your entire life. When you recognize food as fuel, not entertainment, you're no longer a slave to impulse. You, instead, feed your body when it needs fuel, much like you fill your tank when your car is low on gas. You don't overfill your car because today is a "cheat day" or you want to "treat yourself." Besides, we must stop thinking about stuffing poison into our faces as a "treat." The real treat is when we treat our bodies with respect, when we nourish our bodies so we can live well. We can live for the joy of the present moment, not for the next treat. Not to mention, if we have only one "cheat day" a week, that's the equivalent of cheating seven weeks a year. I don't know about you, but I wouldn't be happy if my spouse cheated on me even half that much. And yet we're constantly cheating on ourselves.

Does that mean we can't enjoy our meals? Of course not. But if we're being honest, no matter what we eat, we rarely truly enjoy the food that enters our mouths. Instead, we hit drive-thrus, we eat on the go, we snack out of boredom, and we stuff our faces while multitasking.

Last week, inside the shared break room at my office, I saw a large man watching Netflix on his iPad while devouring an entire pepperoni pizza. Not only was his meal unhealthy, but the expression on his face was not one of joy. If anything, his features conveyed defeat, as if his lunchtime routine was an escape. Even pleasure seemed to be missing from the entire process.*

It may seem bewildering, but I enjoy my meals more now as a "healthy eater" than ever before, and only part of the reason has

---

* Of course I recognize myself in this man. Unchecked, I, too, am impulsive, compulsive, and veer toward easy distractions.

to do with the food itself. Sure, I could talk about how it's possible to make "health foods" taste great,* and I could discuss how good it feels to know I won't experience guilt after feasting on my next meal, but I'd rather take some time to discuss the meals I enjoy the most—and those are the meals I share with others. Instead of turning on the television while snacking, or munching on fast food in my car, I get the most joy from a meal shared at my dinner table.

Exercise as Medicine

While diet is the foundation of optimal health, it's impossible to be healthy from a balanced diet alone. A sedentary person with the perfect diet is still unhealthy.

"Working out" can be intimidating. Walk into any neighborhood gym and you're immediately faced with the paradox of choice.

Should I start with cardio?

What weights should I lift?

How many reps and sets?

What does *that* machine do?

Is today "leg day" or "arm day"?

How do I work my back muscles?

What the heck is my "core"?

When you're overwhelmed, walking out of the gym might feel like the best option. But really, the basic idea of exercise is simple.

Among the experts I've spoken to about this topic—people like

---

* See Max Lugavere's *Genius Foods* as an example.

Ben Greenfield, one of *Greatist's* 100 Most Influential People in Health and Fitness in 2013 and 2014; Dr. Ryan Greene, a Mayo Clinic–trained physician who specializes in human performance; and my wife, Rebecca Shern, founder of *Minimal Wellness*—the key to acquiring a baseline level of physical fitness can be summarized in one word: movement. Exercise needn't be complex; it need only be done. Whether you're hitting the gym or the park, the swimming pool or the lake, the sidewalk or the hiking trails, the key takeaway is that everyone needs regular movement every day to thrive, especially in our increasingly sedentary society, which puts a premium on convenience and comfort over wellness and well-being. Not to mention, it's easier to sleep at night when we get the appropriate amount of exercise.

MINIMALIST RULE FOR LIVING WITH LESS

Gift-Getting Rule

This might sound surprising coming from The Minimalists, but if you want to get better gifts, you must ask for better gifts. Now, that doesn't mean you should ask for more expensive gifts, nor do you need to ask for physical gifts. It means that people who love you want to give you gifts, and that's okay—let them. Instead of saying "no," say "yes" to non-material gifts. Tell friends about the experiences you want to enjoy with them. Tell coworkers about your favorite coffeehouse or local chocolatier. Tell family members about a charity and how they can donate in your name. Wouldn't these alternatives feel better than another pair of cufflinks?

Sleep as Medicine

Matthew Walker, PhD, author of *Why We Sleep: Unlocking the Power of Sleep and Dreams*, acknowledges our collective sleep deficit as a health crisis: "There does not seem to be one major organ within the body, or process within the brain, that isn't optimally enhanced by sleep (and detrimentally impaired when we don't get enough). That we receive such a bounty of health benefits each night should not be surprising." Walker argues that human beings are the only creatures who "deliberately deprive themselves of sleep for no sound reason." Yet we invent countless reasons we "can't" get enough: be it work, recreation, partying, or general busyness, sleep takes the back burner because it's not as exciting as its alternatives, even though without sleep, we can't be our optimal self. A lack of sleep isn't a badge of honor—it is a marker of a chaotic life.

It's impossible to be perfect, especially since many of us face circumstances that impede perfect sleep—newborn children, anxiety, complicated work hours—so it's best to throw perfection out the window. But even in the face of challenges, we can do what we can—we can control the controllable—to improve our sleep. How? Walker has some simple tips, a number of which you can fit reasonably into your nightly routine. Implementing just a few of these practices will improve your overall sleep:

Go to bed and wake up at the same time each day.
Get outside, seek out sunlight throughout the day.
Budget a nonnegotiable eight hours for sleep each night.
Keep your bedroom temperature cool (about 65 degrees).

Hang blackout curtains in the room in which you sleep.

Avoid alcohol and other sedatives (sedation is not sleep).

Keep caffeine to a minimum; avoid caffeine after noon.

Use earplugs and an eye mask to block out noise and light.*

Dim the lights and turn off all screens one hour
    before bed.

Sunlight as Medicine

While excess evening light might hurt our nighttime slumber, especially the blue light found in our glowing screens, it's essential
to get adequate sunlight throughout the day, so much so that sunlight is our fourth type of "free medicine."

You might notice a pattern emerging—all these "free medicines" are inextricably linked to one another: diet to exercise,
exercise to sleep, and of course sleep to light. According to a
Sleep Medicine Clinics study conducted by Jeanne F. Duffy
and Charles A. Czeisler, "The circadian system in animals and
humans, being near but not exactly 24 hours in cycle length,
must be reset on a daily basis in order to remain in synchrony
with external environmental time." And according to Kristen
Stewart, writing in *Everyday Health*, "Because our body clocks,
which control our sleep schedules, are sensitive to light, things
like how much sunlight we're exposed to throughout the day
and what types of light we're exposed to at night affect our sleep
schedules."

We get too much blue light at night and not nearly enough

---

* My wife also uses a white-noise machine because the soothing ambient sound helps
her sleep.

sunlight throughout the day. Because we circulate from our homes to our offices to indoor public spaces—shuttled to each under the canopies of our cars—it has been estimated that Americans spend 93 percent of their time indoors, while our distant ancestors spent virtually all day in the sun. "Either we live in an area with limited sunlight for large portions of the year, or our busy schedules don't allow for more time in the sun," says Justin Strahan, cofounder of Joovv, a red-light-therapy device manufacturer. "Chances are you're not reading this in a park, on the beach, or in your yard. . . . If you're only getting outside for a few hours a week, you likely don't have nearly enough natural light in your life. This equates to a much bigger health risk than most people realize, and can be a root cause of insomnia, fatigue, depression, and other symptoms."

JUST LIKE THE EXCESS STUFF IN OUR LIVES, OUR HEALTH PROBLEMS DON'T GO AWAY WHEN IGNORED— THE CLUTTER AND THE DISEASE MOUNT WITH EACH YEAR THAT PASSES.

So, while it's important to avoid blue light at night—because it negatively affects melatonin production, which helps us stay asleep—it's equally important to seek out light during the day, beginning with first light. People who are exposed to sunlight in the morning not only sleep better at night, but they tend to feel less depressed and stressed than those who don't get much morning light, according to an article in *Sleep Health*, the journal of the National Sleep Foundation. So open those morning blinds when you wake and enjoy your cup of coffee on the patio. Or, better yet, go for a walk around the block as soon as you roll out of bed. You'll feel better, sleep better, and be less stressed as a result.

Succ-stress-ful

Simon Marshall, PhD, an associate professor of exercise and nutritional sciences at San Diego State University, refers to the free "medicines" mentioned in this chapter with an acronym, SEEDS, which stands for sleep, exercise, eating, drinking, and stress management.

With his *SEEDS Journal*, Marshall, who has worked for the CDC and has published more than 100 peer-reviewed scientific articles, focuses on the need for incremental behavioral changes, which are far more likely to stick than a radical, overnight overhaul of one's life:

> For each of these pillars of good health, think of a tiny thing that you can do to contribute to it. . . . [F]ocusing on *small* behaviors builds the correct mindset and contributes to knock-on effects on other changes in that pillar. In short, progress begets progress.

This holds true for minimalism as well. We can't merely simplify once and expect to live the simple life in perpetuity. Minimalism requires incremental changes that occur over time, starting with our relationship with stuff—that is, what we hold on to and what we consume—and then expanding those changes into our other "relationships" (with truth, self, values, money, creativity, and people).

The thing I find most compelling about Marshall's acronym, however, is its final letter: *S* for stress management. While it's critical we take advantage of our "free medicines," it's equally important we avoid the poisons that stress us out.

My friend John Delony, who holds two PhDs, including one in

counseling, compares stress to a smoke detector. He told me that "if your kitchen is on fire, switching off the alarm isn't going to save your house." In that same vein, when we're stressed, we may seek out breathing techniques or yoga poses, which are useful and may calm us in the moment, but when it comes to stress, they only switch off the distress signal temporarily. And if we don't then address whatever is flaring our anxiety, the flames will continue to overtake our lives.

They say "nothing exceeds like excess," but it's also true that *nothing stresses like success.* Wanting success, getting success, retaining success—these are the building blocks of stress and anxiety. In a world caffeinated by twenty-four-hour media, it's difficult to remain calm. But if you're looking to be stressed out, I can think of plenty of ways to increase your anxiety:

Consume more.
Regard everything as precious.
Refuse to let go.
Channel surf.
Peruse social media.
Inhabit the email inbox.
Focus on productivity.
Compare achievements.
Yearn for things.
Forsake sleep.
Forgo exercise.
Hold grudges.
Expand the to-do list.
Hurry.
Take on debt.

Spend more.

Save less.

Say "yes" to everything.

Maybe if we do the opposite—create more, consume less, save more money, shun busyness—we have a chance to restore the calm in our lives, not by removing the battery from the smoke detector, but by tending to the flames that scorch our well-being.

Heartbreak Hallways

In September 2018, shortly before my New Great Depression, back when I felt like I was in peak health, Ryan and I traveled to Brazil to speak at a conference in São Paulo. After our talk, we enjoyed the local cuisine, which included local tap water. Soon, a "food-poisoning event" wiped me out. But unlike typical food poisoning, the effects lingered for weeks, and then months, after I returned to Los Angeles: intestinal pain, rashes, acne, diarrhea, bloating, inflammation, brain fog, hyperosmia, loss of libido, lethargy. Then: a depression so absolute it felt like I was trapped in a giant mason jar left out in the summer sun; I could see relief and freedom beyond the glass, but I couldn't touch it.

Depression seems to hit suddenly. But, if you look closely, there are stages. You don't fall down a hill all at once, even though it feels that way. First comes the sadness. Then, the inability to remain productive. Then, everyday functions become laborious. Eventually, if it gets bad enough, you're searching for "how to tie a noose" tutorials on YouTube.

Suffice it to say, this wasn't just sorrow or even despair; this was my first experience with real, debilitating depression. By

January 2019, I woke up each day wishing I hadn't. It was a stark difference from what I had experienced just a few months earlier, which made it even harder to handle: I'd tumbled from the steepest summit into the darkest valley, and I didn't know my way back. There was an inescapable pall hanging over my life, affecting every aspect of my well-being. My creative output dropped by 90 percent. My ability to contribute to others was muted as I struggled to take care of even myself. And worst of all, my relationships suffered; I felt like a burden on everyone around me: my wife, my daughter, my friends, my coworkers.

> WHILE MINIMALISM STARTS WITH THE STUFF, IT'S ULTIMATELY A STEWARDSHIP PROGRAM FOR ONE'S LIFE.

Because "traveler's diarrhea" usually dissipates within a week or two, my doctors were puzzled. A colonoscopy yielded no answers. Soon, more tests revealed a severe overgrowth of *E. coli* and several other opportunistic bacteria hanging out in my colon, almost certainly from the water I drank in Brazil. Further tests confirmed that the so-called "bad" bacteria (proteobacteria, bacteroidetes, *Bilophila wadsworthia*) had pushed out many of the "good" bacteria (*bifidobacterium*, *akkermansia*, *ruminococcus*), which were now undetectable or nonexistent, creating serious dysbiosis in my gut. Then a PillCam revealed more than a hundred ulcers in my small bowel.

As we work toward a deeper understanding of the problem, I'm reminded of the lessons my mother learned in her twelve-step programs decades ago: "Take it one day at a time," they told her. In my twenties, I'd scoff at trite, one-size-fits-all platitudes like this. But it actually made sense within the context of my suffering.

There are good days, and there are bad days. When you're depressed, the good days are never great; they're merely better than the bad days. And the bad days are often very bad.

But.

This is all part of it. Every adventure is pleasurable; every adventure is painful. That's what makes it an adventure. The pain makes us more alive. If you avoid pain, you avoid life. But through the pain, you learn more about yourself than you ever thought possible.

A trip to the grocery usually isn't an adventure; it's an unmemorable event. With reckless abandon, we stumble through a series of near-life experiences, stacking unremarkable events day after day, and pretend that's living. But it's not. It's a to-do list, a sequence of tasks, a productivity hack. *Living* involves peak experiences and complexities and unnameable emotions that interweave our existence. It requires experiencing the present moment as we walk through life. Joy and pain. Highs and lows. These are the hallways that get us from here to there. It's heartwarming; it's heartbreaking. A meaningful journey is never without pain. Nor is it without joy. It is mixed with both. And sometimes you don't get to decide which experience is around the corner.

The Teleology of Pain

It was Confucius who said, "We have two lives, and the second begins when we realize we have only one." We can comprehend this lesson intellectually, but sometimes it takes a life-altering experience to *learn* this lesson—to truly understand it.

If I've learned anything over the last year, it's this truism: Health is wealth. Moreover, optimal health is real wealth. Or, to put it more profoundly, how about another maxim from Confucius: "A healthy man wants a thousand things; a sick man wants only one." Yes, I knew this before, but only cerebrally. Now, after profound suffering, I understand it viscerally.

I wish I could share an ultimate solution with you, the thing that fixes everything, but I can't. Because I'm still going through it, and the most profound lessons tend to emerge in the wake of trauma. I've learned a lot, but I have a substantial distance to go.

WE HAVE TO BE WILLING TO LET GO SO WE CAN MAKE SPACE FOR A NEW WAY OF BEING.

That's the great paradox of learning: the more we learn, the less we've figured out. And that's okay. We'll never fully figure it out. We'll never "get there." Because there's no *there* there. On some level, we are all lost. How could we not be? We are a crowd of amateurs standing on a giant wet rock that's hurling through infinite, ever-expanding space. And we're running out of time. We act as if life is infinite. Or if we think about mortality, we think of it in terms of life span—how long we can live. But maybe it makes sense to think about *health span* instead. A well-lived short life is markedly better than a life of suffering, or worse, a life of mediocrity.

So, no, I don't have all the answers. But I now understand one thing. If you're reading this and you're healthy, you're already living the dream; everything else—possessions, status, riches, validation—is window dressing. I also know this: On a long enough timeline, the pain is temporary. Every now and then, we have to be broken down to be built up stronger. And that's painful. But sometimes it takes a breakdown to experience a breakthrough.

Rebuilding After a Breakdown

On May 28, 2019, as I struggled with my own problems, a series of fourteen tornadoes devastated my hometown of Dayton, Ohio, a community that had already been hard hit by economic misfortunes, drug overdoses, and other miseries.* The photos of the aftermath were post-apocalyptic: Cars overturned. Downed power lines. Roofs torn from buildings. Gas stations flipped inside out. Even Hara Arena, the 5,500-seat multi-purpose venue where I first saw *Sesame Street on Ice* as a kid, was ripped apart, gutted by 140-mile-per-hour winds.

But perhaps Dayton can benefit from this tornado. While the destruction was catastrophic, and the single death was undoubtedly tragic, few people were physically harmed by the demolishing winds. Everything else—all the material things that seemed so important—was replaceable.

The days and weeks that followed would bring the community together in ways that seemed impossible just a week prior. Churches, community centers, and private citizens opened their doors to the newly homeless. Food banks and soup kitchens received record amounts of food, bottled water, emergency supplies, and monetary donations. Democrats and Republicans set aside their political animus to help those in need. It was as if the tornadoes hadn't simply knocked down physical walls; they had broken down metaphysical barriers within the community.

Because we had the means to do so, The Minimalists contributed to the relief efforts in various ways. Yet it was much more heartening to see the efforts of the people who themselves had been wiped out by the storm. As people got back on their feet, they immediately wanted to help other people who had been affected. The contribution was contagious. It was like one of those

---

* To boot, two months after those tornadoes devastated the city, and just two blocks from my childhood home, there would be a mass shooting that would leave nine people dead and thirty-seven injured.

airline-safety pamphlets come to life: "Secure your own oxygen mask before helping others."

There are two important lessons here.
First, help yourself.
Then immediately help others.

Don't wait for permission—or the perfect circumstances—to help. When an emergency strikes, waiting for permission to act is inimical to progress. Just like you needn't wait for the pilot's permission to secure your oxygen mask, the people of Dayton did not wait for the so-called experts or elites to fix their problem. They took ownership, and then they took massive action. To make a difference, their actions had to be greater than the aftereffects of the disaster. That's the only way we progress—by moving forward, even after a tragedy.

Within a few weeks, temporary shelters were erected, hundreds of homes were restored, and the community was more connected than it had been in years. Unity was the key to getting unstuck.

THE MOST PRO-FOUND LESSONS TEND TO EMERGE IN THE WAKE OF TRAUMA.

If you want to get unstuck, you will have to try new things—sometimes many things—and often they won't work. You will stumble, you will fall, and you will fail your way to progress. Or, as the Irish author Samuel Beckett put it, "Try again. Fail again. Fail better." Our failures compose the best parts of who we are—as individuals, as a community.

It's important to remember that every foundation was once a ditch. Some ditches remain ditches. Others are ripe for a new structure. We get to decide which is which.

Selfishness, Self-Improvement,
Self-Giving, and Serving

I'm intrigued by the word "kenosis," which is derived from the Greek word that means "to empty out." Historically, kenosis refers to the ethic of sacrifice: we experience profound meaning by being subservient to others. In today's terms, I think of kenosis as "self-giving": we feel most alive when we empty ourselves out in the service of other people.

Yes, minimalism often involves an "emptying out" of our homes—removing the excess to make room for others. To empty ourselves, however, we must first possess something worth pouring out. There's a reason those safety pamphlets instruct you to secure your oxygen mask first: if it's easier to breathe, it's easier to help people in need. This is why caring for the self is so important. It's not selfish to act in your own self-interest. Rather, self-improvement is the most effective way to contribute to others.

Selfishness occurs when someone feeds their own pleasure at the expense of others—through dishonesty, contempt, manipulation. Self-improvement, on the other hand, involves caring so much about others that you're willing to improve yourself—you're willing to be a steward of your own well-being—so that you can have enough resources to give. Thus, in a roundabout way, it's selfish not to take care of yourself because you'll never have enough to give if you don't first care for your own well-being.

Contribution shouldn't be confused with "saving" people. A servant is not a savior; a servant is someone who understands that when the world is a better place for others, it's a better place for the servant, too.

The great mystery of contribution is that by giving yourself to others, you *get* more. Not more *stuff*, but more meaning and purpose and joy. You're not only helping them—you're helping yourself. When done with care, giving and self-improvement are self-fertilizing mechanisms: the more you give, the more you grow; the more you grow, the more you have to give. In tandem, these attributes provide a sturdy foundation for a great life.

Greatness isn't measured by ephemera. No one cares how much money Abraham Lincoln had in the bank when he gave the Gettysburg Address, or how much land Seneca owned when he wrote *On the Shortness of Life*, or how many Instagram followers Harriet Tubman had during her thirteen missions to rescue enslaved people. Greatness is measured by our ability to positively influence the world around us. And to do so, we must first care for the self. Because we can't give what we don't have.

Self-Care and the Healing Process

We seem to have a sick-care system, not a healthcare system. As I've demonstrated with my own misfortunes, our society likes to treat symptoms, not problems. We wait until illness strikes to take care of ourselves, when, in reality, the best healthcare is preventative care—that is, taking care of ourselves when we're healthy so we can continue to live healthfully.

"'Self-care' is such an overused term," says Randi Kay, host of the *Simple Self-Care Podcast*, "but it's the best and most straightforward way to describe the healing process." Kay, a native of Fargo, North Dakota, was in her twenties when she first encountered the ideas she would later call "self-care," which she defines as "the act of tuning in to your true needs and then acting accordingly."

By age twenty-six, she'd lost her faith in her religion and her first marriage had collapsed. "I was trying to figure out who I was," she told me. Until then, she had let other people's beliefs and expectations define who she was as an individual. When she started questioning the labels that had been thrust upon her—"Mormon," "wife," "depressive"—her outlook began to change. "I no longer believed what I'd believed. I didn't need an authority to connect me with my spirituality. I didn't need a doctor to tell me to take care of myself."

Although she was diagnosed with depression as a teenager, Kay didn't confront the illness until her twenties, when she "looked inward" and realized she was the foremost authority of her existence. "I had to learn how to trust myself to stave off self-doubt. I had to learn how to listen to my own body." Only then was she able to treat the depression that had been merely kept at bay with prescription medications and therapy. "Those things helped, but they didn't solve the problem. . . . Your body will tell you what's wrong if you listen."

> **WE FEEL MOST ALIVE WHEN WE EMPTY OURSELVES OUT IN THE SERVICE OF OTHER PEOPLE.**

Through a process of self-discovery that included gradual lifestyle changes—diet, hiking, rock climbing, journaling, massage, tissue healing, and even playing live music—she was able to "create a relationship" with herself on *her* terms, and uncover who she wanted to be, one discovery at a time.

"I call it choose-your-own-adventure healing," Kay said. "After my divorce, and after I left the church, I no longer fit the mold I'd created." The structure that once served a critical role in her life no longer did. Because life is fluid, the things that empower us today may disempower us tomorrow. We have to be willing to let go so we can make space for a new way of being. This isn't true only with our material possessions, which we often cling to until they are mere antiquities; it's true throughout all of life's relationships.

Through her exploration and new activities, Kay learned about the mind-body connection. She developed new rituals—yoga, breathwork, bodywork—that brought newfound meaning to her life and replaced the old rituals and labels that had led her to a stressed-out "mediocre life—a life in which I wasn't happy."

OUR FAILURES COMPOSE THE BEST PARTS OF WHO WE ARE—AS INDIVIDUALS, AS A COMMUNITY.

As she healed, she became aware that, for years, she had unwittingly sought out drama and toxicity in her relationships and activities. Instead of enjoying life, she searched for sources of discontent to complain about. She had gotten so used to feeling down that she would create turmoil in her own life so she could keep feeling depressed. It was as if the certainty of depression was better than the uncertainty of a life well lived. "To break the cycle, I had to stop following the depressed-person prescription," she said. "I stopped labeling myself as *depressed* and started doing things I enjoy. And I questioned everything."

When we ask difficult questions, we don't always get the answers we want or expect. Questioning might strengthen faith, or it might move us away from it. Same for material possessions and relationships and career and identity.

When Kay and I spoke on the phone recently, I asked her for some self-care best practices. Here's what she told me:

- Start by figuring out your biggest stressors and pain points and then determine what's keeping you from nurturing yourself. What's screaming the loudest—what's the biggest holdup?

- Life changes will likely be uncomfortable, and that discomfort might make you question everything—those questions are important for fulfillment.
- Self-care is hyper-individualized, not a specific program to follow.
- Habits and rituals that help one person may harm another.
- Modify your self-care to fit where you are, not where you "should" be.
- Self-care is not "go big or go home"—small changes are often enough.
- If what you're doing is not working, be willing to change directions.
- Focus on the *whys*, not the *shoulds*.
- The journey never ends: you may still get burnt out and need to recalibrate.
- Most important: it's *your* adventure, so don't compare it with others' journeys.

Toward the end of our conversation, she alluded to an important link between minimalism and self-care: "People's hurdles with material possessions are similar to their self-care hurdles," she said. "We don't confront our stuff—or our healing—because we have a bag of excuses: 'I don't have enough time.' 'I feel guilty about my past indiscretions.' 'I feel selfish to want to make these changes.' 'I don't know where to start.' 'What will other people think of me?'"

But even the best excuse is still an excuse. If we want to walk away from the mundane lives we've constructed, we have to make some difficult changes. "People don't know themselves," she told me right before we hung up, "and self-care is the best way to get to know the person you want to be."

Coda: Self

Ryan here. Joshua and the experts cited throughout this chapter gave us a lot to consider about our relationship with our self, and now it's time to consider how that relationship is working for you. So, I'd like you to take some time to explore that relationship by way of the following exercises. Sound good? Great! Let's get started.

QUESTIONS ABOUT SELF

1. What are you actually seeking with your current life-style? Why? Is it what you want, or is it what someone else wants?
2. When in your life have you felt your best? What factors contributed to that feeling?
3. What new practices and routines will help you pay attention to your health on a daily basis?
4. What "free medicine" can you incorporate into your health regimen?
5. How can you contribute more to others' well-being?

THE DOS OF SELF

Next, what did you learn about yourself in this chapter? What will stick? What lessons will encourage you to be a better version of yourself? Here are five immediate actions you can take today:

- **Seek gratitude.** Get clear on everything that's remarkable in your life. The more you appreciate what you have, the easier it will be to let go of stress and anxiety. Today, write down the names of ten people who have had a positive effect on your life, and list ten things you are grateful for in your life currently.

- **Pause.** Find ways to pause each day: meditation, walks, breath-work, and other self-care rituals that will help you slow down. Schedule five minutes each day to meditate and twenty minutes to walk. Or schedule any other form of self-care that works for you.
- **Identify habits.** Make a list of the healthy habits you want to adopt.
- **Behave healthfully.** Incorporate a health regimen into your life that works for you. Health is relative, and it will take some time and effort to find the best fit, so start by simply choosing one item on the list of healthy habits and incorporate it into your life today.
- **Get accountable.** Take action each day toward *your* optimal health. There are two things that will help ensure you take action: (1) find an accountability partner, and (2) schedule these healthy activities as commitments on your calendar.

THE DON'TS OF SELF

Finally, let's discuss the pitfalls of self. Here are five things you'll want to avoid, beginning today, if you want to be the best version of yourself:

- Don't let the fear of missing out distract you from momentum, progress, or the present moment. You will always be missing out on something. The real power comes from staying focused and committed.
- Don't let petty concerns interfere with living a meaningful life.
- Don't take your body for granted.
- Don't use food as entertainment.
- Don't make excuses or blame others for an unhealthy lifestyle.

RELATIONSHIP 4 | VALUES

I walked out of the fitting room with a guilty man's shiftiness, a bright-yellow necktie crammed into my pants' pocket. My eyes darted crazily for security cameras. I had just turned eighteen, and my first big job interview was the next day.

My mother had been sober for more than a year and was working for a mail-order catalog company, where she met a guy who knew a guy who was hiring retail store employees for the local telephone company. So I polished my résumé with my work experience—cashier, dishwasher, busboy, waiter, telemarketer—and ironed my only dress shirt and khakis. All I needed was a tie before my interview. But I didn't own one, and I didn't have any money, so I chose to take one from a department store at the Dayton Mall. I knew it was wrong, but was it really a big deal to compromise my values just this once? Besides, was it stealing if I really needed it?

I must have looked nervous as hell to the plainclothes security guard who followed me out of the store. He waited until I had exited before he handcuffed me and read me my rights. "You have the right to remain silent," I heard him say. Then the sound of my thumping heart took over, and I couldn't hear anything. I felt ill.

Small-Bore Compromises

I had the right to remain silent, but what could I say anyway? That I didn't mean it? That I swear I have a good explanation? That I'd like a do-over? I didn't feel compelled to fill the air with bland nattering, so I just stewed in my own shame.

Nothing bespeaks guilt like being escorted through a shopping mall food court in handcuffs. You would think I would have learned my lesson that day and avoided malls for the rest of my life. But little did I know that, a decade later, I would manage more than a hundred retail stores, including a flagship store outside that very mall, living the claustrophobic American Dream. And I got there one small compromise at a time.

I had finished high school a semester early, in December 1998, and spent the beginning of 1999 immersed in audio-recording school. But I soon abandoned my dream to be a studio engineer when I discovered that most make less than minimum wage and are forced to record music they hate if they want to make any money at all. I didn't want to be stuck in the same place as everyone else who grew up around me; I wanted to make real money. Even if I had to work for a soulless corporation, even if the values of that corporation didn't align with my own.

Have you ever seen a school of barracudas attack an object on the surface of the water? It's an incredible sight. They see something shiny and they simply react—just like all the barracudas around them. Barracudas don't have values; they just lunge toward the next shiny object. And we humans tend to do the same. We follow trends, go into debt, apply for jobs we hate just so we can afford the new car that will take us to that same job. We lie, cheat, and steal. We build a life on a foundation of compromises.

But if we're willing to compromise anything, eventually we'll compromise everything. Even our values.

Object A

Most eighteen-year-olds don't know what their values are. Or worse, as in my case, they value nonsense. As a teenager, I craved everything I didn't have: money, possessions, a large home, expensive cars, gadgets, so-called security, power, status, the white picket fence. Thanks to the help of the media, advertising, and peer pressure—not to mention childhood privation—this was an easy trap to fall into.

The French psychoanalyst Jacques Lacan referred to this driving desire as Object A; that is, the thing we think we want—the thing that would make us satisfied if only we could acquire, possess, or achieve it.

The gold watch.
The luxury vehicle.
The designer clothes.
The suburban homestead.
The corner-office promotion.
The move to a new city.
The marriage proposal.
The award or certificate.
The stupid yellow necktie.

We all have our own Object A's, and the most insidious part is that they continue to change throughout our lives until, eventually, the object of our desire becomes the object of our discontent. That smartphone you couldn't live without three years ago is now frustratingly slow and antiquated. That new car you wanted so badly is now just a car payment and a burden. That sailboat that was going to bring you so much freedom on the weekends is now a bottomless money pit. In time, we realize the things we wanted aren't the things we want.

When I spoke with the philosopher Peter Rollins about desire, he said, "While it's different for everyone, Object A is the object that you think will fix everything. It's the object that destabilizes your life: that person you *have* to be with, or that job you want more than anything else, or that city you *have* to move to in order to feel alive." In its most extreme cases, Object A is, as Rollins puts it, "the thing for which you'd be willing to set fire to your entire existence—you'd be willing to destroy your health, your relationships, everything—in order to get it."

> IF WE'RE WILLING TO COMPROMISE ANYTHING, EVENTUALLY WE'LL COMPROMISE EVERYTHING.

But maybe that's not as extreme as it sounds. Maybe we all make tiny sacrifices day after day until our life is one giant compromise. As we age, we let our health go, we stop exercising and eating healthfully; we put on a few pounds each year. We forsake the people we love because we choose to spend more time with coworkers and clients while we advance our careers. We give up on our dreams because dreams aren't as "practical" as a white picket fence and a sport utility vehicle and a monthly debt payment. So, strangely, we actually do set fire to our entire existence—a slow burn—in order to get momentary pleasure, even if it makes us miserable in the long run.

Ergo, the problem isn't desire; the problem is the belief that the next milestone will bring with it everlasting joy—even though we know, from experience, it won't. We've all earned a trophy or moved to a new neighborhood or started a new relationship or acquired a coveted new possession just to be let down on the other side of our desire.

"Another way to think about Object A is to think of it as something that doesn't exist," Rollins explained. "It's an incarnation." He claims that human beings are structurally prone to think there's an absolute that will fix us. "Whether it's millions of dollars, a relationship, or a religion, that's the incarnation of Object A. But whenever you get it, you're always a little dissatisfied."

Many people and products promise to deliver Object A to us—they say they can deliver us peace and comfort and a satisfaction so great we'll never want for anything else—but these promises are not unlike the promises of a duplicitous guru. Eventually, they will let us down. And, according to Rollins, when Object A lets us down, the pendulum often swings in the opposite direction: "If monogamy was your Object A, you may seek out polyamory as soon as you're unsatisfied with your relationship. Or, if you're a conservative Christian, you might become a hippie when your religion is no longer living up to your expectations—and vice versa. There's always a new place to go when this place fails to deliver."

FROM MONEY AND POSSESSIONS TO STATUS AND SUCCESS, THE THINGS YOU DESIRE USUALLY WON'T PROVIDE THE SATISFACTION YOU ANTICIPATE.

Whatever our Object A is, it is, by definition, guaranteed to disappoint. And yet we continue to seek happiness through our personal Object A's. There are three reasons this happens to all of us: our interests adapt to our environment, we conflate pleasure with contentment, and our surface desires do not match our deepest values. Let's examine these realities one at a time.

The Hedonic Treadmill

Before moving to the city for college and, subsequently, a well-paid job as a research scientist, Luke Wenger lived a fairly modest existence, growing up on a farm in northeast Kansas. Wenger, a Packing Party Case Study participant whom we briefly introduced in the "Relationship with Truth" chapter, acknowledges that he'd let life get in the way of living. "No matter how strong you think your values are," he said in the middle of his unpacking experiment, "it's easy to compromise [those values] when you're surrounded— bombarded—daily with the temptation of creature comforts."

As soon as Wenger was employed as a scientist, his regular paychecks enabled him to fill his apartment with all the things he ever wanted. Or, at least, the things he was told by advertisers and marketers and society to want. "But, every time, the satisfaction from those purchases was short-lived," he said, "and I kept spending more and more, collecting more and more, all in a vain effort to find happiness."

According to the theory of Hedonic Adaptation, also known as the Hedonic Treadmill, our desires continue to change shape as we navigate through life. Like Luke Wenger, as we become accustomed to new changes—both positive and negative—our expectations adapt to our new circumstances. Although the term itself was coined in 1971, the concept of Hedonic Adaptation has been discussed by philosophers for centuries. Many famous thinkers on this subject—from Epicurus to Yang Zhu—have observed that individual humans seem to have a hedonic (or happiness) set point, and that, even though we might experience a jolt of happiness with each new change, our long-term happiness is not significantly affected by impacting events.

For example, if you lose a limb in a car accident, it will almost certainly make you unhappy. But, in time, you'll heal, and you'll adapt to your new circumstances, and, happily, you'll experience happiness again. Conversely, if you win the lottery, you'll probably experience a great rush of pleasure and excitement. But, eventually, that feeling will wear off, and you'll return to your previous baseline, regardless of how many commas reside in the balance of your bank account.

The same is true for less extreme examples. From money and possessions to status and success, the things you desire usually won't provide the satisfaction you anticipate. Which means we must measure satisfaction differently if we want to understand how to feel fulfilled as humans.

The Well-Being Continuum

As a teenager, in the years before I exited the Dayton Mall in handcuffs, I didn't realize there was an entire scaffolding upon which I could build a meaningful life. Sure, I knew "right" and "wrong" as concepts, but I set all that aside because I wanted ephemeral pleasure, instant gratification, immediate results, even if it cost me happiness and contentment and joy in the long run. This pattern continued throughout my twenties and was only amplified by my increased purchasing power.

In fact, that's the real problem. We confuse pleasure with other, more meaningful forms of well-being. We use four distinct terms—pleasure, happiness, contentment, and joy—interchangeably, although I'd argue they have major differences that, when understood, help us increase our overall well-being. To make these abstractions more concrete, let's look at the various ways we experience food as an illustration.

Pleasure. When you eat a piece of birthday cake, you experience a burst of pleasure as the processed sugar and fat and gluten dance on your taste buds. The pleasure doesn't last long, though, so you go for a second bite, and then a third, and so on, until you're stuffed. This is pure pleasure. But even though you're full, your body is confused because you just gorged on empty calories, and you didn't get any of the essential micronutrients, elements, or minerals you need to thrive. Let's be clear: there's nothing wrong with pleasure. We all want to feel good. The problem occurs when we forsake higher forms of well-being to experience pleasure—when pleasure is the goal, rather than a by-product. When our primary diet is cake, we become malnourished. The same can be said for almost all forms of pleasure. When we seek only pleasure, we miss out on life's essential mental, physical, and emotional nutrients. A few bites won't kill us, but let's not pretend it's "good" for us, either. There is no merit in pleasure alone. And somewhat paradoxically, pleasure is often the enemy of happiness.

Happiness. If pleasure is consuming a piece of cake, then happiness is eating an enjoyable, healthy meal. Happiness occurs when you make a momentarily beneficial decision. When you eat a balanced meal that contains all the nutrients you need to flourish, you experience happiness, albeit briefly, because you made a satisfying decision. That decision might not always be as pleasurable as pure pleasure—and, at times, it might even be painful (think of your most intense gym workout)—but you feel happy in the moment because your decision aligns with the person you aspire to be. Both pleasure and happiness are fleeting, which is precisely why neither is a noble goal. But if you live a life that's congruent with your values, you will experience happiness. Hence, happiness is not the goal—living a meaningful life is, and happiness is a beautiful by-product.

Contentment. To extend our food metaphor, if happiness is a healthy meal, then contentment is a consistent, well-balanced diet. Just as there's a giant delta between a healthy meal and a healthy lifestyle, there's also a big difference between happiness and contentment. Sure, you might have a "cheat day" a few times a month, but contentment arises from a series of nourishing decisions over a protracted period of time, not a single "good" or "bad" decision. It's a side effect of a well-lived life. Of course, contentment requires a deeper understanding than mere happiness, but its payoff is markedly higher.

Joy. The highest form of well-being is joy, and it occurs only when other people are involved. You might experience pleasure, or even happiness, from your lunch today, and you might feel content with your overall dietary lifestyle, but you can experience joy if you share a meal with someone you care about. They say "giving is living" because you are living your best life when you're interacting with—and contributing to—the world around you. A person who is driven by joy, instead of mere pleasure or happiness, makes it their life's mandate to bring joy to others. That's real living! Nearly all of life's peak experiences occur on the other side of contribution.

Joy is also different from the other forms of well-being because it makes room for negative emotions, too. With pleasure and happiness, there's no room for sadness or frustration or disappointment. But because joy doesn't strive for immediate satisfaction, it is possible to experience the full range of emotions—including pain and grief and regret—and still experience joy. Joy doesn't stop at mere satisfaction; it strives for fulfillment and tranquility.

Sure, joyous experiences might also be pleasurable, but they are so much more than that. There is an automaticity to joy that doesn't require continuous yearning the way pleasure does. Think of some of the most joyous times in your life. When were they? Who was there? There's a strong chance that all of these experiences involved other people, either directly or indirectly. A concert. A book club or meetup group. Sex with the person you love.

Unfortunately, we often settle for pleasure because it's immediate and easy, or we endlessly pursue happiness when, in an ideal world, we would seek a life of contentment and joy, a life of repeated intentional decisions that align with our values and benefit others. The clinical psychologist Jordan B. Peterson, who is a professor at the University of Toronto, once remarked that instead of happiness, a more virtuous aspiration is to "be the strongest person at your father's funeral," suggesting that a life of virtue strengthens our character and is far more fulfilling, even in its most difficult moments, than a life built upon perfunctory pursuits.

> IN TIME, WE REALIZE THE THINGS WE WANTED AREN'T THE THINGS WE WANT.

In the introductory chapter of this book, I said that every possession I own must serve a purpose or bring me joy. I chose those words carefully. It's not enough for a material item to simply offer pleasure, or even happiness, because then I could always find a new excuse to acquire more. Instead, my possessions must act as tools that augment my life (serve a purpose), or they must serve the greater good (bring joy). Otherwise, the stuff just gets in the way.

There is, however, a place where pleasure, happiness, contentment, and joy intersect. Today, in the English-speaking world, when we speak of "pursuing happiness," we're often talking about what

Greek and Roman Stoics called *ataraxia* or what the ancient Greeks, in general, referred to as *eudaemonia*. *Ataraxia*, which is generally translated as "unperturbedness" or "tranquility," was first used by the Greek philosopher Pyrrho, and eventually the Stoics, to describe a lucid state of robust equanimity characterized by ongoing freedom from distress and worry. Similarly, *eudaemonism* is a system of ethics that bases moral value on the likelihood that good actions will produce contentment. Meaning it's not only desirable, it's ethical to feel pleasure and happiness and contentment and joy when our actions align with the best version of ourselves.

Now, of course, most people treat these terms as synonyms (and rarely even mention *ataraxia* or *eudaemonia*), and that's acceptable in everyday discourse. But if we start thinking of these states as different levels of well-being—and as a staircase toward fulfillment and tranquility—we can begin to make better decisions that affect our contentment and joy, without substantially affecting our pleasure or happiness. In time, those better decisions will lead to a better life.

MINIMALIST RULE FOR LIVING WITH LESS

Seasonality Rule

Look at your possessions. Pick something. Anything. Have you used that item in the last ninety days? If you haven't, will you use it in the next ninety? If not, it's okay to let go. That's why some people call this the 90/90 Rule. What's particularly useful about this rule is that it covers every season. Let's say it's March and you're getting ready to embark on some spring cleaning. Pick up the first item you see in your closet, basement, or storage unit. Maybe it's an old sweater. Are you using it right now (in the spring)? Have you used it in the last ninety days (in the winter)? Will you use it in the next ninety days (in the summer)? If yes, keep it. If not, say goodbye!

Drunk Shopping

A recent survey found that "drunk shopping" is an estimated forty-five-billion-dollar-per-year industry. Apparently, 79 percent of tipsy consumers have made at least one drunk purchase, and the average drunk shopper spends $444 each year making inebriated buying decisions.

I would argue, however, that nearly 100 percent of us do this. We may not be drunk on alcohol when we shop, but we're frequently under the influence of instant gratification, so much so that we make purchasing decisions we know are antithetical to our values—just to feel the dopamine rush of the moment.

We ignore our budgets.

We buy things we don't even want.

We make purchases to impress others.

We set aside our values for short-term gain.

I know because I've done all these things.

When our taste for possessions or pleasure is stronger than our values, we sacrifice fulfillment for transient gains. That's certainly what happened to me the day I was arrested for shoplifting. Truth be told, I could have borrowed a necktie from a friend, or arrived at my interview without one at all, and I would've been okay. But the story I told myself was that I needed this right now, that I needed it so much that it didn't matter if I sacrificed my values to get it. I hadn't had a single drink, but, in a way, I was shopping under the influence. My decisions were impaired by a misguided attitude: *I must have this, and I must have it now!* And because I didn't know what my values were, it was an easy compromise to make.

Of course, this happens to everyone at some point. We search for shortcuts or act on impulse, and the world around us boosts the signal of temptation. It's not only drunk shoppers who are impaired; our children are also intoxicated by instant gratification.

Think about the last time you left a museum. You were probably forced to exit through the gift shop. It's consumerism's last gasp. And, sadly, it works. Every time my daughter bounds through the knickknacks, tchotchkes, and souvenirs, she begs to bring one home.

"Can I get something? *Pleeeease!*"

"What do you want?"

"I don't know—*anything!*"

That's what consumerism does to everyone. We don't know what we want, but we know we want more, and we want it now. We don't even stop to think about it—to question what might add value to our lives, or what might get in the way. But if we don't question everything we bring into our lives, we'll allow anything in.

The message of minimalism, then, is simple: If you didn't need it five minutes ago, you probably don't need it now. And even if you do, it wouldn't hurt to wait.

If I tell my daughter to ask me tomorrow whether she can buy that useless widget, she almost always forgets. That's because we remember only that which is meaningful, and all the ephemera dissipates into the ether.

Understanding Our Values

It is beneficial to understand your values—they illuminate the direction in which you must travel to experience a fulfilling life. Your values help you make the decisions you actually want to make, including deliberate choices about consumption. If I would have gotten clear on *my* values, I could have made better decisions and avoided the embarrassment and guilt and shame that accompanied my arrest. That wasn't the person I wanted to be. But then again, I didn't know who I wanted to be—because my values were hazy at best.

Thus, I spent the next decade careening from one hapless decision to the next, even if, ostensibly, I had my life together. I may have had the house in the suburbs, the twin Lexuses, the tailored suits, the respectable career—but those supposed achievements masked a lifetime of unchecked poor decisions. And because I didn't know who I wanted to be, those decisions moved me away from being the best version of myself. I moved slowly in the wrong direction at first, but, as I grew more discontent throughout my twenties, it was as if I was running away from the life I desired.

HAPPINESS IS NOT THE GOAL— LIVING A MEANINGFUL LIFE IS, AND HAPPINESS IS A BEAUTIFUL BY-PRODUCT.

In time, through repeated missteps and struggle, I realized that no matter how fast I traveled, I'd never reach my destination if I was headed the wrong way. To figure out the right direction, I had to determine my own values.

If I've learned anything throughout my four decades on this planet, it's this: the most genuine way to live is to align your short-term actions with your long-term values. You want to make your future self proud of your present self. Otherwise, you'll speed from one pleasurable experience to another, which might feel pleasant in the moment, but it will leave a devastating void.

There are at least two reasons people don't understand their values: First, we don't stop to question what they are, and so our values are shaped by pop culture, the media, and the influence of others. Second, we don't understand that some values are more important than others.

If you're reading this, you're already making progress against that first hurdle: you're questioning your values. Bravo! As you're pondering, though, it's equally important to understand that not all values are created equal. Some are, in fact, not values at all, which means they get in the way of what's important. That's why I separate my values into four contrasting categories: Foundational Values, Structural Values, Surface Values, and Imaginary Values. Let's look at them one at a time.

Foundational Values

Every home must be built on a sturdy foundation. You can own a beautiful house, but it will sink into the ground if its foundation isn't solid. The same is true of our values. While most people have different values overall, we tend to share five similar Foundational Values:

- Health.
- Relationships.
- Creativity.

- Growth.
- Contribution.

These are the unshakable principles by which I live my life. So whenever I'm feeling unfulfilled, I check to see whether I'm neglecting any of them. You may have others as part of your foundation, but these five are nearly universal. A decade ago, in an effort to better understand our foundations, Ryan and I wrote our first book, *Minimalism: Live a Meaningful Life*, about these five shared values. Instead of reprising that entire book, I will simply summarize each of the Foundational Values in the following sections.

FOUNDATIONAL VALUE 1: HEALTH

Imagine winning the lottery, finding a perfect match in your significant other, paying off your debts, moving into your dream home, and not needing to work another day in your life. Now imagine waking tomorrow with a sharp pain in your gut. You leave your beach house, drive to the doctor's office in your luxury vehicle, and wait for her to tell you what's wrong. "You have less than a year to live," she says. "And you likely won't be able to do much more than get out of bed after today." Oh, the heartache. You finally got "everything you ever wanted," but your failing health immediately took it away, and your possessions couldn't do a thing for you. Without your health, you're unable to enjoy even the simplest things in life.

FOUNDATIONAL VALUE 2: RELATIONSHIPS

Imagine winning the lottery, getting into the best shape of your life, paying off your debts, moving into your dream home, and not needing to work another day in your life. Now imagine waking tomorrow and having nobody to share your new life with. No friends. No family. No loved ones. Oh, the heartache. You finally got "everything you ever wanted," but there's no one to enjoy it with. Without worthwhile relationships, you are unable to live a meaningful life.

FOUNDATIONAL VALUE 3: CREATIVITY

Imagine winning the lottery, getting into the best shape of your life, finding your soul mate, establishing the most meaningful relationships possible, paying off your debts, moving into your dream home, and not needing to work another day in your life. Now imagine waking tomorrow, and the next day, and then the next, with nothing to do, nothing to fuel your fire. Oh, the horror. There are only so many TV shows you can watch, or vacations you can take, before you realize passion is missing from your life. You will not feel fulfilled—you will not feel passionate about life—if your life lacks creativity. This is frequently the root cause of that empty feeling so many people experience.

While we'll explore creativity—and what prevents us from being creative—later in this book, I'd like to take a moment to discuss the concept of "passion." When Ryan and I originally conceived of the five Foundational Values, passion was third on this list. But one could argue that what we really meant was creativity.

If you search the Internet today, you'll find no shortage of "experts" who want you to "follow your passion." There are at least two problems with this misleading advice. First, it presupposes you were born with a preexisting passion—as if you were meant to be an astronaut, accountant, or actor. And second, the concept of passion has been overused and mistreated by so-called influencers over the last two decades, so much so that it has lost its meaning. Did you know that the Latin root of passion means "to suffer"? Do you think these Internet authorities are actually telling people to "follow their suffering"? Of course not. It's easy to encourage someone to follow their passion, but that advice is too simplistic.

Life doesn't contain these sorts of absolutes. No one has a predetermined destiny, nor a singular preexisting passion waiting to be uncovered. There are dozens, even hundreds, of things you can do with your life—unlimited creative opportunities to fuel your passion. In this manner, creativity fundamentally fulfills the same needs as passion, but it's a better descriptor of this Foundational Value.

FOUNDATIONAL VALUE 4: GROWTH

Imagine winning the lottery, getting into the best shape of your life, finding your soul mate, establishing the most meaningful relationships possible, paying off your debts, moving into your dream home, cultivating the creative project that makes you the most passionate, and discovering your life's mission. Now what? Visit the nearest lake and fish every day? Sit on the couch and bask in the bluish glow of your television? Of course not. You want to continue to enjoy your newfound life—the one with the improved health, improved relationships, and newly discovered creativity. Thus, you must continue to improve; you must continue to grow. Turns out, the old saying "if you're not growing, you're dying" is brutally true.

Of course, not all growth is beneficial. A bicep after a month in the gym is a type of growth. But so is a tumor. So we better choose deliberately how we want to grow, or we'll grow according to the dictates of everyone else. Our society has developed a particular narrative since the Industrial Revolution, one that says we must explore *never-ending* growth, which might sound appealing at first, but it's not the type of growth I'm interested in. What I'm focused on is *intentional* growth.

Never-ending growth says we must grow at any cost; intentional growth happens when we grow in accordance with our values. Have you ever made a "one-time" compromise that led to a series of greater compromises? I have. I've literally lied and stolen to get what I wanted. But then I didn't stop with the first indiscretion. I'd lie to cover up the previous lie, and then I'd need to tell an even bigger lie to cover up the cover-up. What a tangled web. This often happens when we compromise, even though there's nothing intrinsically wrong with compromise itself. In fact, most relationships require continually meeting in the middle. The problem occurs when we compromise what we desire to get what we want today. It's harder to stick to our principles—to avoid the allure of the shortcut—but it's important if we want to grow with intention.

NEARLY ALL OF LIFE'S PEAK EXPERIENCES OCCUR ON THE OTHER SIDE OF CONTRIBUTION.

Never-ending growth forsakes people for profitability; intentional growth doesn't pretend money is irrelevant, but it doesn't allow the profit motive to run the show, either. Ryan and I run two profitable businesses—The Minimalists in Los Angeles, California, and Bandit Coffee Co. in St. Petersburg, Florida—but money is not the primary driver for either. We focus on *adding value* to our readers, listeners, viewers, followers, clients, and customers without undermining our values. We treat our employees fairly and pay them fair wages. We focus on quality, not quantity. We don't run advertisements on any of our platforms. We don't sell our audience's data to third parties. And we don't send spam or junk to anyone—ever. As a result, people trust us, and they are willing to support our work, be it the books we write or the coffee we roast. Sure, we may not squeeze every nickel out of either business this quarter, but it's easier to sleep at night knowing our decisions match our values, and we feel better about the long-term prospects of both enterprises when their growth isn't predicated solely on padding our wallets.

Never-ending growth worries about competition and increased expectations; intentional growth contemplates cooperation and higher standards. During my corporate days, we fixated so heavily on imaginary targets. My retail stores were responsible for tracking twenty-nine different performance metrics on a daily basis, which meant that, even on a "great" sales day, we could always find something to make us discontented. We do this in our personal lives, too, don't we? We look at the scale in our bathroom and pretend its readout is a proxy for well-being. We look at the numbers on our bank statement and pretend they're a proxy for happiness. We look at the material possessions in our home and pretend they are a proxy for completeness. These expectations only grow in time. What was once a grand hope becomes commonplace as our expectations expand, creating chaos along the way. The antidote to this chaos is a bit of a paradox: to restore order in our lives, we must lower our expectations and raise our standards. UCLA head coach John Wooden famously discouraged his players from looking at the scoreboard. Instead, he encouraged them to commit to playing *their* best. Consequently, Wooden's teams won ten championships in a twelve-year period, and he went on to become one of the winningest coaches in NCAA history—not because of his expectation of winning, but because of his high standards.

Growth is a critical component of living well—as long as it's intentional growth—because continual improvement makes us feel alive and brings purpose to our actions. Think of all the improvements you've already made in your life. Didn't many of them seem unfathomable five or ten years before? How were you able to make those changes? Chances are you made them not through a giant leap, but through incremental modifications over an extended period of time. Sure, some changes can be huge and immediate—ending a relationship, quitting your job, moving to a new city—and occasionally these giant leaps are necessary. But most growth comes from baby steps—because those baby steps allow you to eventually take the giant leaps.

FOUNDATIONAL VALUE 5: CONTRIBUTION

Imagine winning the lottery, getting into the best shape of your life, finding your soul mate, establishing the most meaningful relationships possible, paying off your debts, moving into your dream home, cultivating the creative project that makes you the most passionate, discovering your life's mission, and finding new ways to grow every day. Now what? Stand atop your mound of money, basking in your success?

Hardly.

Whether you call it giving or altruism or service, the final Foundational Value is contribution, which perfectly complements the previous value. Growth and contribution create a regenerative sequence: the more you grow, the more you can help others grow; the more you help others grow, the more you grow in return. Intentional growth feels great, but contribution can feel even better because we'll often do more for the people we love than for ourselves. That's because humans have an intrinsic need to contribute to others. While there can be many ways to serve others, it is beneficial to learn how to contribute most effectively to the world around you. According to William MacAskill, a Scottish philosopher, ethicist, and originator of the effective altruism movement, "Effective altruism is about answering one simple question: how can we use our resources to help others the most? Rather than just doing what feels right, [effective altruism uses] evidence and careful analysis to find the best causes to work on." In other words, giving is nice but constructive contribution is even nicer.

If you contribute wisely, "you can have a tremendous positive impact on the world," MacAskill claims. "This is such an astonishing fact that it's hard to appreciate. Imagine if, one day, you see a burning building with a small child inside. You run into the blaze, pick up the child, and carry them to safety. You would be a hero. Now imagine that this happened to you every two years—you'd save dozens of lives over the course of your career. This sounds like an odd world, but current evidence suggests that this is the world that many people live in. If you earn the typical income in the United States, and donate 10 percent of your earnings each year to the Against Malaria Foundation, you will probably save dozens of lives over your lifetime."

> **WE CONFUSE PLEASURE WITH OTHER, MORE MEANINGFUL FORMS OF WELL-BEING.**

But, of course, writing a check isn't the only way to get involved. People without the financial means to donate to charity can find ways to serve the people in their local and global communities: serving food at soup kitchens, homeless shelters, and food banks; building homes with Habitat for Humanity; tutoring children who need help with their schoolwork. There are countless needs waiting to be met, not by the perfect savior, but by *you*, the imperfect person who's simply willing to help.

When Ryan and I left the corporate world in 2011, after being on this planet for thirty years and barely contributing at all, we finally made time to serve several worthy causes. Over the past decade, The Minimalists have built two orphanages, provided relief to the victims of Hurricane Harvey, supported the survivors of the Orlando and Las Vegas mass shootings, funded a high school for a year in Kenya, installed clean-water wells in three countries, constructed an elementary school in Laos, and purchased thousands of mosquito nets to fight malaria in Africa. At the time of this writing, we are raising money to build a nonprofit grocery co-op on the west side of Dayton, which is one of the largest food deserts in the United States. I inform you of these projects not to boast or be self-aggrandizing but, rather, to show you it's possible to go from zero giving to contributing greatly in a short span of time. All it takes is a willingness to help others.*

Whether you're writing checks or helping others with your hands (or both), the most effective way to contribute is to find a contribution method that inspires you to keep giving. Your contribution muscle grows as you serve others, and as you continue to give, you'll begin to experience a newfound purpose—one that informs you that life isn't about *you* personally; it's about *us* as a community.

MINIMALIST RULE FOR LIVING WITH LESS

One In, Ten Out Rule

Being a minimalist doesn't mean you'll never buy anything new. It means you'll do so intentionally, and you'll let go deliberately—or you could do both simultaneously. That's why we created the One In, Ten Out Rule. Based

---

* If you'd like to get involved with one of The Minimalists' future projects, you can sign up for our free newsletter at minimalists.com.

on the one-in, one-out policy used to manage the number of people in one building at any one time, this rule helps control what new items you buy and what items you keep because for every new item you acquire, you must get rid of ten things you own. Want that new shirt? Ten articles of clothing hit the donation bin. Want that new chair? Ten pieces of furniture make it to eBay. Want that new blender? Ten kitchen items get axed. When employed regularly, this rule will reshape your everyday consumption habits.

Structural Values

Once a foundation is established, a framework is erected. While every house has a frame, each home is different: some are made with steel and bolts; some are built with wood or brick; others are formed with concrete or cement. The same is true with your values. Your Structural Values make you who you are—they are your *personal* values. Below are a handful of my Structural Values with a personal definition for each*:

- Autonomy: freedom from external control.
- Enoughism: capacity to discern how much is enough.
- Humility: clarity of self; lack of ego.
- Mobility: unfettered by geography.
- Quality: better but fewer; the result of intention.
- Restraint: ability to avoid impulse.

---

* This is just a snapshot. For a comprehensive list of my values, visit minimalists
.com/v.

- Sincerity: earnestness free from deceit or hypocrisy.
- Solitude: time alone, not interacting with others.
- Vulnerability: courage to act irrespective of outcome.

As you gain experience, your Structural Values may change slightly over time, but much like your home, the structure tends to remain the same once it's built. Unless, of course, you embark on a serious remodeling project, which is always a possibility. When I left the corporate world at age thirty, I took a wrecking ball to my old values and constructed a new life based on new Structural Values.

Surface Values

After your foundation is set and your frame is in place, your home is beautified by its exterior. While this facade is not as critical as the structure itself, what's on the surface makes your house interesting and unique and enjoyable. You may even say it's what makes a house a home. The same is true with your Surface Values.

These *minor* values play an essential role in adding variety and diversity to your life—you might even think of them as your personal interests. But just because they are minor, that doesn't mean they don't have a major impact on your overall satisfaction; they are minor only relative to the more important values listed above, but they are a crucial component of a well-rounded life. Here are a few of mine at the moment:

- Aesthetics.
- Art.
- Cleanliness.

- Design.
- Meditation.
- Music.
- Reading.
- Writing.

As your interests change, your Surface Values may shift dramatically from month to month, year to year, decade to decade. Just as you might keep your house feeling fresh by repainting or incorporating new plants, you can keep your life feeling fresh by making sure your minor values match your current interests and desires. If one stops adding value, it's no longer of value, so let it go with abandon. You can always pick it up again in the future if you change your mind.

Imaginary Values

Say you've built a magnificent home on a solid foundation with a sturdy structure and even a beautiful facade. That's the equivalent of living a meaningful life. Unfortunately, that's not what usually happens. If we spend any time at all contemplating our values, we usually obsess over our Imaginary Values, which aren't even part of our value hierarchy. Imaginary Values are merely obstacles that get in our way. They are like a fence around the home we've constructed; we can't get in unless we eliminate the barrier. Here are a few of the Imaginary Values that sometimes prevent me from feeling fulfilled:

- Busyness.
- Comfort.

- Email.
- Productivity.
- Public opinion.
- Social media.
- Television.

As we gain more experience, our Imaginary Values change. There will always be new obstacles because once we're content, we're good at distracting ourselves with shiny new objects and offerings. We build well-decorated prison cells adorned with ephemera and then complain about our self-imposed incarceration.

But we must break through our obstacles. It was the author Ryan Holiday who showed us that "the obstacle is the way," and if I were to append his message, I'd say this: the only way to live a meaningful life is to get our Imaginary Values out of the way and then prioritize our higher-order values accordingly.

How to Use These Values

Everyone is different. My Structural Values might qualify as your Surface Values, or even your Imaginary Values—and vice versa. And that's okay—ideal, even. Our differences make life interesting. Imagine how boring things would be if everyone was exactly like me, or exactly like you.

It's also worth noting that our Surface Values sometimes become our Imaginary Values, and, if we're being honest with ourselves, even our Structural Values can become Imaginary Values as we reprioritize our lives. This is natural. As we get clear on what we want, we often discover that the things that served us yesterday get in the way today.

To help you identify your own values, we've included a Values

Worksheet at the end of this book.* Once you've completed this worksheet, review it with someone you trust. And if that person is willing, review their worksheet with them. You'll soon discover that once you understand *your* values—and the values of those closest to you—you'll understand how to interact with them more effectively, which will improve your relationships and help you both grow in exciting, unexpected ways. At the beginning of each year, my wife and I sit down at our kitchen table to review our Values Worksheet together, which not only helps me better communicate with her; it helps me understand how I can be the best version of myself.

Coda: Values

Hey! It's Ryan again. Wow! Joshua gave us plenty to reflect upon when it comes to values, huh? So are you ready to jump into some exercises that will help you better grasp your values? Fantastic! Please take the time to contemplate what each exercise is asking you. Afterward, you'll appreciate how much more you understand and value your values.

QUESTIONS ABOUT VALUES

1. What is your Object A? Why?
2. How are you currently compromising your values and holding yourself back?
3. When it comes to changing your life to align with your values, what frightens you—and why?

---

* You can download and print additional copies of the Values Worksheet at minimalists.com/resources.

4. What do you understand to be the differences between pleasure, happiness, contentment, and joy?

5. How will your future self express gratitude for the way you are living your life today?

THE DOS OF VALUES

Next, what did you learn about your values in this chapter? What will stick? What lessons will encourage you to better align your actions with the person you want to be? Here are five immediate actions you can take today:

- **Understand your values.** It is crucial to write down all of your values, even the imaginary ones. Use the Values Worksheet on page 321 or visit minimalists.com/resources and download a free printable copy.

- **Find a partner.** Choose someone with whom you can review your values. Ask them to participate with you. Reviewing your values with someone will provide accountability, reinforce your values, and inspire you to live up to what you value.

- **Get clear.** After you've completed the worksheet and reviewed it with your accountability partner, get clear on what values you are currently ignoring and/or compromising. How will you ditch the compromises and start taking actions and making decisions that align with your values?

- **Identify obstacles.** What are your biggest obstacles? Write them down, and then make a plan for how you will address them. If you get stuck, you may want to ask a friend or family member for guidance—or consult a professional (a therapist, doctor, or coach, for example).

- **Recognize consequences.** What are you sacrificing when you don't live up to your values? Write down the consequences of those sacrifices.

THE DON'TS OF VALUES

Finally, let's consider what's getting in the way of your values. Here are five things you'll want to avoid, beginning today, if you want to be the best version of yourself:

- Don't chase perfection. Perfection can't be acquired, and if we chase it, we will forever be let down. However, we *can* take consistent actions that create incremental changes.
- Don't chase pleasure and happiness. When we do, we never experience true joy. Instead, we want to focus on living a meaningful life. When we live this way, pleasure and happiness become byproducts.
- Avoid high expectations. Instead, hold yourself to higher standards.
- Don't let immediate satisfaction or immediate dissatisfaction control you.
- Don't compromise your values.

RELATIONSHIP 5 | MONEY

I got my first credit card the summer I turned eighteen, and I spent the next decade spending. My shiny new MasterCard made it easy. If I couldn't afford something, that was fine: finance it! Most purchases were aspirational, as if attempting to buy my way to the next tier of success. "You can't make money without spending money" was the occult mantra I'd heard at business meetings and conferences, and, boy, did I take it to heart, even though I never really understood what it meant. It just sounded nice—a simple justification for financial mismanagement. I wasn't living beyond my means, I told myself; I was living within the means of my future self. I wasn't reckless; I was just spending the amount of money I'd be able to make after the next promotion, pay raise, annual bonus, or commission windfall. Until then, my credit cards would bridge the gap.

When my first card maxed out, it was easy to get another, and then another, and then several more over the years until, eventually, I had fourteen pieces of maxed-out plastic in my wallet, everything from Visa and Discover to Diners Club and Macy's, each of which made my purchases hassle-free, or so I thought, because I could acquire new clothes and home decor and a catalog of impulse purchases without spending *my* money. At least that's how it felt each time I swiped.

It was as if "I'll use my credit card" had become my de facto slogan. Unconcerned with the future harm caused by debt and interest rates and the anxiety associated with both, I used credit for almost every purchase. And it only got worse—not better, as I thought it would—as I made more money.

The temptation of debt has a way of erasing our identities, replacing them with the vast struggle to be like everyone else. I got my first promotion at age twenty-two, the same year I built my first house. I bought a Lexus at twenty-three. A second Lexus at twenty-four. A Land Rover at twenty-five. Each time, I thought satisfaction was around the bend. But as I rounded the corner, the adrenaline faded, and the only thing in the foreground was yearning. Yearning for something better, something different, something to fill the void. I was digging a ditch one shovelful at a time. And I wasn't alone.

Financial Dysfunction

Julie Hamilton, a Packing Party Case Study participant from Madison, Wisconsin, found herself and her family swept up in the pursuit of more: "I was helping my husband run several small businesses, and we were so focused on success and the realization of our American Dream—the house, the cars, the possessions—that we ultimately found ourselves smothered by it all." In the middle of her family's unpacking experiment, Hamilton admitted that she and her husband felt as though they were "suffocating from stress." It took simplifying for the Hamiltons to understand that the life they'd been leading wasn't sustainable; that the financial burden of endlessly pursuing more had broken them.

Millions of Americans are living paycheck to paycheck, and according to a recent CFSI survey, 72 percent of Americans are financially unhealthy. Sometimes we are nudged unwillingly into debt by unforeseen medical expenses, but often we make repeated careless decisions that surround us with heaps of debt over time.

THE TEMPTATION OF DEBT HAS A WAY OF ERASING OUR IDENTITIES, REPLACING THEM WITH THE VAST STRUGGLE TO BE LIKE EVERYONE ELSE.

I did the latter—and became a victim of my own reckless choices. Not only was I one of those financially unhealthy folks, but, even though I was earning nearly $200,000 a year by my late twenties (in Dayton, Ohio, mind you), I was also one of the 44 percent whose expenses exceed their income. By many measures I *appeared* prosperous, but really, I was suffering from "financial impotence" a decade before Neal Gabler coined that term in *The Atlantic*, explaining that the condition "has many of the characteristics of sexual impotence, not least of which is the desperate need to mask it and pretend everything is going swimmingly."

Like the Hamiltons, that's what I did. I pretended to be successful. But my attempts to mask my financial woes were like trying to paint a burning house—a few extra coats were never going to extinguish the fire. How could I *not* have noticed the flames? You'd think I would have been alarmed by the billing statements singeing my mailbox each week, but I compartmentalized my indiscretions, and my debt left burn marks. I was living a lifestyle that wasn't joyous or virtuous—the gradual descent into living to work, not working to live. How miserable was I willing to be to impress the people around me?

And to make matters worse, I often encouraged others—friends, family, employees—to go into debt: *You deserve that sports car, that grand piano, that kitchen remodel!* It was a perverse way to repackage my failures as favorable outcomes because if enough people lived like me, I was vindicated, right? Misery encourages others to pull up a chair and stay awhile.

A portrait of financial dysfunction, I made good money but spent even better money, and as I approached age thirty, I had a mortgage payment, a second-mortgage payment, several car payments, a credit-card consolidation loan from my early twenties, and a stack of new credit-card payments, not to mention my regular bills and living expenses. To boot, I had two separate student-loan payments, but no college degree to show for it (don't ask). I was one misstep away from seeking out the modern-day equivalent to loan sharks—payday lenders—which is where our society's most desperate people often turn. And many of us are far more desperate than you may realize.

Did you know that one in four Americans would need to borrow or sell something to pay for an unexpected expense of $400? That is also roughly the same percentage of American adults who have no retirement savings, according to a recent report from the Federal Reserve. And approximately the same number of people—25 percent—say they have skipped *necessary* medical care in the last year because they were unable to afford the cost. (That says something about both our opaquely priced medical system, which could be better regulated to remove price gouging, as well as our inability to save money.)

Debt is stripping us of our freedom, our security, our identity. Our creditors are holding the American Dream hostage. And the New American Dream is to become debt-free.

In a magazine interview a few years ago, a reporter asked me whom I thought of when I heard the word "successful." My answer was not Steve Jobs, Bill Gates, or Kim Kardashian. Nor do I think of the old American Dream—the big house, the cars, and the debt associated with opulence—as my definition of success. When I think of success, I think of my friend Jamar Hocker in Cincinnati. Why? Because he knows you might be able to purchase fugitive pleasures, but financial freedom is not for sale. Although he is an outstanding father, husband, high-school teacher, and real estate investor, those things alone don't make him successful. What makes Jamar successful is that he's living the New American Dream: he is joyous, healthy, and debt-free; he has full control of his life; and he doesn't derive his self-worth from external factors—all of which makes him one of the most successful people I know. Sure, Jamar works hard, but that work isn't designed to amass more possessions—he works to increase his freedom, while most of us work hard to become broke.

Most People Are Broke

There are many reasons for our individual financial crises, including medical emergencies, job loss, and predatory lending. And of course, we can't forget about inflation—in the last decade, home prices have gone up 26 percent, medical expenses have increased 33 percent, and college costs have surged 45 percent—and so we've gotten into more and more debt to keep up with our rising expenses. While it's easy to spread the blame, we must also take ownership of our own actions. Every time we sign on the dotted line, every time we spend recklessly, every time we bring home something we can't afford, we are asking our future self to take responsibility for our current decisions.

During the summer of 2018, The Minimalists embarked on a Money and Minimalism speaking tour with Dave Ramsey's team of Ramsey Personalities. Host of the third-largest talk-radio show in America and author of several best-selling books, Ramsey has helped millions of Americans get out of debt and change their financial futures. While spending time at the headquarters of Ramsey Solutions outside Nashville that summer, I had the opportunity to learn more about why so many people from the richest country in the world are broke.

"If you want to win with money, figure out what most people are doing, and then run in the other direction," Ramsey said in a rant about financial negligence, speaking energetically in aphoristic sentences—more financial poetry than prose. The following is verbatim:

Most people are broke.
Most people look good, but they're broke.
They spend more than they have coming in.
They don't act their wage; don't live on a plan.
They don't have money set aside for emergencies.
They don't agree with their spouse on spending.
They hope the government will care for them in retirement.
Most people are stupid with money; they spend like they're in Congress.
The bankruptcy rate is at an all-time high; foreclosures are rising again.
Most people are living paycheck to paycheck.
Credit-card debt continues to climb.
We have more than a trillion dollars in student-loan debt.
The average car payment is nearly $500 over eighty-four months—that's stupid.

Normal in America is broke and stupid.

You don't want to be normal.

You want to be weird.

Weird is contrary.

And when the culture has lost its way,

the best thing you can be is a contrarian.

What I appreciate most about Ramsey's financial soliloquies is they come from a place of love, albeit *tough* love. Sure, he might rattle you if you're one of the 16 million people who listen to his show each week, but he does so because he cares. If this isn't apparent through your speakers, it's obvious when you spend time with him. After making all the same stupid decisions most of us have, Ramsey himself struggled with financial dysfunction until, eventually, when he was broke and broken, he had to file for bankruptcy and start over. But he rose like a phoenix from the ashes of financial ruin, and he has spent the last three decades applying what he learned to help people get out of debt and reclaim their resources.

A few years ago, I wrote a quasi-satirical essay called "11 Signs You Might Be Broke," which was modeled on Jeff Foxworthy's famous "You Might Be a Redneck" routine.* I won't rehash all the arguments from that piece—"you might be broke if you're living paycheck to paycheck," "you might be broke if you have a monthly car payment," "you might be broke if you have credit-card debt" are a few—but I'd like to summarize its thesis: being broke is okay; being broke without a plan to break the cycle is not. You see, we've all been broke or broken at some point in our lives. True, we all need money to live, but, as Tyler Durden says in *Fight Club*, you are not the contents of your

---

* If you're interested, you can read the entire essay at minimalists.com/broke.

wallet. What's more important than income is how we spend the resources we have. I personally know broke people who make six (or even seven) figures. I also know families who live on $30,000 a year but aren't broke at all—because they deliberately live within their means. Real wealth, security, and contentment come not from the trinkets we stockpile, but from how we spend the one life we've been given. Yet it's difficult to enjoy that life when we're anchored by debt, which means we must raise the anchor if we want to move toward better living. Debt-free is the new pay raise.

Getting Out of Debt

Besides respecting Ramsey's much-needed brand of tough love, I also appreciate that his advice is eminently actionable. In his best-selling book *The Total Money Makeover: A Proven Plan for Financial Fitness*, which has more than eight million copies in print, Ramsey outlines a universal plan—the very plan he used—to get out of debt and achieve financial freedom. He calls this plan the Seven Baby Steps:

Baby Step 1: Save $1,000 for your starter emergency fund (and build a budget).

Baby Step 2: Pay off all debt (except the house) using the "debt snowball."

Baby Step 3: Save three to six months of expenses in a fully funded emergency fund.

Baby Step 4: Invest 15 percent of your household income in retirement.

Baby Step 5: Save for your children's college fund.

Baby Step 6: Pay off your home early.

Baby Step 7: Build wealth and give.

These simple steps—specifically Baby Steps 1 and 2—also guided me personally out of six figures' worth of debt. How? First, I had to save $1,000 as fast as I could—an emergency fund to cover life's unexpected events: car repairs, medical expenses, and other actual emergencies. This first step was momentous because I didn't want to dig a deeper hole while I was working my way out of debt. Next, it was time to establish a budget. I used Ramsey's "envelope system" at the time, but if I were to do it again today, I'd use his free budgeting app, EveryDollar, to track my monthly expenses.

DEBT-FREE IS THE NEW PAY RAISE.

Once I had my emergency fund and my budget set, it was time to start methodically paying off my cars, credit cards, and student loans. Following Ramsey's plan, I sold two cars and cut up all my credit cards, and then I listed all my debts, putting them in order by balance and then paying them off, one by one, from smallest to largest (hence, the "debt snowball"). It took me four years of rigorous work—radically reducing my spending, eating at home, even delivering pizzas to earn extra money—to become debt-free. I had to create better spending habits because *you can't spend your way out of debt*. But now that I have zero debt, and I've experienced all the benefits of financial freedom, I'm never going back.

Living without debt has enabled me to contribute more than ever. Living without debt has allowed me to walk away from the corporate world. Living without debt has helped me consume less and create more. Living without debt has made it easier to travel the world. Living without debt has encouraged me to invest in my future. Living without debt has filled me with a calmness I never felt while indebted. Living without debt has convinced me that there's no such thing as "good" debt.

It wasn't only Dave Ramsey who helped elucidate the financial crises that are happening in households across America. While on tour with Ramsey's handpicked team, I had the opportunity to discuss money, debt, and investing with a handful of America's top financial experts: Rachel Cruze, Anthony ONeal, and Chris Hogan, all three of whom we'll meet in this chapter.

Childhood Lessons About Money

During our Money and Minimalism event in Nashville, Rachel Cruze, coauthor of *Smart Money Smart Kids*, explained that our adult money habits start when we're children. "I was six months old when Mom and Dad filed for bankruptcy," Cruze said, which might suggest a childhood filled with struggle and money problems. After all, our children are always learning from us—sometimes from our words, but usually from our actions.

Was Cruze destined to repeat her parents' mistakes? Not in this case. Luckily, her father is Dave Ramsey, and the behaviors he and his wife, Sharon, modeled for Cruze and her siblings changed dramatically after they hit rock bottom. "I was only six months old, so I had no concept of money," she said. "I didn't know how it felt to be broke or what it meant to be wealthy. . . . Some might say I was born right at the worst time: the crash.

"But," Cruze added, "I see it differently. I think I was born at the perfect time: the fresh start." She wasn't old enough to see her parents lose everything; instead, she witnessed the slow rebuilding and all the lessons that accompanied that process. Of course, it wasn't easy. Her family was the first-ever family to go through the Dave Ramsey plan.

"After my parents' bankruptcy, they could have gone right back into the old habits that got them into trouble in the first place," Cruze said, and by all indications, she's correct. According to *Debt .org*, repeat filers are responsible for 16 percent of all bankruptcy cases. But that's only part of the story because almost everyone has some debt: a recent YouGov survey showed that 70 percent of U.S. adults are indebted, including 78 percent of Gen Xers, 74 percent of Baby Boomers, 70 percent of Millennials, and 44 percent of Gen Zers. It wouldn't have been surprising if the Ramsey family, given their previous behaviors, would have gotten out of their hole just to dig another in the years that proceeded their bankruptcy.

After speaking with Cruze, it became clear that many of our financial problems stem from our childhoods and our parents' own mishaps with money. The key to breaking the cycle, then, according to Cruze, is to teach all kids, starting as young as age three, about finances by encouraging them to *earn money*—not *get an allowance*—by doing chores, and then show them how to allocate their earnings appropriately.

Cruze suggests that all children, ages three to eighteen, divide their income across three key areas: spending, saving, and giving. "Give each child three specific envelopes: one named 'spend,' one named 'save,' and one named 'give.' Have them write those words— big and bold—across each envelope, and then encourage them to decorate them however they want. Every dollar they earn—or receive as a gift—needs to be spread across these envelopes. If they have five dollars, one goes into the 'give' envelope first; two go into the 'save' envelope; and then, finally, two go into the 'spend' envelope." This might be the most basic form of budgeting, but Cruze says it helps kids build solid spending habits. As I was writing this section, I began trying this approach with my six-year-old daughter. While I can't tell you whether she'll grow up to be the next Warren Buffet, I can assure you it's the only time I've seen her enjoy math.

> MINIMALISM ISN'T FOR EVERYONE— IT'S FOR ANYONE WHO'S DISCONTENTED BY THE STATUS QUO.

Wouldn't you have benefited from these simple lessons as a kid? I know I would have. As a matter of fact, Cruze's simple kids' budget is more comprehensive than my own budget when I was at the peak of my corporate career. I had learned about budgeting by my mid-twenties, but I chose to ignore what I knew was best. Why? Well, we often dismiss the lessons we learn to fill our life with shiny new objects. And it is this kind of short-term thinking that gets us back into debt.

Under the Influence of Impulse

It's that time of year again. The time of year when people go into debt. Of course, it doesn't matter whether you're reading this in December or June or somewhere in between: it's always the time of year when people go into debt. That's what we do. And that's why we're broke.

We purchase gifts with credit cards.
We buy jewelry with "no money down."
We assume eighty-four-month vehicle loans.
We take on thirty-year (and even forty-year) mortgages.

We even finance furniture. Furniture!

Come on.

I walked into a furniture store recently because my wife wanted to look for a new throw pillow. As we meandered the maze of coffee tables and couches and credenzas, I saw the same sign again and again, strategically placed on various pieces of furniture: "Take me home today! Financing available."

This is what it's come to? We feel as though we need everything we want, and we need it right now. And we needn't budget, we needn't save, we needn't prioritize our expenses—because we can let our future selves sort it out. Someday.

How has that worked out so far? Are you grateful for your past self's reckless spending? Are you happy with the lack of planning? Are you content with the trail of debt left in the wake of all the things your former self purchased under the influence of impulse? I know I'm not. It took me years to become debt-free, and I'm not going back—because I'm no longer willing to deny my future self joy by pleasing myself today.

Truth be told, if we need to finance a thing—be it a sofa or an SUV—then, by definition, we can't afford it. So instead of going into debt, perhaps we consider going without. Not forever—just until we have enough money to cover the full purchase.

Until then, we can still sit on that outmoded couch. We can make do with that lumpy mattress. We can use the cosmetics already lining our bathroom shelves. We can go shopping in our own closets for the clothes we don't wear. We can drive that old minivan until it croaks.

Frankly, if we want a new thing, we can wait until we can afford it. Maybe then, when we've got that bundle of hard-earned cash in hand, we'll realize we don't actually want the object we coveted while standing in the store.

Otherwise, we'll act on impulse; we'll gratify our desires instantly. If we succumb to the temptation of debt, we might even feel a spark of pleasure at the checkout line, but that flame will soon be extinguished when the first monthly bill arrives.

MINIMALIST RULE FOR LIVING WITH LESS

Wait for It Rule

With the advent of online shopping and one-click purchases, it's easier than ever to add to your hoard. To prevent impulse purchases, The Minimalists created the Wait for It Rule, aka the 30/30 Rule. If something you want costs more than $30, ask yourself whether you can make do without it for the next thirty hours. (If it's $100, wait thirty days.) This extra time will help you assess whether this new thing will truly add value to your life. Often, after deliberating, you'll find that your life will be better without the widget, so you can forgo the purchase altogether. If you do acquire the item, though, you'll feel better about the acquisition because you brought it into your life with intention, not in the impulse of the moment.

A Minimalist Economy

If everyone immediately stopped spending their money, our economy would crash, right? Yes, this goes without saying. Consequently, one of the biggest (supposed) arguments many people have against minimalism is that if everyone became a minimalist, then we'd all be doomed: we'd no longer be able to "stimulate" the economy, the financial system as it stands today would collapse, and no longer would we have the wealth necessary to purchase cheap plastic crap from the big-box store at the edge of town. There are several problems with this framing—some obvious, some a bit more abstruse.

First, no informed person would argue that we should stop spending money or that we must stop consuming. As stated in this book's introduction, consumption is not the problem—consumerism is the problem. Consumerism is compulsory, vapid, pernicious, impulsive, unfocused, misguided. Worst of all, it is seductive: consumerism's shiny facade promises more than it can possibly deliver because love, contentment, and tranquility cannot be commodified, and the truth is that once our basic needs are met, the acquisition of trinkets does little for our well-being.

> **USING CONSUMERISM TO STIMULATE THE ECONOMY IS LIKE FIXING A CRACKED MIRROR WITH A HAMMER: IT ONLY WORSENS THE PROBLEM.**

Well, then.

Using consumerism to stimulate the economy is like fixing a cracked mirror with a hammer: it only worsens the problem. Yes, trade is an important part of any society. Circumventing consumerism, however, doesn't imply that minimalists sidestep commerce. Rather, minimalism is predicated on intentionality, which means we minimalists spend our money more deliberately.

Minimalists invest in experiences over possessions: travel, concerts, vacations, theater. We can all spend money without acquiring new material things.

Minimalists buy new possessions carefully.

To do so, we must ask better questions:

Will this thing add value to my life?

Can I afford to buy it without going into debt?

Is this the best use of this money?

Minimalists support local businesses. Small, independent shops tend to be less motivated by profit. Sure, they need to make money to keep the lights on, and there's nothing wrong with that, but earning a buck usually isn't the primary concern of the neighborhood bookstore, restaurant, or bike shop. They are in business because they are passionate about their product or service, and they want to share that passion with their patrons. Passion begets greater quality and better service, which makes the money they earn even more well deserved.

Ultimately, minimalists aren't interested in "stimulating" the economy. Stimulation is ephemeral. We'd rather improve our economy's long-term health by making better individual decisions about consumption, getting involved in our community, and supporting local businesses that care. If more people do this, whether they're minimalists or not, we'll build a stronger economy, one that's predicated on individual standards and community interaction, not a false sense of urgency and skewed thinking and the mindless stockpiling of junk we never needed in the first place.

Student Debt

Speaking of skewed thinking, it's baffling how many lending institutions will loan five or even six figures' worth of debt to eighteen-year-old children. I guess it's not *that* surprising, though, since these loans are guaranteed by the United States government. So what do these institutions have to lose? Literally nothing. But it's odd that we as a society expect kids to select the career path they want to pursue for the rest of their lives, and then we advise them to borrow heaps of money to pursue that path. This line of thinking dramatically limits the ability of young adults to explore new options, and when people are unable to easily change their mind about the work they want to do, they feel stuck—confined by the debt that stems from the path a former version of themselves chose. Do you see a pattern here? If we don't choose carefully today, we always end up paying for it—with interest—tomorrow.

Even worse, we encourage young adults to spend money they don't have on a degree with virtually no return on investment: fashion design, art history, liberal arts, music, communications. But how many great communicators actually earned a communications degree? How many fashion designers, artists, and musicians got their big break with their diploma? Conversely, how many dog walkers and baristas have master's degrees, or even PhDs?

Don't get it twisted. I wouldn't discourage anyone from learning about fashion or art or communication; I would simply question whether it makes sense to accrue debt to do so. We frequently conflate *schooling* with *education*, but we don't need a lectern and a lecture to learn something new. In the real world, we are all students, and there is no substitute for real-world experience. Not even the most prestigious universities can give you that.

Sure, some professions require a degree. I mean, you wouldn't visit a self-taught surgeon, a YouTube-trained dentist, or a DIY dermatologist, would you? But even when it comes to such vital professionals, we rarely care about the institution they attended. If you're like me, you have no idea where your accountant, lawyer, or massage therapist went to school. What matters more than their alma mater is their knowledge, communication skills, bedside manner, personality, and skill set. I'd rather have a kind, talented nurse from Ohio State over a grumpy one from Yale a hundred times out of a hundred.

Anthony ONeal, the author of *Debt-Free Degree*, with whom The Minimalists shared a stage in Birmingham, Alabama, during our Money and Minimalism tour, discussed with me the impact of the decisions we make as we transition into adulthood. "Every parent wants the

> **THE QUICKER WE UNTETHER FROM DEBT, THE SOONER WE'LL EXPERIENCE FREEDOM.**

best for their child," he said. "Many parents accept that college is essential to their child's future success, but most struggle to pay for it and end up turning to student loans. That's why the average college graduate walks away with thirty-five thousand dollars in student debt and no clue how much that debt will actually cost them."

With his anti-student-debt diatribe, ONeal doesn't seem to be trivializing the importance of the college experience, but he wants parents and college students to see the big picture: when it's all said and done, "your degree should help you land a job," and you can earn that degree without debt. Everything else is secondary.

ONeal taught me that, contrary to popular belief, you can graduate from college completely debt-free: "I've helped thousands of students who have gone to college without a single student loan," he said. How? ONeal calls it "*finding* money *for* school and *saving* money *on* school." Grants, scholarships, and selecting an affordable university are the three legs upon which a debt-free degree is built.

Did you know there are more than 10,000 scholarships and grants out there, essentially free money that's waiting to be grabbed? I know this only because ONeal has a Scholarship Search tool on his website, anthonyoneal.com, which helps students find the grants and scholarships that are most appropriate for them. ONeal told me a story about a high-school student named Jimmy. During his junior year of high school, he applied for nearly a hundred different scholarships and grants. Suffice it to say, he was disappointed when more than 80 percent of his applications were denied. But several got approved, and when Jimmy did the math, he realized he'd earned more than $400 an hour just for filling out scholarship applications. Where else can a high-school student earn that much money?

Other than *finding* money for college, you can *save* a considerable amount if you pick the right school. Did you know you can save $66,000, on average, by attending an in-state community college your first two years instead of a reputedly prestigious private college? After which you can transfer to any university of your choice and still graduate with their diploma.

To be clear, if you want to graduate debt-free, there's more nuance than finding scholarships and an affordable school. Everything adds up—getting good grades in high school, scoring well on the ACT and SAT, taking college courses during the last year of high school, setting up college-savings accounts, taking some online classes, applying to work-study programs, living at home while attending college—but, ultimately, there is already a blueprint to get through college without strangling your future self with debt. All that might not sound as sexy as the college experience in *Van Wilder*, but graduating without debt sets you up for a life of financial freedom.

Budgeting and Investing in the Future

It was a cloudless summer evening in Louisville, Kentucky. The sky, polluted only by city lights, was the color of an overripe plum, and the line in front of the Mercury Ballroom, a historic Tudor-Gothic theater in the heart of downtown, stretched down the street and around the corner. Chris Hogan, an NFL-sized man with kind eyes and a sonorous, voice-of-God baritone, stood in the greenroom, wiping sweat from his brow, as he prepared to join The Minimalists on stage to discuss the principles in *Everyday Millionaires*, his latest book based on the largest study of millionaires ever conducted. Hogan says he wrote the book to "destroy the millionaire myths that are keeping everyday people from achieving financial independence." He and his research team surveyed more than 10,000 people with a net worth greater than a million dollars, and they discovered how these high-net-worth people reached their financial status. "The formula might surprise you," he said. "Millionaire status doesn't require inheriting a bunch of money or having a high-paying job. No. The path to becoming a millionaire is paved with ordinary skills—skills that you either already have or that you can learn. If you thought you could never become a millionaire, think again."

That formulation sounded odd to me at first. I mean, who thinks they can actually become a millionaire? Isn't that a pipe dream? "The people who become millionaires aren't trust-fund babies," Hogan told me. "They are regular, everyday hardworking people." Of the 10,000 millionaires he surveyed, the top three professions were engineers, accountants, and teachers. "These are people who, on average, aren't earning six figures—they are the people you live beside, or work beside, and they don't flaunt [their hard-earned wealth]." Hogan and I agreed, however, that having a million dollars in the bank is not the goal. "Achieving financial freedom, so you can live—and give—like no one else, is the goal," he said. You want your money to work for you so you don't have to keep working for money once you're retired.

Hogan was perspiring backstage not because he was nervous— quite the opposite. You could tell from his jovial tone and broad smile and some other unnamable thing—what some people might call an aura—that he was passionate and energized and ready to inspire the crowd, not with a cheesy motivational speech, but in a concerned-about-the-state-of-your-future, fatherly sort of way. In his first book, *Retire Inspired*, Hogan helped people understand that "whether you're twenty-five or fifty-five, you don't have to retire broke, stressed, and working long after you want to." To prove this thesis, he created the R:IQ—the Retire Inspired Quotient—a retirement calculator available at chrishogan360.com that pairs with his book to take the guesswork out of retirement planning.

> **WE FREQUENTLY CONFLATE SCHOOLING WITH EDUCATION, BUT WE DON'T NEED A LECTERN AND A LECTURE TO LEARN SOMETHING NEW.**

"Retirement isn't an age—it's a financial number," Hogan claims. "Most people fail to invest in their dreams, but they willingly invest in five-dollar cups of coffee, two-hundred-dollar gym shoes, three-hundred-dollar jeans, thousand-dollar phones, three-thousand-dollar computers, and fifty-thousand-dollar cars that are all outdated within two years, or used up in two minutes." Yet 60 percent of Americans have less than $25,000 saved for their own retirement. Those numbers are more than statistics to Hogan;

he has spent thousands of hours talking to thousands of regular people who struggle with money—particularly with saving for their future. "Behind every statistic are real people with real names, real faces, and real families. I've walked with them, laughed with them, and cried with them. I've seen the fear in their eyes—the distress of people who hit their senior years with no money and are suddenly unable to work." If that sounds anything like your situation, Hogan has a message for you: "I want you to change. In fact, it is time for you to change."

That change begins with a change in mindset. "Retirement is not an old-person thing," Hogan said. "I want you to think of retirement as a 'you are free to do whatever you want' thing, unburdened by the money problems most people have." After several decades working in the banking and finance industry, Hogan joined Ramsey Solutions and has been a financial coach to some of the biggest names in Hollywood, professional sports, and entertainment. Surprisingly, many of the so-called rich are struggling with money, too. "I've seen people 'do stupid' with money like you couldn't believe," he said.

Why? Because, according to Hogan, these people aren't dreaming big enough, or they are dreaming about other people's dreams. Thus, Hogan's first step toward financial independence in retirement is to dream big: "I want you to dream in high definition." He says it's important to make a dream list, and be as thorough as possible. If you get crystal clear about what you want out of retirement—down to the last detail, including where you'll live, how you'll spend your days, and how you'll contribute to your community—then you'll be able to figure out how much money you need to get there. Conversely, if you don't know where you're going, you'll fishtail your way to nowhere.

"All these years of working kneecap to kneecap with people from all walks of life have taught me one fundamental truth: most of these folks lack a plan." Hogan often repeats the dictum, "If you have a dream without a plan, it's just a wish." He knows that having a plan sounds simple, but "it is the one glaring omission that so many of us seem to overlook." So, what does a respectable retirement plan look like? "You can't sit on the couch, *hoping* to win with money—you must start with a budget."

While we outlined the idea of budgeting earlier in this chapter, let's expand on the concept using Hogan's "three key steps of budgeting." First, start with your income. "You have to begin with what you earn—all of it: the side projects, bonus money, every single penny," Hogan says. Second, separate your needs from your wants (use the No Junk Rule in our "Relationship with Stuff" chapter as a guide). Finally, make a plan for every dollar you earn (use the free budgeting app EveryDollar as a blueprint for building your budget).

Once you have a budget, put all your effort toward eliminating debt. "You can't retire indebted," Hogan tells the people he coaches. That means: no loans, no car payments, no mortgage—completely debt-free. In fact, Hogan recommends paying off all debt, except for your home, before investing any money in retirement plans. "After you eliminate all debt except your home and build up a fully funded emergency fund, you should budget to invest fifteen percent of your income into your retirement plans." He recommends employer-matched 401(k) or 403(b) accounts, Roth IRAs, and mutual funds when investing your money. Personally, since I'm self-employed, I put 20 percent of my income, every single month, into a SEP-IRA (Simplified Employee Pension) and into S&P index funds, both from Vanguard.

While any of these investment vehicles—401(k), mutual funds,

IRAs, and index funds—have the best chance to get you safely to retirement, not all investments are "good" investments.

Five Investments to Avoid

Whether or not you use Chris Hogan's and my investment strategy, I'd be remiss if I didn't warn you about the investments I personally avoid. Of course, I'm not a licensed wealth manager, but this advice aligns perfectly with that of the experts I've interviewed, including Hogan, Ramsey, and others. Some of these so-called investments might sound like exciting opportunities, but if you park your money in the wrong places, it's like throwing stacks of cash into a paper shredder.

Cash-value life insurance. Cash-value plans, such as whole life or universal life, are horrible investments. You don't "invest" in car insurance or health insurance, so why would you invest in life insurance? If you have dependents, then yes, you need life insurance (unless you are wealthy enough to self-insure), and your best bet is always term life insurance. Personally, I have a twenty-year term life policy that equals ten times my annual income. That way, if I were to die unexpectedly, my wife and daughter wouldn't have to worry about paying the bills. I have the same thing for my business—a twenty-year-term "key man" policy—so if I croak, Ryan will have enough money to run our business and continue sharing our message after I'm gone.

Individual stocks. Unless you are an expert day trader, individual stocks pose too much risk to the average investor. Even if your employer offers a "special" rate for their stock, I wouldn't invest my money in any single stock, not even with reputable companies like Apple, Google, or Tesla; it's simply too high-risk for my taste. I want my money to grow over time, preferring to "get rich slowly" rather than "get rich quick," the latter of which almost always leads to a perilous outcome.

Gold, silver, and precious metals. Like individual stocks, these metals are too fraught with risk when compared to index funds. Even worse, gold and silver are commodities, and commodity prices are often manipulated by speculation rather than supply and demand.

Annuities. Variable annuities—or any annuity for that matter—are generally foolish investments, especially since there are so many other solid options available. More often than not, annuities are rife with fees and penalties and surrender periods, not to mention low rates of return. No thanks!

Low-interest-yielding investments. If you're investing for greater than five years, then low-interest-yielding investments, such as CDs, individual bonds, and the like, are poor investments because the interest earned usually doesn't outpace inflation. These are great options, however, if you're saving for less than twelve months because they reduce your overall risk.

Seven Investment Myths Debunked

I know planning for retirement can seem overwhelming, and when we're overwhelmed, we begin inventing stories about why we can't invest or why we should wait. Well, you *can* save for retirement— and you needn't wait. I'd like to allay your fears by addressing a few of the worries—nay, myths—I've heard throughout my years of helping others establish retirement accounts.

Myth 1: I'm too old to save for retirement. During my corporate days, I frequently hired employees who were older than I was—often by two or three decades—with no retirement-savings plan. Fear had long ago set in, and they figured it was too late. They were stuck; they had missed their opportunity. Not true. While it is true that you're better off starting at age twenty-five than at fifty, it is also true that you'll be better off starting at age fifty than at, say, seventy. Then again, seventy is a better start than ninety, isn't it? The past is the past. We must stop peering at the rearview and instead look ahead toward the horizon. As long as you're still breathing, it's never too late to start. It's never too early, either.

Myth 2: I'm too young to save for retirement. Too young? No way! If you're younger than thirty, you have it made! Young people, no matter your tax bracket, have a significant opportunity to become truly wealthy thanks to the power of compound interest. Someone who invests $25,000 by age twenty-five with a 12 percent rate of return will have more than $2 million by age sixty-five—even if they don't add another dollar after age twenty-five. Conversely, if that same person waits until age thirty, they will have to contribute more than three times as much to achieve the same outcome. The lesson? Compound interest is the best way to grow your money over the long haul—so start while you're young.

Myth 3: I don't make enough money to save for retirement. Actually, there's no reason you can't retire a millionaire. That's right: virtually everyone, even minimum-wage earners, has the opportunity to be a millionaire when they retire. It sounds too good to be true, but the math proves otherwise: a twenty-five-year-old who sets aside only $23 per week will retire with more than a million dollars if the money is invested properly (12 percent rate of return). Okay, so maybe you're not twenty-five anymore—me, either! And maybe we can't bank on a 12 percent rate of return every year. That's all right—we simply need to adjust accordingly.

Myth 4: Inflation will hurt my retirement nest egg. This is the only myth that is partially true. However, it's irrelevant. While it is true $100 ten years from now will probably have less buying power than $100 today, the flip side of that coin is also true, and considerably more salient: your $100 ten years from now will be worth infinitely more than your friend's $0 invested. In fact, solid investments are the only way to outpace inflation. It is better to invest your $100 than to keep it in a bank or under your mattress.

Myth 5: I'd rather spend my money on something else. When intentions are good, this excuse occasionally sounds like the most compelling reason to avoid saving for the future. True, we sometimes cling selfishly to money, using our income to purchase the trinkets of ostensible success—new cars, upgraded gadgets, and all the accoutrements of consumerism—but frequently we want to use our money to contribute beyond ourselves: charities, nonprofits, and loved ones in need. Contribution is certainly admirable, and I want you to be able to contribute generously, but I've found the best way to help others is to help yourself first—the best way to give generously is to have more to give. If anything, investing in yourself *first* helps you flex your giving muscle.

Myth 6: The stock market isn't safe. Translation: you don't understand the stock market. That's okay: I don't completely understand it, either. The only people who must have an advanced understanding of the market's intricacies are stock brokers, day traders, and fund managers. Rather than allocating several hours a day to learn the nuances of mutual funds, index funds, and the S&P 500, I choose to use an investing service like Vanguard that takes the guesswork out of investing. It is true that any investment introduces risk into the equation, but long-term investing in the stock market has proven to be the best way to grow your retirement savings. Over the last thirty years, including 2008's steep decline and subsequent Great Recession, the market has averaged a rate of return of nearly 11 percent. Even when you account for 1929's Great Depression, the market has averaged greater than 9 percent growth over the past 100 years. Investing in the market is the most stable positive-growth investment one can make in the long term.

Myth 7: I don't have enough time or knowledge to manage my retirement savings. It's true, you and I will likely never have as much financial wisdom as the experts, but that's precisely why we must seek out tools developed by trusted, reputable experts. Although I'm usually a do-it-yourself kind of guy, I didn't DIY my investment strategy. Instead, I did my research and found online investment tools that allow me to control my money without being overly controlling. I don't want to constantly scrutinize my investments—tweaking and reacting out of fear every time the market goes up or down—but I don't want to fly blind, either. Rather than piloting the plane myself, I put the best possible pilot in the cockpit. For me, that means trusting Vanguard with my retirement accounts. For the folks at Ramsey Solutions, it means finding an Endorsed Local Provider—a local

broker "with the heart of a teacher" at endorsedlocalprovider.com—
and allowing them to manage your retirement accounts.

MINIMALIST RULE FOR LIVING WITH LESS

Selling Deadline Rule

Have you ever tried to sell something, but it just won't sell? Perhaps you posted it on Craigslist or Facebook, but no luck. Maybe you didn't do a good enough job with the photos or description, but more than likely, you priced the item too high because it's hard to accept it's no longer worth what you paid. We're all victims of the sunk-cost fallacy. That's why we created the Selling Deadline Rule, which acts as a shot clock for getting rid of possessions that no longer serve you. Whenever you attempt to sell an item, give yourself thirty days to do whatever you can—online auctions, yard sales, consignment shops, shouting from the rooftops. Throughout the month, gradually lower the price. If you're unsuccessful after thirty days, donate the item to a local charity.

Money Is Not the Root of Evil

Money seems to be the biggest point of contention in most relationships. We quarrel, quibble, and squabble over household spending. And illogically, our interactions seem to grow even more contentious as we get more money.

I read an observational study a few years ago about the differences between our closest primate ancestors—bonobos and chimpanzees. While neither use currency, they behave very differently when it comes to one of their most precious resources: food. Like human babies, the youngest bonobos and chimps are both eager to share their bananas with others, but their proclivities bifurcate as they grow older. Bonobos remain generous and they continue to share their bananas with the rest of their family and friends well into adulthood. Chimps, on the other hand, hoard their bananas and will even use violence to fight off others who attempt to take one for themselves.

What's even more fascinating is that even when bonobos are persuaded by humans to hoard, they continue to be generous. Researchers gave bonobos the opportunity to keep a pile of bananas for themselves while a fellow bonobo watched from behind a gate. But the altruistic bonobos always chose to open the gate and share their excess with friends. According to the researchers, chimps would never do this. They'd rather bicker and argue and even fight if necessary. Sound familiar?

> **IF YOU DON'T KNOW WHERE YOU'RE GOING, YOU'LL FISHTAIL YOUR WAY TO NOWHERE.**

We adult humans tend to act more like chimps when it comes to our finances. Money destroys marriages, ends friendships, and breaks up business partnerships. This is why money gets a bad rap. But it doesn't have to be the boogeyman. Unlike our primate ancestors, we can *choose* how we behave with our resources. Instead of clinging to everything, we can channel our inner bonobo.

Money isn't bad or evil—it is merely an amplifier. Money won't necessarily improve your life, but it will amplify your existing behaviors. If you have foolish habits, then more money will make your life considerably worse. (Think of all the lottery winners who end up destitute.) And if you're already a generous person, then more money can help you be more caring and considerate. Regardless of your past behavior, the choice is yours today: Are you going to be a chimpanzee or a bonobo? Choose carefully—your relationships depend on it.

The Poor Minimalist Myth

"I grew up minimalist—it was called being poor." If I had a tchotchke for every time I heard someone parrot this hackneyed line, I'd have a storage locker full of useless junk. I don't know whether these naysayers are bad-faith cynics or they're simply confusing poverty with minimalism, but either way, I find this line of thinking odd, especially since these same critics often claim that minimalism is only for wealthy people, or that it solves only First World problems, and so it's not applicable to people who live below the poverty line. I'm not sure what to do with this kind of bipolar reasoning, so let's address it from both sides to clear up any confusion.

We've already established that minimalism, at its core, involves using our limited resources intentionally. Who wouldn't benefit from that? I, too, grew up poor, and so did Ryan, and we certainly weren't minimalists, but we definitely would have benefited from being more deliberate with our (very) limited resources. In fact, my impoverished childhood self would have benefited even more than my supposedly rich adult self who stumbled into minimalism at twenty-eight. Ditto for Ryan.

But let's set that aside for a moment. Let me pretend we don't get frequent emails and letters and tweets from aspiring minimalists, from Kalamazoo to Kenya, who have next to nothing but who still struggle with desire and the ceaseless tug of consumerism. Let's pretend that minimalism hasn't helped those people like they say it has. And let's pretend that minimalism solves only First World problems.

Okay.

What's wrong with that? Are the problems of the First World not worth solving? Are people with money not allowed to question their stuff? Are we supposed to alienate and divide people based on their income?

Look, minimalism isn't for everyone—it's for anyone who's discontented by the status quo. It seems to me that 50 percent of the Western world isn't bothered by consumerism and the excesses of modernity, and it's not my place to convince them to jettison their stuff. But the remaining half of the population has a vast opportunity in front of them. Whether rich or poor, young or old, black or white, man or woman, anyone who feels hollowed out by the endless pursuit of more can find a better life with less.

Final Thoughts on Money

Money isn't everything, but it's also not nothing. As a minimalist, I'm not opposed to having money—I'm opposed to having money problems. I won't tell you how to live your life. I exposed my own financial mistakes and lousy decisions throughout this chapter so that you can learn from my blunders. I tend to avoid sweeping, one-size-fits-all solutions, but when it comes to money, this is the one chapter in this book that carries with it universals that can work for everybody.

Have a budget.
Establish an emergency fund.
Spend less money than you make.
Get out of debt as soon as you can.
Other than a mortgage, never go into debt again.
Invest in your future self by saving for retirement.

Use your resources to contribute to others' well-being.

If you need a car loan, you can't afford that car.

If you must use a credit card, you can't afford that thing.

Most purchases are unreasonable if you're in debt.

Even if you need a degree, you don't need debt.

Teach kids about saving and giving when they're young.

You cannot buy a meaningful life—you can only live it.

While we're all different ages and genders and come from different backgrounds, I can't think of a single person who wouldn't benefit from implementing these principles in their life. For nearly a decade now, I've purchased Dave Ramsey's book *The Total Money Makeover* by the case and have handed it out to friends and family and even strangers who ask me about getting out of debt. Too often we're waiting for someone else to set us free—for the government to wipe the slate clean, for our future self to make more money, for a relative to die and leave us enough cash to pay off our debts. But even if we were to abolish everyone's debt, and everybody started with a clean slate tomorrow, we'd eventually be back in a world of debt if we didn't change our behaviors—because money doesn't buy better habits. There are no financial saviors out there, so we better save ourselves. The quicker we untether from debt, the sooner we'll experience freedom.

Coda: Money

Hi, friend—Ryan here once again. Joshua gave us a lot to think about when it comes to how we're dealing with our finances. Now let's explore how you're doing with respect to this important relationship. I've got some exercises prepped and ready to go for you below.

QUESTIONS ABOUT MONEY

1. Describe your relationship with money. Is it healthy or unhealthy? Why?
2. What stress, if any, do you experience regarding money?
3. What nonessential expenses are busting your budget?
4. What plans, if any, have you made for retirement?
5. What changes will you make to improve your spending habits and your relationship with money?

THE DOS OF MONEY

Next, what did you learn about your relationship with money in this chapter? What will stick? What lessons will encourage you to get out of debt and invest in your future? Here are five immediate actions you can take today:

- **Adjust your approach.** In your journal, briefly describe what money means to you: What does money provide for you? What do you want it to provide? How does money control your life? How much money do you think you need to be happy? What could you do for others with money? After you've written your thoughts, consider whether your current approach warrants any adjustments, and then write down what actions will affect those positive changes.
- **Unravel your influences.** How was your attitude regarding money formed? To explore this, first write down the mistakes you've seen people around you make with their finances,

followed by the fruitful decisions you've seen people make. What's your first memory involving money? What entertainment are you consuming that might influence your view of money?

- **Locate your freedom.** Write down what financial freedom looks like for you. Be clear on when you'll get out of debt, when you'll retire, where you'll live, how you'll spend your days, and how you'll contribute to your community.
- **Form your budget.** Create a budget today. Financial freedom is not obtainable without one. Here's how you create a budget:
  - Create a spreadsheet for budgeting or download a budgeting tool like the free app EveryDollar.
  - Identify every source of income for the month: paychecks, bonuses, side projects, yard sales, and any other ways you earn money.
  - Write down what's essential, what's nonessential, and what's junk. (If you need guidance, see the No Junk Rule in the "Relationship with Stuff" chapter.) Then start budgeting for only the things you need. Nonessentials can certainly be included later, but only if you can afford them.
  - Use your budget tool to assign every dollar you have coming into your household. When assigning your dollars, use the Seven Baby Steps to help guide your allocation.
- **Simplify your spending.** Start spending your money like a minimalist. Minimalists buy new possessions intentionally. To do so, we must ask better questions: Will this thing add value to my life? Can I afford to buy it without going into debt? Is this the best use of this money?

THE DON'TS OF MONEY

Finally, let's discuss what's getting in the way. Here are five things you'll want to avoid, beginning today, if you want to improve your relationship with money:

- Don't continue poor spending and saving habits.
- Don't take on financial burdens you can't afford.
- Don't talk yourself into going into debt.
- Don't deprive yourself permanently of "nonessentials" that add value to your life. You can bring them into your life by budgeting and saving for them appropriately.
- Don't forsake your long-term financial health for short-term gains—you don't want to sacrifice future security for momentary pleasure.

RELATIONSHIP 6 | CREATIVITY

I got my first *real* job at thirteen, the summer between junior high and high school, spinning cotton candy at Americana, a discount amusement park on the outskirts of Middletown, Ohio. But my first *ever* job was a decade earlier, in the mid-'80s. We had just moved to American Village—a bland apartment complex composed of dozens of brown-brick buildings separated by thin landing strips of brown grass—twenty miles south of Dayton. Our one-bedroom unit was entirely beige, the carpet and walls and appliances all shades of monotony.

A couple weeks before my fourth birthday, I asked to buy a G.I. Joe action figure at the local Hills department store. Mom explained we didn't have enough money to both pay our bills and purchase the plastic man I wanted, so we'd have to wait till Friday for the toy soldier. Being that I was only four and I didn't understand money or commerce or delayed gratification, I figured I could help. That afternoon, I marched down to our apartment's main office and told them I needed a job. After she realized it wasn't a joke, the woman behind the counter smiled and then whispered something to her coworker before returning her benevolent eyes to me.

"Okay, if you pick up all the litter around our buildings, we'll give you a dollar a week," she said.

"Two," I said.

"Excuse me?"

"I'll do it for two dollars a week."

Neither woman could contain her laughter. Was this little boy negotiating his salary?

"Two dollars, huh?" she said.

"One for my mom to pay the bills, the other so I can buy toys."

"Bless your heart," she said, and then shook my hand to seal the deal.

Every weekend that summer, I dropped off a small trash bag filled with dozens of glass bottles and food wrappers and scraps of paper, and every weekend, I returned home with a dollar for my mom—and a dollar for me.

Let's ignore that I was grossly underpaid and that we were probably breaking several child-labor laws, and let's focus instead on the wisdom I absorbed that summer. While I didn't learn about budgeting or inflation or sound financial principles, I picked up many valuable lessons that formed a foundation for my aspirations. I learned about the payoff from drudgery. I learned it's impossible to have the peaks without the valleys. I learned about earning an income by creating value. And I learned about not sitting around and relying on others.

Most important, I learned about the power of asking. You see, had I not been willing to ask for that first "job," then not only would I have missed out on my first taste of earning income, but I would have missed out on the knowledge gained through the experience itself.

It turns out that any creative endeavor—be it writing a book, opening a yoga studio, or baking a cake—is ultimately just a series of questions. All creativity is birthed from continuous questioning, and our creations merely answer those questions.

> Who would benefit from this?
> What makes my solution interesting or unique?
> Where is the greatest need for my perspective?
> Why hasn't this problem already been solved?
> How can I better serve others with my creativity?
> What's the thing I can't not do?

All great art—as well as every great leader—attempts to answer these questions (and many others). Creativity is most effective and powerful and heartfelt when it answers questions. Of course, those answers take on different forms depending on the brand of creativity. Some creatives solve problems with films and books and broadcasts, others through business or volunteering or just listening. No matter how you use creativity to solve problems, questions will always be found at the core. And as we create, and our creations peel back the layers of questions, better questions emerge.

Everything's Creative

Minimalism won't necessarily help you be more creative, but removing life's excess often helps people uncover their creative side. For the longest time, I led two separate lives: professional JFM and personal JFM. There was Corporate Me—prim and proper, ostensibly flawless. And then there was Creative Me—totally flawed. The two mixed about as well as glass rubbing against concrete. So I kept them segregated: Corporate Me didn't talk about his love for writing, and Creative Me loathed himself for hiding his creativity from the world. It was almost as though each was ashamed of the other.

What I didn't realize, however, was that both were creative. As I climbed the vocational ladder, Corporate Me learned about leadership and business management and public speaking and countless other skills that would serve my future creations. Although it didn't seem like I was being creative at the time, I was *creating* a more knowledgeable version of myself, and I was helping people solve problems. What's more creative than that?

When you think of a typical "creative" person, you may imagine famous artists like Agnes Martin or Michelangelo, or writers like Mary Karr or F. Scott Fitzgerald, but I'd posit that most pursuits are at least somewhat creative. My brother, Jerome, for example, fabricates countertops at a factory in Cincinnati; he may not be a traditional artist, but he's certainly a creator. My wife, Rebecca, is a dietitian who works with people one on one to develop personal nutrition plans to improve their lives; she's not creating a physical good, but she's nevertheless a creator. My friend "Podcast Shawn" Harding edits The Minimalists' books, essays, and podcast episodes; while he's not the author of our work, he plays a pivotal role in the creative process, and thus he's a creator, too.

> **OUR GLOWING SCREENS HAVE GOTTEN IN THE WAY OF EVERYTHING, AND WE'RE ADDICTED TO OUR DISTRACTIONS. SCROLLING IS THE NEW SMOKING.**

Bottom line: you're a creative if you create something that solves problems or adds value to others. It's no more complicated than that. This is important, because creativity is an essential part of living. To create something worthwhile, though, we mustn't simply talk about creating—we must create. Unfortunately, a bevy of roadblocks get in the way. That's when minimalism steps into the picture—to help us clear the obstacles from the path so we can create.

Avoiding Procrastination

I was an aspiring writer for many years. I didn't write much, but I *aspired* daily. Bricklayers, carpenters, and many other creatives understand they must put in the work—literally brick by brick—if they want to build anything of note. But for some bizarre reason, writing is one of the few professions in which people expect to learn via some vague paranormal process, without doing the actual work. Perhaps it's because we writers possess an unrealistic affinity for perfection, and the sentences situated on the page are never as great as the perfect screeds in our heads.

So we procrastinate.

In my twenties, I was a champion of procrastination. I deployed every excuse I could get my hands on: too busy, too tired, too early, too late, too distracted, and dozens of other "toos." It was like I owned a Rolodex filled with apologias, always ready to evade the drudergy of creating. Many of my excuses were valid—I really was busy, I really did have other things to do—but even the best excuse is still an excuse.

Some writers take the excuses even further by claiming "writer's block." That was a go-to for me. But it's a peculiar justification, isn't it? Think about it. I've never heard about a nurse who calls off work because of "nurse's block." No, nurses and doctors and retail workers simply show up, even when they feel tired and uninspired, because that's what's necessary. Now, one might contend that those aren't creative fields, but I'd argue otherwise. These professionals help people solve problems, which is the heart of creativity.

All creatives must show up if they want to create. You see, just like "nurse's block" or "bricklayer's block," "writer's block" does not exist—unless you force it into existence. Of course, professional writers and artists and creators—the ones who make a living from their craft—know there is only one effective remedy for procrastination.

Sit in the chair. Those four words changed my creative life. The problem isn't a blockage—it's a willingness to sit down and do the work. I had to learn to show up every day. Both literally and figuratively, I had to learn how to sit in the chair, distraction-free, each day, until it was habitual. Some days produce gold, but most produce sediment. That doesn't matter, though. The only thing that matters is that I sit down each morning and create. We don't learn via osmosis—it takes work. The same is true with any creative pursuit.

In my twenties, I wanted to create something of great import, but I only wanted the end result, and I did not want what was required to achieve it. The effort. So I procrastinated. It was the opposite of minimalism. Instead of simplifying and getting to the essence of creativity, I cluttered my days with diversions. My hands and mind stayed busy, but not creative. I distracted myself to avoid the work.

Avoiding Distractions

We can't talk about creativity without talking about distractions—because our relationship with creativity is inversely proportional to our relationship with distractions. On the surface, we tend to think of minimalism as a form of decluttering, but perhaps we'd be better served if we thought of it as de-distractioning. Not only does our stuff get in the way of a more creative life, but once we get rid of the excess, we begin to notice just how much time we've been wasting pacifying ourselves with distractions. And in the modern world, we can't talk about distractions without talking about our biggest weapon of mass distraction: technology.

"I definitely got caught up in the quest for the latest and the greatest when it comes to tech," said Jerome Yost, a Packing Party Case Study participant from Emmaus, Pennsylvania. "The newest smartphone was never new enough for me. And there was always a new feature or capability that made me feel like the phone I had was inadequate, even though it did everything I needed it to do—and then some." Throughout his unpacking experiment, Yost began to realize that he had been distracting himself with technology, not using it to better engage with the world around him but to *avoid* the real world, to be pacified by the synthetic.

This isn't a new problem. Two thousand years ago, the Stoics worried about distracting themselves by reading too much and not engaging with the physical world. Today, reading a book seems like an extravagance. Indeed, I'm delighted you made it this far. Six out of ten people read only a headline before commenting on an online article; imagine how that stat plummets when we're talking about reading an entire book. You're one of many thousands of people who purchased this book, but one of the few who avoided a cornucopia of distractions to make it this far. Why is this the case? Because Jerome Yost isn't an anomaly. Our glowing screens have gotten in the way of everything, and we're addicted to our distractions. Scrolling is the new smoking.

> JUDGMENT IS BUT A MIRROR THAT REFLECTS THE INSECURITIES OF THE PERSON WHO'S DOING THE JUDGING.

Imagine you're eating dinner with a friend at your favorite restaurant. Amid the sounds of utensils and dishes and mastication, you hear the muffled ring of the mobile phone in your friend's pocket. Most people wouldn't stop the conversation to answer their phone in front of you. Even if it was an emergency, they would step away from the table to take the call. Why, then, don't we extend the same consideration when it comes to text messages, emails, and social-media posts?

Look around the next time you're in line at Chipotle, Whole Foods, or 7-Eleven—our addictions are showing. A generation ago, nearly everyone casually puffed cigarettes throughout the day. Today, indoor smoking seems nutty, but it's been replaced by the captivating glow of our six-inch screens.

Now look around again.
Take in the room, breathe.
Why isn't anybody smiling?

Maybe it's because we check our smartphones 150 times a day. Or maybe it's because we tap, swipe, and click on our phones 2,617 times, which results in us using our gadgets as much as twelve hours a day on average. To make matters worse, 86 percent of smartphone users check their phones while speaking with friends and family, and 87 percent of Millennials say their smartphone never leaves their side.

If the goal of our technology is connection, then why do we let our devices create a smokescreen between us? There's been much talk about "building a wall" lately, but perhaps we've already built one—an attention barrier between us and the people in our everyday lives. Or, as comedian Ronny Chieng recently observed, "Every night in America is like a competition to see how many screens we can get between our face and the wall."

Personally, to tear down this glowing barrier, I've been trying something different as of late: anytime I must respond to a message—at home, at the office, or at the local burrito joint—I simply say, "Please excuse me while I step outside to take this message," just like I would if I needed to make a call.

It sounds silly at first, but this choice forces me to prioritize that which is urgent versus that which is important. When scrutinized, our urgent tasks are rarely important. Plus, my friends respect my good manners, and they almost always extend the same courtesy back to me. This type of intentionality is a valuable step toward reducing distractions. But, truth be told, it may not be enough. Many of us must go further to declutter our digital lives.

Digital Declutter

Eliminating distractions is easier said than done. In his book *Digital Minimalism*, Cal Newport, a professor of computer science at Georgetown University, asked 1,600 people to participate in a "digital declutter" experiment. "In my experience," Newport writes, "gradually changing your habits one at a time doesn't work well—the engineered attraction of the attention economy, combined with the friction of convenience, will diminish your inertia until you backslide toward where you started." He instead recommends a rapid transformation—"something that occurs in a short period of time and is executed with enough conviction that the results are likely to stick." Enter: the digital declutter.

Newport asked his participants to set aside thirty days to "take a break from optional technologies." While each person got to determine their own rules, optional technologies can include "apps, websites, and related digital tools that are delivered through a computer screen or a mobile phone and are meant to either entertain, inform, or connect you." According to Newport, social media, Reddit, video games, YouTube, and even text messaging are examples of the types of "new technologies" we need to evaluate when preparing for a digital declutter; our microwaves, radios, and electric toothbrushes are not. In short, what is distracting you? Remove that for a month.

During that month-long break, knowing that tech withdrawal can feel unpleasant, Newport implored participants to explore and rediscover analog activities and behaviors they find satisfying and meaningful. "For this process to succeed," Newport writes, "you must also spend this period trying to rediscover what's important to you and what you enjoy outside the world of the always-on, shiny digital." Newport claims that participants are more likely to succeed if they "cultivate high-quality alternatives to the easy distraction [technology] provides." These alternatives might include reading books, having coffee with friends, writing, painting, attending community events, planning family outings, listening to music, going to concerts, playing sports, and unearthing other pastimes that have fallen by the wayside since your life has grown inundated by a barrage of interminable pings, notifications, alerts, updates, and other interruptions.

After the break, Newport had participants reintroduce optional technologies starting from a blank slate: "For each technology you reintroduce, determine what value it serves in your life and how specifically you will use it to maximize this value." To do this effectively, he recommends asking a vital question: Does this technology directly support something I deeply value? If not, don't bring it back. "The fact that it offers *some* value is irrelevant—the digital minimalist deploys technology to serve the things they find most important in their life, and is happy missing out on everything else."

Productivity expert Tanya Dalton calls this removal of the superfluous "the joy of missing out." In her book of the same name, she writes, "Doing less might seem counterintuitive, but doing less is more productive because you're concentrating on the work you actually want to be doing." For me, this is the most compelling argument for digital minimalism. When we stop conflating distraction and busywork with productivity and efficiency, we're able to accomplish something profound and meaningful with our creativity.

Our tech has us *doing* so much that we rarely make time for *being*. We're attempting to fill every interstitial zone with more work. Every downtown scene is the same: heads tilted downward, faces lost in glowing screens, technology turning people into zombies. We live in a busy world, one in which our value is often measured in work rate, output, yield—the rat race. We are inundated with meetings and spreadsheets and status updates and rush-hour traffic and tweets and conference calls and travel time and text messages and reports and voicemails and multitasking and all the trappings of a busy life. Go, go, go. Busy, busy, busy. Get. Things. Done.

Americans are working more hours than ever, but we are actually earning less. *Busy* has become the new norm. And if you're not busy, especially in today's workplace, you're often thought of as lazy, unproductive, inefficient—a waste of space.

But for me, "busy" is a curse word. Whenever someone accuses me of being busy, my facial features contort, and I writhe in mock pain. I respond to their accusation the same way each time: "I'm not busy, I'm focused."

Henry David Thoreau wrote, "It is not enough to be industrious; so are the ants. What are you industrious about?" If I were to amend his quandary, I'd say, "It is not enough to be busy; so is everyone else. What are you focused on?" There is a vast difference between being busy and being focused. The former involves the typical tropes of productivity: anything to keep our hands moving, to keep going, to keep the conveyor belt in motion. It is no coincidence we refer to mundane tasks as "busywork." Busywork works well for factory robots and other automatons, but not so great for people who are attempting to do something worthwhile with their waking hours.

Being focused, on the other hand, involves attention, awareness, and intentionality. People sometimes mistake my focused time for busyness because complete focus apes many of the same surface characteristics as busyness. Namely, the majority of my time is occupied. The difference, then, is that I don't commit to a lot of things, but the tasks and people to which I commit receive my full attention. Being focused doesn't allow me to get as much accomplished as being busy; thus, the total number of tasks I complete has gone down over the years. Yet the significance of each undertaking has gone up—way up. This year, for example, I'll accomplish only a couple creative milestones—publish this book, teach a writing class*—but those efforts will receive all of me. And everything else I do will support those endeavors, directly or indirectly.

> **ANY CREATIVE ENDEAVOR—BE IT WRITING A BOOK, OPENING A YOGA STUDIO, OR BAKING A CAKE—IS ULTIMATELY JUST A SERIES OF QUESTIONS.**

This might not look good on a pie chart next to everyone who's tallying their metrics—and it requires saying "no" to almost everything else—but it certainly feels better than being busy just for the sake of being busy. Sure, sometimes I fall back into the busy trap that engulfs our culture. But when I do, I make an effort to

---

* Visit howtowritebetter.org for details.

notice my slip-up, and then I course correct until I'm once again focused on the worthwhile aspects of creative life. It's a constant battle, but it's a battle worth fighting.

MINIMALIST RULE FOR LIVING WITH LESS

Don't Upgrade Rule

When it comes to consumer electronics—smartphones, laptops, tablets—you're presented with the newest "upgrade" every other week. Advertisers spend billions of dollars to get you to lust over their new releases. Your current device—the one that was supposed to satisfy you—is now the object of your displeasure. But you needn't play that game—you don't *have* to upgrade. Sure, sometimes a thing breaks or wears out, and when that happens, you are left with at least three options: go without, repair it, or replace it. *Going without* is almost taboo in our culture, but sometimes it's the best option because you're forced to question whether you need that thing, and occasionally you discover life is actually better without it. Of course, you can't always go without, but you can usually *repair* your broken item without replacing it. You wouldn't buy a new car just because the brake pads needed to be changed, would you? Same goes for many household items. And as a last resort, you can replace things, but even when you do, you can do so responsibly by purchasing used items; you can even "downgrade" and still have what's necessary to live a fulfilling life. Not only is this approach better for the environment, it's often better for you, too.

Removing Distractions

While I'm not a Stoic—and I'm certainly not a Luddite—I enjoy conducting stoical experiments. You see, creativity requires a certain amount of distraction-free time—or "deep work," as Cal Newport calls it—and to get there, I frequently remove potential distractions for a period of time to determine whether they add real or imaginary value. Then, if I decide to bring a former hindrance back into my life, I'm able to use it more deliberately. Let's review some of the distractions I've removed over the last decade and how those deletions have benefited my creativity.

Television. Shortly after my first marriage ended, I moved into a recently remodeled apartment in Dayton. Every time Ryan visited my new home, he'd point to the empty bracket on the wall and ask, "What size TV are you going to get?" Initially, I responded with "I don't know" and pondered whether a fifty-five-inch was big enough. But as the days turned into weeks, I realized I didn't miss my television, and I was, in fact, better off without it because every night when I returned home from work, I couldn't switch on my biggest distraction and get hypnotized by its flickering glow. Instead, I had to engage in something more productive—like writing, reading, or exercising—or I had to turn to other divertissements. That's the funny thing about distractions: when you eliminate one, the others become more obvious. And in today's intrusion-heavy world, we have countless diversions to turn to.

Home Internet. After living without a television for a year, I moved into a smaller apartment in an effort to allocate any extra income toward paying off debt. Ryan helped me move all my furniture on a Friday, and when I called the cable company that afternoon to transfer my Internet service, they told me they couldn't schedule the technician for several days. "Okay," I said, "I'll call you back when I'm in front of my calendar." Then something unexpected happened: I had the most productive weekend of my adult life. After I unpacked my belongings and cleaned my new apartment, I wrote for several hours each day, I called a few family members to catch up, and I even read a book. Without the obstructions of television and home Internet, I was finally doing the things I *aspired* to do—the things that required rigor or discipline to get done. Turns out that discipline shows up when the diversions disappear. So I never called the cable company back. If I needed to use the Internet, I would do so at work, at coffee shops, or at the library down the street. That way, I had to plan my online activities in advance, which made little time for goofing off. And even when I wanted to blow off steam—say, watch YouTube videos or browse social media—I'd have to plan that in advance, too.

Smartphone. After removing the interference of TV and the Internet from my home life, the amount of time I spent creating increased exponentially—so much so that I finally started on the writing career I had always claimed I wanted. After setting up a blog and finishing the novel I'd been working on since age twenty-four, I was now writing every day—first thing in the morning, after work, even on the weekends—which eventually gave me the confidence to take the biggest creative risk of my life: I walked away from my corporate career to pursue writing full-time.

Within a few months, I discovered one other distraction that followed me everywhere—to coffee shops, to friends' houses, even into my bed at night: my smartphone. It was as if I was carrying a distraction machine in my pocket. Yes, I had eliminated television and the Internet from my home, but had I *really*? Or were versions of those distractions now in my pocket? So I locked my phone in a drawer for two months—and I learned a lot about my habits in the process.

Besides learning that pay phones are virtually nonexistent these days, I learned about a special kind of loneliness. You see, once you've removed television, the Internet, and a phone from your life, you've eliminated your main pacifiers, and you're finally forced to confront the twitch that propels many of your impulses. Without the glowing screens to entertain and amuse me, I was confronted by thunderous silence. You learn just how loud your thoughts are when you turn down the volume of everything around you.

"When you bought your first smartphone, did you know you would spend more than 1,000 hours a year looking at it?" Seth Godin, author of nineteen best-selling books, asked this question on his popular blog. "Months later, can you remember how you spent those hours?" Godin concludes that, "If we wasted money the way we waste time, we'd all be bankrupt."

Two months without the constant buzz of a phone also helped me understand that we, as a society, have weird expectations. Before ditching my smartphone, I felt pressure to respond to text messages, email, and social media constantly throughout the day.

Our expectations vary dramatically from person to person. You might expect a response in an hour, someone else might expect one in ten minutes, another person the same day. These expectations are arbitrary, and when I eliminated my ability to respond immediately, I was able to form my own expectations, instead of letting the world dictate my response time. Soon, without the banality of cursory text conversations, my face-to-face interactions became more meaningful. When I spent time with my closest friends and loved ones, I had more to discuss in earnest, and because those conversations felt deeper, I enjoyed them more than usual.

With my phone absent from my pocket, I also learned that "downtime" is a misnomer. Once upon a time, we had precious moments in which we could find momentary solace: airports, checkout lines, waiting rooms, and other transient sanctuaries. No longer is this the case. Now everyone seems to be on their phones during these fleeting moments: they are attempting to be more *productive* or *interactive*, but perhaps stopping and thinking would be more *effective* than checking email or social media one more time—especially if we want to create something meaningful.

Finally, distractions or no, I realized that the world goes on. Without a cellphone, without the Internet, without a television, the Earth keeps spinning. You can test anything for a short period of time to see whether it's right for you. There wasn't a single time when I truly *needed* my phone during those two months. Sure, there were times when it was inconvenient, when I had to fight through the frustration—but that was a small price to pay to deprogram the twitch.

Reintroducing Tools, Not Distractions

Because minimalism is not deprivationism, I reintroduced the phone into my life after two months. But it returned in a different capacity. Today, I use it for GPS, phone calls, the dictionary app, a memo pad, and a handful of useful applications. And yes, I still send the occasional text message—but not when I'm with other people, and certainly not when I'm standing at a urinal. (There's a time and a place for everything.)

Moreover, to avoid the most common surface distractions when

I'm alone, I've turned off all notifications, deleted all social media, and removed any distracting apps from my phone, including anything I haven't used in the last ninety days. I regularly switch my phone to "do not disturb" unless I explicitly need to use the device, and I partake in The Minimalists' Screenless Saturdays, during which my wife and I shove our phones in a drawer and spend the day together without screens. I even set the phone's display to grayscale because, according to Tristan Harris, a former design ethicist at Google, the tonal change makes the apps on your phone less enticing, which prevents endless checking and scrolling. Imagine all those Instagram photos and YouTube videos drained of their captivating bursts of color.

Do you wonder whether we're living in a dystopian future when Gopi Kallayil, a chief evangelist at Google, refers to our smartphones as our "seventy-ninth organ"? Is it even scarier now that MRI scans have revealed that the gray matter in a phone addict's brain physically changes shape and size similar to a drug user's brain? Personally, if I'm going to have a phone, I'd rather have it as a tool than as a brain-altering appendage.

But, of course, our tools are only as good (or bad) as the person using them. A chainsaw can cut down a rotting backyard tree, preventing it from impaling a neighbor's house. Or that same chainsaw can be used to hurt our neighbor, to chop him up into tiny pieces. A can of paint can beautify a home's facade. Or one might use it to graffiti the walls at an otherwise pristine public park. The same goes for technology. We can use Twitter and Reddit and YouTube to enrich our lives and the lives of others, to communicate and share in ways we've never been able until now. Or we can get stuck in social media's Bermuda Triangle, careening from Facebook to Instagram to TikTok, lost in the meaningless glow of our screens.

We can use our smartphones to photograph gorgeous land-scapes, message loved ones, or map out directions to a distant national park (or—*gasp!*—to make phone calls). Or we can use that same device to twitch: to incessantly check email, thumb through an endless stream of status updates, post countless selfies, or partake in any other number of non-value-adding activities, all while ignoring the beautiful world around us.

Bottom line: It is up to us to determine how we use our chainsaws, paint cans, and technology. Our tools are just tools, and it is our responsibility to ask critical questions about how and why we use them. Because to become a Luddite is to avoid an entire world of possibilities, a better world that's enriched by the tools of technology. If we use them intentionally, we can change the world with these tools. Or we can cause a lot of harm. It's an individual choice, the world is at our fingertips, and it's up to us to act accordingly.

> MINIMALISM WON'T NECESSARILY HELP YOU BE MORE CREATIVE, BUT REMOVING LIFE'S EXCESS OFTEN HELPS PEOPLE UNCOVER THEIR CREATIVE SIDE.

Over the last decade, I've reincorporated some of my former distractions into my life at various intervals, although my time without them helped me bring them back more deliberately—not as distractions, but as tools. I lived without a television for nine years, until the apartment I moved to in Los Angeles came with one mounted to the wall. To be frank, I wish it hadn't. But because it's there, my family and I use it from time to time. However, I have three rules that make even TV viewing more intentional: schedule viewing at least twenty-four hours in advance, don't watch more than three hours per week, and never watch television alone.

I have a similar challenge with home Internet these days. After five years without it, my circumstances changed, and my wife and young daughter decided they needed it more than I didn't. But, happily, we can have it both ways: all I have to do is ask them to hide the Wi-Fi password from me, and *poof!*, no Internet for me (but Ella can still enjoy *Wild Kratts* on her tablet every weekend).

How about you? What distractions are preventing you from creating what you want to create? If you're not sure, go back and review your Imaginary Values from the "Relationship with Values" chapter. Those are typically our biggest distractions. What would happen if you removed them from your life for a day, a week, a month? There's only one way to know for sure.

Creators, Not Consumers

We often think of ourselves as consumers, which is true to an extent, but we are creators first. We've made tools and structures and artwork for millennia. But our modern consumerist society has conditioned us to think we're merely clients and buyers and shoppers, and as a result, many of us have let our creative muscles atrophy.

We humans create for two reasons: expression and communication. Which means that when we stop creating, we lose the ability to effectively express ourselves, and we're unable to successfully communicate with others.

When done thoughtfully, creativity is an act of love. In fact, there are few acts as loving as creating something meaningful for others. According to Ken Coleman, nationally syndicated radio host, career coach, and author of *The Proximity Principle*, loving creations accomplish three things: equipping, encouraging, and entertaining. Coleman calls these pillars of creativity the three E's. "Whether it's a piece of art or a self-help book, your creations should *entertain* people enough that they want to experience more," Coleman told me. "They should also *encourage* people to take some sort of action, big or small. And they should *equip* people with knowledge or experience—helping them walk away from the painting or movie, or whatever the creation is, with more useful information than what they arrived with."

Personally, I've made my living as a writer for ten years now, but I've also grown vehicle-agnostic throughout that decade. When I started writing fiction in my twenties, I wanted only to become an author, to write books and nothing else. Then I became an author and discovered I also enjoy other creative endeavors: blogging, podcasting, public speaking, filmmaking. You see, being passionate about writing doesn't mean I'm passionate *only* about writing. In fact, many of the skills are transferable. Often, writing is the best medium to communicate or express an idea or feeling—it's the best way to equip, encourage, and entertain others. More times than not, though, it's best to find the most appropriate channel for the message. I still write most days, but I *create* every day, because creating makes me feel alive. When it's going well, I can feel it on my nerve endings.

Create Value, Not Content

It seems that everyone today is a "content creator." But why? While I'm an advocate for creativity, I'm not a fan of simply creating to create—that wouldn't be very minimalist of me. *What* you create is just as consequential as creating, and because volume is not indicative of merit, I avoid creating "content." Opt instead to create value, to solve people's problems, to entertain, to communicate something worthwhile, to express something visceral, to produce something meaningful, to make something that will stand the test of time. Just like it's important to make conscious choices as a consumer, it's equally important to create consciously. Otherwise, you're just adding to the noise.

Think of the most egregious examples of noisemakers—advertisers, cable-news stations, social-media "influencers"—what do they have in common? Two things: vapidity and the profit motive. Now, as you know from the previous chapter, I'm not anti-money, but the outcome needn't be income. As a matter of fact, forcing yourself to make money from a hobby is a great way to kill your love for that creative pursuit. This fact was glaringly apparent when I spoke with Paul Johnson, a singer-songwriter who goes by the stage name Canyon City, about his journey from playing music as a hobbyist to making it his career.

Johnson had been playing guitar since he was a kid, but when he moved from Fargo to Nashville at age eighteen to pursue his dream, he quickly discovered he was compromising his creative integrity to appease decision makers in the music industry. "I was finally paying my bills from music," he told me. "I signed a record deal and was making commercial music for corporations, but it wasn't the music I wanted to make."

After a few years of recording jingles and soulless "content," Johnson's dream job had turned into a nightmare. "It sucked all the joy out of music," he said. "It was like the thing I loved most had died, and I was responsible for killing it." So Johnson did something unexpected: he stepped away from making music professionally, got a job hauling lumber at Home Depot, and started making music again as a hobby. "When I removed the pressure of making money from my music, the love eventually returned," he said, "and that's where Canyon City was born." It's no coincidence that, after returning to his craft for the love of creating, rather than the love of a paycheck, Johnson eventually made a full-time living from music again. The difference is that now he does it on his own terms, and money is not the motive—it is a by-product.

Good businesses make money; great businesses make a difference. The same is true with creatives. Although I don't chase income with my creative pursuits, money tends to show up when you use your creativity to entertain or aggressively solve other people's problems. Eventually, when you're skilled enough, people are eager to pay you for the value you create. Perhaps the artist Shepard Fairey said it best: "I charge three cents for my two cents." Of course, you can do that only when people find value in your creations.

Be Prepared for Criticism

When it comes to sharing your creations with the world, you'll find people who enjoy your unique perspective, but you'll also find dissenters. Once it's public, your creation will be reviewed, analyzed, and evaluated. That's natural. When this happens, please understand that there's a difference between criticism and feedback: criticism illuminates problems; feedback provides solutions. Thus, we must seek feedback from trusted people because it makes our work better, but we must avoid criticism from naysayers because it clutters the path to creativity.

Whenever you create something meaningful, you will be critiqued. And no matter how close to perfect your creation is, it will be judged.

"That lighting looks creepy."
"This book is stupid."
"Don't quit your day job."

Judgment is but a mirror that reflects the insecurities of the person who's doing the judging. Most criticism is nothing but an unsolicited discharge of personal preference. And because you didn't ask for it, you aren't required to respond. Better yet, it's best not to fire back. Instead, click delete or mute or block and move on to the next creation.

MINIMALISM IS NOT DEPRIVATIONISM.

If you do this with enough frequency, the calluses you form will help you shape the next creation without worrying about its reception. This type of fearless creativity—combined with rigorous trusted feedback—is crucial for constructing an opus worthy of your pride.

After all, what's the alternative? Respond to every cavil, niggle, and jab? If you do that, you'll lose sight of what you hoped to create in the first place, and you'll only end up feeding the seagulls. Seagulls? Yes. Ryan and I refer to Internet critics not as trolls but as seagulls, because they fly in, crap on you and your work, and then fly away. And just like seagulls, they're usually too simpleminded to understand the implications of their own actions. Truth be told, most critics bring nothing to the table: they simply project their own insecurities and add zero value to the conversation. And if we listen to them, their toxicity permeates our thoughts, making it difficult to create anything of value. So, you have two choices: either create and be criticized, or hide from meaningful work because you're scared of a little bird poop. Personally, I'd rather cover my head and craft something worth criticizing.

It's worth mentioning, however, that there are professional critics who add value to the conversation. But even a well-considered critique of your art usually isn't for *you*; it's for the consumers of the creation. I've had countless outlets write effusively about my creations, and I've also been panned by critics a great number of times. That's fine: we can't expect everyone to like everything we do. What I've learned from a decade of the public spotlight was summed up masterfully by the popular radio host Charlamagne tha God: "You're never as good as they say; you're never as bad as they say, either." Keep this in mind when you're creating. Avoid the criticism because it's not for you. Instead, seek feedback from people who want to help you make your work better.

The Instruments of Creativity

We sometimes confuse the instruments of creativity with creativity itself. We attempt to locate the pencil Hemingway gripped to write his stories, the camera Coppola held to direct her films, the guitar Hendrix strummed to record his songs. But owning Jimi Hendrix's guitar does not make you Jimi Hendrix. Ditto for the implements of Hemingway and Coppola. Yes, many creative pursuits require tools, but the *specific* tools aren't as important as you might think, and they can even get in the way of the work when we place too much emphasis on them. This is one of the areas in which minimalism expands our creativity.

Rather than seek out the perfect notebook, pen, and keyboard to write my books, essays, and grocery lists, I simply *write*, regardless of what tools are available to me. Many of my best lines have been scribbled on a napkin with a dull pencil. In fact, I'd argue that constraints breed creativity. Have you ever watched a director make a masterpiece of a film, or a musician record a classic album, just to follow it up with a creative flop? Because they had few resources at their disposal during the first project, they were forced to rely on their talent and skills, but, when given a functionally infinite budget, they turned to elaborate tricks, throwing money at their problems instead of solving those problems creatively. This happens in many creative pursuits. When we start looking for financial solutions to creative problems, our creativity suffers.

Unlimited resources can stifle creativity. Thus, when we create, we must first reach for the most powerful tools—the tools that are in every creative person's toolbox: questions. Asking questions stimulates creativity like nothing else. So, if you want to nurture your creativity, ask questions often.

What am I attempting to express?
What am I trying to communicate?
What problems do I want to solve?
What questions do I hope to answer?
How will this add value to other people?
How will this equip, encourage, and entertain others?

These questions will undoubtedly lead to more questions, and that's good news because your curiosity will propel your creativity more than any shiny new object ever could.

The Birthplace of Creativity

"Where do you get your ideas?" is a common question among aspiring creatives. But I've always found it funny because that question conjures images of retail stores or storage lockers or top-secret government facilities that house creative concepts. When faced with this question, I respond the most honest way I can: "From life."

MINIMALIST RULE FOR LIVING WITH LESS

Photo-Scanning Party

Like most people, you've probably let your photos go unchecked over the years, and now those overstuffed boxes and photo albums are collecting dust in your basement or closet. Sounds like it's time for a Photo-Scanning Party! First, invite a few friends over, order some food, and then sit at your kitchen table together. Thumb through all your photos and discuss the memories they trigger. Set aside your favorites. Second, use a portable photo scanner to save your favorite photos to a memory card. Third, upload your photos to the cloud. That way, if anything happens to your home—flood, fire, robbery—they're all safe and secure online. If you're feeling brave, you can shred the physical photos after they're uploaded. Finally, instead of hiding the photos in your attic or garage, display them throughout your house using a few digital picture frames.

For a detailed discussion about scanning photos, listen to "Hidden Clutter," episode 272 of *The Minimalists Podcast*.

Experience begets creativity. I wrote fiction throughout my twenties, likely because my own life was so banal—so remarkably unremarkable—that I wasn't living a life worth writing about. As a result, most of the stories I wrote, even the ones that were completely made up, weren't worth reading. Over time, however, I created some changes in my own life that were worth sharing—walking away from a corporate career, getting divorced, jettisoning most of my possessions, fostering new relationships, exploring new hobbies—and I observed these changes by putting my life lessons on the page. If I were a stand-up comedian, I probably would have found ways to tell jokes about my pain and sorrow. If I were an architect, I might have used my personal struggles to inform the designs of my houses. Ditto for any creative profession: we use the events in our lives, and the happenings of the world around us, to inform our creations—both directly and indirectly.

No, that doesn't mean Martin Scorsese was in the mob or Jim Carrey was an actual pet detective. Rather, these creatives expressed life's profundities through their work, and they used different latticeworks upon which to hang their creativity. Artistry and vision manifest differently for each creator, but the end result is the same: the struggles of life tend to find their way into every creation.

We all aspire to create—it's a human need—but we can't create in a vacuum. Instead, we must live a life that's worth sharing. Not a flawless or seamless life, but a life in which everything is left on the field, a life we learn from so that others can gain knowledge from our experiences. In short: writing is great, but don't write stories in lieu of living them.

Perfectionism Is the Perfect Villain

Voltaire once advised, "Don't let the perfect be the enemy of the good." It's true that, when creating, we all want to put our best foot forward. We want to be able to look in the mirror and honestly proclaim, "I did the best I could, given the resources I had at the time." But our expectation mustn't be perfection.

The best you can do changes over time. My best writing twenty years ago would be mediocre today, although I wouldn't have gotten to today without years of mediocrity. That might sound discouraging at first, but I'd like to posit the opposite: you have permission to be "good enough" today. Or, as the author Becky Beaupre Gillespie writes, "Good enough is the new perfect."

In this respect, creating is much like visiting the gym. You may desire to be fit and muscular, but the only way to make that happen is to keep showing up, day after day, and building on the previous days' progress. You may never develop the "perfect" physique—just like you may never paint the perfect painting or build the perfect smartphone app—but your personal best will continue to get better as you put in the hours.

Doing the real work is better than the perfect idea that's trapped in your head. "No matter how many hours you spend attempting to render something flawless," writes Elizabeth Gilbert in her book *Big Magic: Creative Living Beyond Fear*, "somebody will always be able to find fault with it. (There are people out there who still consider Beethoven's symphonies a little bit too, you know, loud.) At some point, you really just have to finish your work and release it as-is—if only so that you can go on to make other things with a glad and determined heart. Which is the entire point."

Celebrating and Sharing Creations

Okay. Let's say you've gotten to the point where you're ready to share your music or drawings or software with the world. You've put in the hours and drudged through the drudgery, you've solicited feedback from trusted confidants and used it to improve your creation, and you've looked in the mirror and acknowledged that while your finished work is not perfect, it's the best you can do at this point in your life. That's wonderful. Congratulations!

Take a moment to reflect on what that means. Look around: How many people do you personally know who have written a book or recorded an album or painted a painting? Five? Fewer than that? If you're like most people, there's a good chance you're the only person in your immediate circle who has actually done what you've done and seen it through to its completion. This is something you can be proud of. Your new creation has the ability to be an asset for the rest of your life. Nothing can take that from you—not a job loss or a family emergency or tough economic times. The thing you created is forever yours, an asset for life, even if it were to sit in a drawer for the next decade. Which it won't. Because creativity deserves to be shared.

The Virus of Virality

So, what are you going to do with that new thing you created? Ideally you'll share it with people who are interested in it, right? But how do you find those people? How do you connect with an audience? How do you let the world know about your creation?

To answer these questions, we must first discuss one of the biggest misconceptions that we, as a society, have: in order to share your work with the world, you must "go viral." In today's online-driven world, virality is so enticing that almost every creative person wants it. The overnight success. The secret formula. The magic pill. The path of least resistance is endemic in our current culture. But I want to encourage you to look for something else.

The desire to go viral is counterintuitive. We avoid viruses throughout the rest of our lives—we wash our hands, cough into our elbows, and avoid sick people—but when it comes to reaching an audience, we seek out the viral moment, not realizing that this kind of attention is also an illness. Viral content is but a well-crafted soundbite, which is, by definition, devoid of substance. Soundbites have immediate appeal, but lack staying power.

Think about it.
What actually goes viral?
Instagram butt photos.
Worldstar fight videos.
YouTube car crashes.
Incendiary tweets.
Vacuous controversies.
Inane arguments.
TMZ headlines.

Most of the viral moments we witness are gone just as fast as they arrived, and their brief footprint didn't add to the greater good. And even when the rare high-quality book or album or TED Talk does, indeed, go viral, that was never the point. Its spread was merely a consequence of exceptional craftsmanship.

Have you, at any point, stopped to consider why we strive for virality? Is there a reason we try to create the viral video, the overshared blog post, the retweeted tweet? Or are we all just Pavlov's dogs, drooling on command for a morsel of attention?

Maybe I'm allergic to the magic pill, but my own overnight success didn't happen, ahem, overnight. It occurred one creation at a time, the slowest of slow burns. As far as I can tell, I've never had anything go viral. And yet, I don't need to go viral, and neither do you. Sure, going viral would undoubtedly send a shedload of people your way—clicks and views and comments—but is that the kind of attention you want? Are they an engaged audience? Are they going to stick around? Is it a reciprocal relationship? Or is going viral more like throwing a party with an open bar? Of course people will make an appearance, but what will keep them there when the free booze has run dry?

There is, however, an alternative. Instead of going viral, I focus on one thing, and one thing only: adding value. Habitually, before every tweet I send, every podcast I record, every book I write, I ask myself, "Will this add value?" If not, then it's not worth sharing, no matter how much attention it may garner. Real creatives don't create for attention; they create because they can't *not* create.

When it comes to reaching an audience, adding value is the only way to gain long-term buy-in, and it's one of the few ways to build trust. When people trust you, they are eager to share your message with the people they love because human beings are intrinsically wired to share value with others. Trust—not virality—is the best strategy to spread your work. Without it, the exit is just a click away.

Creatives as Businesspeople

The present day is the most exciting time in history to be a creative person. No longer are you beholden to the gatekeepers; no longer must you compromise your art. For the first time in history, thanks to the online world, *you* are in control. I know this firsthand. When I wasn't happy with the publishing landscape in my twenties, I took matters into my own hands: I refused to wait for someone else's permission to publish my work.

When the gatekeepers said *no*, I said *yes* to myself. Over the last decade, Ryan and I have independently published four books, three of which were best sellers; we've toured internationally; and we've established an audience larger than most traditionally published authors'. And, until recently, we've done it all on our own. That's because we're not *just* creatives, and neither are you.

You see, there was a time when a creative was just a creative. During those times, an author like myself focused solely on writing the best book they could write. Someone else would edit, lay out, design, market, sell, and publish the book, which was a deal that most authors were fine with, at least partially, because it was the only option available—it was the only way to reach an audience.

WHEN WE START LOOKING FOR FINANCIAL SOLUTIONS TO CREATIVE PROBLEMS, OUR CREATIVITY SUFFERS.

Today there are other options, and even creatives who operate within the traditional system would benefit from taking control of their own promotional efforts. Of course, for creatives who are independently releasing their work, this is doubly true. In order to succeed—apart from the outside chance of being "discovered" and showered with money—it's best to view yourself as an entrepreneur, a creative businessperson. This perspective allows a creative person to look at each business challenge as an opportunity to enhance their work and get it to the right people. Administrative tasks—like updating social media and selling—become one more part of the creative process, which they are, if you're doing them well.

It might sound scary at first, but it's actually empowering. No more excuses, no more waiting around to be selected, no more blaming failure on someone else. You are in charge of your quality, your design, your distribution, your destiny. You must create, and then you must find your own audience, because no one else is going to do it for you.

Coda: Creativity

Ryan here, ready to join you again for a deeper dive. I hope Joshua's exploration of creativity got you excited to discover what fulfills you creatively. Ready to find out? Great! Let's go through the exercises I've outlined to help you locate what fuels your passion.

QUESTIONS ABOUT CREATIVITY

1. How is procrastination affecting your life?
2. How are distractions getting in the way of your creativity?
3. Do you consider yourself *busy* or *focused*? Why?
4. What would you like to focus on more? Why?
5. How often do you get out of your comfort zone?

THE DOS OF CREATIVITY

Next, what did you learn about your relationship with technology and creativity in this chapter? What will stick? What lessons will encourage you to avoid distractions and create something meaningful for the world? Here are five immediate actions you can take today:

- **Find your creativity.** It's important you get clear on what you want to create in your life. Write down five things you'd like to create. To help you with this list, ask yourself these questions:
  - How can I better serve others?
  - What problems do you want to solve?
  - Where is the greatest need for a solution?
- **Concentrate your creativity.** Now you need to explore your ideas further to help narrow down what creation you're going to focus

on. For each idea you've already written, now jot down the answer to these questions:

- What makes this creation interesting or unique?
- How will this add value to others?
- What steps are necessary to implement my creation?

- **Cultivate your creativity.** Now it's time to choose one creative endeavor to cultivate into a passion. If one of your five creative ideas isn't jumping out as the top choice, throw them into a hat and choose one randomly. (Before grabbing one, think about which one you hope comes out of the hat—that's the one you should choose.)

- **Remove your distractions.** Now that you have chosen a creation to work on, it's time to get focused. To do this, you must set up boundaries between you and whatever is getting in the way of creating. To help set these boundaries, write down what distractions take up most of your time (commitments, technology, social media, and the like). Be honest. Then, for each distraction, write down the answers to these questions:

  - Do you *need* this distraction in your life? If so, why?
  - How much time are you dedicating to this distraction now? What would be a more appropriate amount of time?
  - If you say *no* to this distraction, what can you say *yes* to that truly matters?

- **Practice your creativity.** Since you have freed up time by removing distractions from your environment, you can now fill that time with creating. Write down the answers to these questions to help you form a plan to create more:

  - How often will you create? Can you commit to a daily practice?
  - Who will hold you accountable?
  - When will you start?

THE DON'TS OF CREATIVITY

Finally, let's discuss what's getting in the way. Here are five things you'll want to avoid, beginning today, if you want to improve your relationship with creativity:

- Don't attempt to cultivate a passion with money as the primary goal.
- Don't focus on going viral. Instead, focus on gaining people's trust and adding value.
- Don't let perfection become the enemy of creation. No creation is perfect, not even the ones created by professionals.
- Don't worry about the brand name of the tools you are using to create. The tools are only as creative as the user.
- Don't focus on criticism. Instead, focus on creating.

RELATIONSHIP 7 | PEOPLE

You can't *change* the people around you, but you can change the *people* around you. If I could travel back in time and give one piece of advice to my young self, I would hand him a sheet of paper with that sentence written on it.

We understand the indispensable role of other human beings when we are children: our mothers feed us, our fathers care for us, our siblings teach us, our friends interact with us, our families love us. But with each year that passes, new desires and pursuits build barricades between us and the people in our lives. Let's face it, we started social distancing way before the pandemic of 2020. By puberty, we begin to covet cars and clothes and contraband, inching us away from our companions and relatives. In our twenties, we enlist in careers that create yet more distance, working hard to avoid the hard work of living well. And as we grow older, we accumulate accoutrements and artifacts, isolating ourselves with more square footage. We fill our homes with stuff, but we feel empty amid the clutter.

To fill the self-constructed holes in our Swiss-cheese hearts, we lust for exciting new relationships that may not share our values, surrounding ourselves with people who bring out the worst in us. Before we know it, we're all grown up, but we haven't matured much. Puzzled, we look around—by age thirty or forty or fifty or older—and wonder why we've encircled ourselves with the possessions and people that pointillate our vacuous lives. If we want to escape this quagmire, we must honestly assess the relationships we've established, including the toxic ones.

Hence, the opening line of this chapter.

Too often, we try to *change* people—attempting to mold them into someone else, someone they aren't, someone who fits our ideal version of a friend, lover, or family member—instead of seeking out new, empowering, supportive relationships that enable us to grow and thrive and be the best version of ourselves. Naturally, this tension leads to quarrels that leave little room for compassion and affection, let alone prosperity. In time, toxicity permeates the entire relationship, and the tiny spats and passive-aggressive behavior mount until, one day, after one too many unnecessary escalations, we've had enough of the toxic relationship, and then we say or do something we can't take back. It's no coincidence that many romantic relationships end with the intensity of war. Angry words turn into shouting, which turns into punched walls and objects hurled across the room.

The acute reader will notice that each of this book's relationship chapters began with the word "I." That is, until this chapter, which began emphatically with "You." This decision was deliberate: I wanted the book's format to mimic our own lives. You see, I'd planned on writing a relationship book, but I realized that the things that screw up our interpersonal relationships are usually our internal relationships. Before we can focus on cultivating meaningful relationships with others, we must first recognize our own issues.

That's not an excuse to treat people poorly until you've mastered the six internal relationships in your life. On the contrary. Minimalism allows us to eliminate the excess stuff so we can sort through the excess baggage in our heads and hearts. As we improve our relationships with the truth, with our self, with our values and money and creativity, we begin to form the best version of ourselves,

A TOXIC PERSON IS ENTITLED TO NOTHING.

which creates the groundwork for improving our relationship with others. If we don't do this—if we don't work to understand ourselves—we're inadvertently punishing the people around us by not living up to our potential.

Different Personalities

According to Carl Jung's theory of personality differences, first published in his 1921 book, *Psychological Types*, people can be characterized by their "preference of general attitude." In 1962, Isabel Briggs Myers, founder of the Myers & Briggs Foundation, published the Myers-Briggs Type Indicator (MBTI) personality inventory, a standardized test to make Jung's theory "understandable and useful in people's lives."

Myers, and her mother, Katharine Briggs, developed their personality test to identify and describe the "sixteen distinctive personality types that result from the interactions among the preferences." That is:

Favorite world: Do you prefer to focus on the outer world or on your own inner world? This is called Extroversion (E) or Introversion (I).

Information: Do you prefer to focus on the basic information you take in, or do you prefer to interpret and add meaning? This is called Sensing (S) or Intuition (N).

Decisions: When making decisions, do you prefer to first look at logic and consistency or first look at the people and special circumstances? This is called Thinking (T) or Feeling (F).

Structure: In dealing with the outside world, do you prefer to get things decided, or do you prefer to stay open to new information and options? This is called Judging (J) or Perceiving (P).

By simply reading these descriptions, you may be able to identify your personality type; to be sure, though, you can take the full test at myersbriggs.org.

If I were to simplify this theory, I'd present it like this:

Some people are introverts (I), others are extroverts (E).
Some people are detail oriented (S), others are "big picture" (N).
Some people are thinkers (T), others are feelers (F).
Some people are planners (J), others are spontaneous (P).

When you determine your preference in each of the four categories, you'll have your own personality type, which is usually expressed as a code with four letters.

Personally, I'm an ISTJ (an introverted, detail-oriented, thinking planner). Now, does that mean I should spend time only with people who share similar personality traits? Definitely not. Ryan, the other half of The Minimalists, is literally my exact opposite:

ENFP (an extroverted, big-picture, feeling, spontaneous person). My wife, on the other hand, has a personality that's closer to mine: INTJ (an introverted, big-picture, thinking planner).

None of these personality traits are "right" or "wrong," but, regardless of whether you give any weight to the MBTI itself, it's useful to understand *your* predisposition because it will help you better interact with others. Similarly, acknowledging others' unique personalities—rather than trying to configure their personalities to fit yours—will help you appreciate their perspectives and make your relationships richer and stronger. I find this especially true with introversion and extroversion.

Introverts and Extroverts

For years, I didn't grasp my own penchant for solitude, so I let societal norms dictate my interactions. Although I'm an *extreme* introvert, my behavior throughout my teens and twenties was that of an extrovert. The career I chose forced me to be a "people person," spending nearly all of my waking hours actively engaged with others in meetings, on phone calls, and on the sales floor. The only time I had to myself was in the bathroom—door locked and hiding from the chaotic world, if just for a moment. To make matters worse, I'm socially competent, which people tend to mistake for extroversion. This is so common that there was even a period of time I talked myself into thinking I was, indeed, an extrovert. But that's like an Alaskan salmon talking himself into being a German shepherd—even with the nicest dog collar, that fish isn't going to bark. It's not in his nature, just like extroversion isn't in mine. Consequently, I felt drained by the ceaseless interactions.

I'm confident the opposite would have been true for Ryan. If he were to live a life of solitude, he'd be miserable without scores of people to constantly talk to, interact with, befriend. That doesn't mean he doesn't appreciate a quiet moment every now and then, but quietude is not his default setting. A German shepherd might be able to swim, but he can't breathe underwater.

Of course, nobody is 100 percent introverted or 100 percent extroverted. Both personality traits exist on a continuum. Introverts are, by and large, quiet, reserved, shy, passive, silent, reliable, calm, and rigid, while extroverts are talkative, sociable, outgoing, lively, touchy, optimistic, active, and assertive. But truth be told, you could describe me with characteristics from both sides: I'm reserved, reliable, and rigid like a typical introvert, but I'm certainly not shy or passive. And while I'm not talkative or even remotely outgoing, I'm often optimistic and assertive like the average extrovert. The point being that none of us fit neatly into a specific personality type. But if you know yourself well enough, you'll be able to adjust your life, and your interactions with others, to better fit your personality—instead of trying to stretch your personality to fit someone else's expectations.

Frankly, I used to think there was something wrong with me. Throughout my twenties, I followed societal norms, doing all the things you're supposed to do to be a normal, functioning member of society: going out with coworkers after work, spending every evening and weekend with friends, killing time with small talk. Always engaged. Always on. Never alone. But, as this constant interaction wore me out, I wasn't pleasant to be around. It felt oddly lonely to never be alone.

Then, as my twenties twilighted, I discovered I was more affable whenever I carved out time for myself. Today, I spend copious amounts of time alone. In fact, I don't know anyone who has more alone time than me: walking, writing, exercising, reading, ruminating. In the process, I've learned to enjoy the sound of silence, to sit quietly and hear what's going on not only around me, but inside me. Yet the greatest benefit of prolonged solitude is that, when I do decide to immerse myself in social situations—be it dinner with friends, a date with my wife, or a book-tour event with thousands of readers—I'm more pleasant to be around. Not only do I benefit from my alone time, but everyone around me benefits, too, because we all get the best version of me.

I don't, however, recommend more alone time, or more social time, to anyone. What works for me may not work for you. I know Ryan would suffer if my routine was thrust upon him. He's the life of the party: naturally charismatic, funny, and likable. As an extrovert, he gets his energy from other people, and time alone exhausts him. The opposite is obviously true for me. So classifying his approach, or my approach, as right or wrong misses the point. It depends on your personality. Besides, even with extreme personality traits, there are no absolutes. Even I, a borderline ascetic, would detest perpetual solitary confinement. Just as Ryan, with all his charming extroversion, occasionally needs a break from his social lifestyle.

The Three Relationships

People sometimes use the word "relationship" to connote a physical or intimate relationship. But, for the purposes of this chapter, your relationships are anyone with whom you interact—friends, partners, spouses, lovers, roommates, coworkers, acquaintances. All of these folks can be considered your relationships, and whether

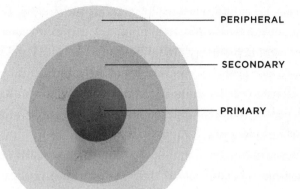

PERIPHERAL

SECONDARY

PRIMARY

they're healthy, neutral, or toxic, each of us has three distinct groups in our life: primary, secondary, and peripheral.

Your *primary* relationships are your closest relationships. This group most likely includes your significant other, immediate and close family members, and extremely close friends. These are the five or so main characters in the movie of your life, and they are, by far, your most significant relationships.

Your *secondary* relationships consist of folks similar to your primary group, except these relationships are less significant for a variety of reasons. Secondary relationships might include your close friends, your boss, your favorite coworkers, and your extended family members—your supporting cast.

Chances are the vast majority of the people in your life will fall into the third group—your *peripheral* relationships—which includes most coworkers, neighbors, community members, acquaintances, distant family members, the majority of your Facebook friends, and the like. These are the minor characters (and, occasionally, the extras) in your life's cast.

But just because someone resides in one of these groups, that doesn't mean the relationship is inherently healthy. In fact, some of the largest obstacles in life are the toxic people who have crept into our cast. Thus, it is crucial to understand which roles which people play in your life so you can reprioritize your relationships and surround yourself with people who support the person you want to become—not drag you toward *their* ideal version of you.

If you make a list of all the people in your life and label each relationship as *healthy*, *neutral*, or *toxic*, there's a good chance you'll find scores of people in your primary and secondary groups who likely don't belong there. It is up to you to decide which role these people play in your life (or whether they'll play a role at all).

THE MOST LOVING THING YOU CAN DO IS BE HONEST WITH OTHERS, EVEN IF THAT MEANS LOVING THEM FROM A DISTANCE.

Unfortunately, we tend to prioritize relationships out of proximity and convenience. Which means we end up spending most of our precious time with people in our peripheral group. These aren't "bad" people necessarily, but we have only twenty-four hours in a day, and if we spend most of those hours with coworkers and acquaintances, we forsake the people closest to us, which isn't fair to them and, ultimately, isn't fulfilling to us.

It is important to remember that your relationships will not remain static. People will veer in and out of your life and switch relationship groups as you grow and they grow. Many people who were especially relevant to you ten years ago are far less relevant today, right? Likewise, your future relationships will continue to shift, change, and grow. New friends will be made, current relationships will fade or strengthen, and some will end altogether. It's critical that you play an active role in this process—you want to be engaged in your relationship selection. In the following sections, we'll explore how you can seek out new empowering relationships, how you can repair and strengthen your current relationships, and how you can let go of toxic relationships to make room for the people who will help you live meaningfully.

Finding Empowering Relationships

I saw my wife naked for the first time about two minutes into our first date. Because it was my birthday, and Rebecca knew I was a minimalist, she thought a couples massage would be an appropriate experiential gift. (The other options were horseback riding and kayaking, both of which I turned down because it's disingenuous to pretend I like things I don't actually like.)

When the two of us walked into the massage parlor, we were greeted by two therapists, a large man and a small woman, both in cult-white scrubs, standing next to twin massage tables in the middle of an otherwise empty room. A Zen-garden playlist and central air conditioning filled the space with a cool serenity. "Go ahead and get undressed to your comfort level," the woman said. "We'll be back in two minutes."

As soon as they exited, I looked at Bex with a wide-eyed smile that said, "Well, you're the one who set this up," and then slid off my shoes.

She shot back an embarrassed glance and an accompanying shrug that communicated, "I didn't realize we were going to get undressed in the same room."

I raised my eyebrows to say, "But you knew it was a *couples* massage!"

She shrugged again and removed her top. And then I undressed to *my* comfort level (naked), trying not to gawk as Bex stripped down to *her* comfort level (panties). She looked so stunning that if she would have caught the contorted expression on my face, she might have mistaken it for a reaction to something offensive.

This is both a poor example and a good example of how to meet new people. While it's generally a bad idea to get naked the first time you hang out with someone, it is important to be honest about your preferences from the start. I could have impersonated a man who likes riding horses or floating down rivers, but that would have established a synthetic sense of who I am, leading to false expectations for Bex and, ultimately, a counterfeit connection. Instead, I was up-front about my preferences, and I asked the same of her, to simply be candid about who she was and what she wanted. That way, if our preferences clashed, we wouldn't have to experience the slow decline of an artificial alliance.

YOU CAN ESTABLISH A BOUNDARY WITHOUT ERECTING A FENCE.

These days, in our ever-connected world, there isn't a "best way" to meet new people. Although I've known Ryan since middle school, and I've known my friend Podcast Shawn since our corporate days, almost all of my primary and secondary relationships were formed within the last decade, and even those relationships vary widely in terms of how we met. Months before our birthday date, Rebecca and I first encountered each other at a grocery store in Missoula, Montana, where we were both living at the time. I happened upon my friend and business partner Colin Wright thanks to Twitter. I made contact with Joshua and Sarah Weaver, the husband-and-wife duo with whom Ryan and I now own a coffeehouse in Florida, after they read our book *Everything That Remains*. I came across the philosopher T.K. Coleman after hearing him on an obscure podcast. And I've started dozens of other worthwhile relationships on dating apps and at meetup groups and conferences and as friends of "friends" on Facebook or Instagram. The modern world has presented us with more ways than ever to meet new people.

The commonality between all of my newer relationships has little to do with *how* we met, and has everything to do with *why* we met, and *why* we grew close: we share similar values. No, we're not carbon copies of one another—in fact, most of my friends have different religious, political, and lifestyle beliefs, as well as diverse backgrounds, ethnicities, genders, sexual orientations, and socioeconomic statuses—but we've grown close because we have a strong foundation upon which we've been able to build a thriving relationship. This is true even though many of these people live in other states or even on other continents and we may not see each other regularly.

I've found that the key to establishing and fostering new, empowering relationships is threefold.

First, the most enriching relationships coalesce around shared values, not beliefs or ideologies or interests. If you have similarities outside your values, that can be nice, but our differences can also make the relationship stronger because those differences encourage us to challenge each other, in good faith, which helps us solidify our own viewpoints, or change them altogether.

Second, quality is always greater than quantity. It is possible to have a close connection with someone you see only once or twice a year, as long as your time together is meaningful. Conversely, it's possible to be stuck in a middling relationship with someone you encounter every day of your life. One could even argue that these lackluster relationships are more likely because we tend to take people for granted when they're eternally nearby. That's not always the case—you can be intentional with any relationship—but it's harder to appreciate someone who's never absent. This is why Bex and I spend more than half our time apart. The distance brings us closer together.*

Finally, every relationship requires reciprocity. That is, you must add value to—and get value from—the other person if you want the relationship to grow. Every relationship—friendship, romantic, or otherwise—is a series of gives and takes. Instead of thinking of it as simple reciprocity, though, I like to imagine that every relationship has an Us Box. For the relationship to work, both people must contribute to—and get something from—that box. If you give but don't get, you'll feel exploited. And if you only take but don't give, you're a freeloader. Yet if both people give what they can, the relationship will grow, although it may never be an even split. A relationship is not a transaction, so we needn't behave transactionally. Rather, we contribute what we *can*, and that may not be the same as what the other person can give. Sometimes, depending on our circumstances, we have the ability to *give* more to the relationship. Other times, we need to *get* more. The key is to be honest about what we can contribute to, and what we need from, the relationship. If we can do this—if we can set standards and then meet them through our actions—our relationships will flourish.

There have been times in my life where I've had the ability to be the primary contributor to a relationship—or to a particular part of a relationship. This book is a good example of that dynamic. While Ryan and I are equal partners in The Minimalists, I'm responsible for 90 percent of The Minimalists' blog and book writing. Conversely, Ryan fills in the gaps in other areas of our

---

* Bex and I dive deep into the details of our unconventional relationship on our podcast, *How to Love,* which is available at howtolove.show.

business—areas that aren't necessarily my strong suit. While he and I don't keep a ledger of duties, nor do we tally our exact individual contributions, it all works out in the end because we're both willing to contribute to the best of our ability.

There are other situations, however, in which I haven't been able to be the main contributor. A few years after I started dating my wife, my health took a turn for the worse. At that point, I was unable to contribute as much as I could previously: I couldn't work full-time and thus earned less income; my ability to parent was significantly diminished; and I couldn't participate in normal activities like travel, attending events, and grocery shopping. As a result, Bex had to pick up some of my slack. Which is exactly what she did. And then some. But she didn't just hold things together while I was ill, she contributed more than her fair share, going out of her way to take care of me, finding doctors and potential solutions, and, perhaps most important, taking the time to *understand* what I was going through. She understood that my shortfalls weren't by choice, that I wasn't neglecting our relationship, but that I simply wasn't the best version of myself during that snapshot of time. With her support, my health has improved immensely. Since my nadir, in the summer of 2019, it feels as if I've crawled out of a deep crater in the middle of the desert. Now that I'm above ground again, I might still be in the desert with a great distance ahead of me, but at least I'm headed in the right direction. I was humbled by my illness, and without Rebecca's support, I might still be crawling around the floor of that hollow basin. As my health continues to improve, I'm once

> YOU CAN'T *CHANGE* THE PEOPLE AROUND YOU, BUT YOU CAN CHANGE THE *PEOPLE* AROUND YOU.

again able to contribute more to the relationship—perhaps not as much as I once did, at least not yet, but more and more with every month that passes.

How to Be Yourself

Now, you might be thinking, "Of course I want empowering people in my life, but how do I know whether a relationship is supportive or toxic, growing or dying?"

The short answer is:

You probably already know.

If you're wondering whether a relationship is toxic,
it probably is.

A relationship is toxic
when it's very harmful or unpleasant
in a pervasive or insidious way.

Does the relationship constantly make you feel
sad, agitated, or upset,
anxious, angry, or scared,
guilt-ridden, chastened, or regretful?
Then there's a good chance it's toxic.

But when a relationship is truly outstanding,
you don't wonder at all.
You just know.
It's outstanding.
It literally stands out.

But why? What makes a relationship worthwhile, and how do you get there? It's tempting to look for a shortcut. Take the magic pill. Let the algorithm decide. Swipe right. But, of course, there are no shortcuts—there are only direct routes.

The most direct route to a solid relationship is the tried and true: just be yourself. Yes, I know, that sounds like trite bubblegum-wrapper advice. But here's the deal. You want people to love you for who *you* are, not who you portray yourself to be. A relationship is not a product, and you are not a salesperson. Which, for the longest time, is what I thought I was. I believed I had to convince others to like me and love me and care about me by pretending to be a different version of myself. Over time, I realized that's not only disingenuous, it's futile. Instead of posing as a gregarious, outdoorsy, crowd-loving guy, I could've just been my pleasant, affable, warm self.

Deep down, how you see yourself is the way everyone else will see you. If you don't like yourself, how can others like you? Sure, you can trick them for a period of time—you can even trick yourself—but, ultimately, you will know better. And it will eat you alive.

To be yourself, you must first know yourself. Today, I don't profess to like camping (or horseback riding or kayaking). I do things differently, honestly, representing myself for who I am, not some idealized figurehead I think others want me to be. I'd never ask you to do things you dislike, and if you're my friend or lover, I expect the same from you. This works only if we're honest with each other.

If you're exhausted by the prospect of being someone you're not, here's the solution: be the best version of *you*—your unexaggerated self—and then surround yourself with people who love you for who you are, in sickness and in health.

The people you surround yourself with will contribute greatly to your joy. Your relationships might not change you, but they will bring out the best—and the worst—in you. So we must choose wisely. No longer is it wise to spend time with people just because "we've always known each other" or because you happened to share a series of childhood events or a common interest. No, the strongest relationships are built upon a foundation of shared values. To get there, you'll need to learn how to set boundaries and communicate effectively.

Boundaries and Communication

At first, it might seem like setting boundaries is one of the last things you'd want to do to foster intimate and open relationships— as if constructing boundaries means you're not willing to let people in. But you can establish a boundary without erecting a fence.

Dr. Henry Cloud, a coauthor of the book *Boundaries: When to Say Yes, How to Say No to Take Control of Your Life*, says that "having clear boundaries is essential to a healthy, balanced lifestyle." According to Dr. Cloud and his coauthor, Dr. John Townsend, "boundaries define who we are and who we are not," showing others what you are personally responsible for. It's sort of like having your own property line around your well-being.

Although the physical world is filled with distinct boundaries— the partition around a cubicle or the walls in your apartment, for instance—it's equally important to construct physical, mental, emotional, and spiritual boundaries in our relationships. As stated by Drs. Cloud and Townsend:

- Physical boundaries help us determine who may touch us and under what circumstances.

- Mental boundaries give us the freedom to have our own thoughts and opinions.
- Emotional boundaries help us deal with our own emotions and disengage from the harmful, manipulative emotions of others.
- Spiritual boundaries give us renewed awe for the mysteries of the world.

You can set boundaries without pushing people away. In fact, your boundaries are a way to bring people *into* your world, to politely let them know what's acceptable and what isn't. You need boundaries to prevent mishaps, miscommunications, and misunderstandings. Healthy boundaries with your parents, significant other, children, friends, coworkers, and even yourself are necessary to protect your relationships from needless harm. So, just like you don't feel guilty for having a front door on your home, there's no need to feel guilty about your boundaries. Much like your front door, well-constructed boundaries keep the undesirables out so you can welcome in only the most appropriate relationships.

Possibly the best way to set appropriate boundaries is through constant and effective communication. Before you can communicate your boundaries, though, you must first define them. If you were building a new house, you'd need precise specifications to get the job done. Similarly, you must identify the specs of your personal boundaries for each relationship in your life.

What are your physical boundaries? Maybe you like to hug everyone, or maybe you don't even want to shake hands. Neither choice is "right" or "wrong."

What are your mental boundaries? Maybe you want to keep your opinions to yourself, or maybe you want to share your political beliefs on YouTube. Again, one boundary isn't more "correct" than the other.

What are your emotional boundaries? Maybe you prefer to be polite and receptive, or maybe you feel the need to be blunt even if it repels some people. Only you know what's natural for you.

What are your spiritual boundaries? Maybe your religion, or lack thereof, is a private experience, or maybe you're eager to proselytize. Either way, do you.

Knowing your boundaries will help you get a grasp on what you're willing to accept, as well as what you need to reject, to live congruently.

> WE ACCUMULATE ACCOUTREMENTS AND ARTIFACTS, ISOLATING OURSELVES WITH MORE SQUARE FOOTAGE. WE FILL OUR HOMES WITH STUFF, BUT WE FEEL EMPTY AMID THE CLUTTER.

Now, it's worth keeping in mind that your boundaries will change over time. Just as you haven't had the same property line your entire life, you're not going to maintain the same boundaries as your relationships change and grow. Plus, your boundaries will become more specific as you communicate them with others.

Marshall Rosenberg, the author of *Nonviolent Communication*, says that "much of how we communicate—judging others, bullying, having racial bias, blaming, finger pointing, discriminating, speaking without listening, criticizing others or ourselves, name-calling, reacting when angry, using political rhetoric, being defensive or judging who's 'good/bad' or what's 'right/wrong' with people"—could be classified as "violent communication." Instead of communicating through these means, Rosenberg recommends a four-step process of "nonviolent communication" that includes our observations, feelings, needs, and requests:

- Consciousness: a set of principles that support living a life of compassion, collaboration, courage, and authenticity.
- Language: understanding how words contribute to connection or distance.
- Communication: knowing how to ask for what we want, how to hear others even in disagreement, and how to move toward solutions that work for all.
- Means of influence: sharing "power with others" rather than using "power over others."

Over time, as we put this process in place in our own lives, we find that we lose the need to judge or persuade people, opting instead to communicate from the heart. And as we learn to communicate better, we also learn how to strengthen our connection with others.

Repairing and Strengthening Relationships

Every other Wednesday, my wife and I take the day off from work, just the two of us, together. Sometimes we have grand plans that involve museums and hikes and coastal road trips, but usually we do nothing more than bring a couple books to our favorite breakfast spot, where we'll read and converse and just spend time together, uninterrupted by the everyday pull of life. It's a sort of reset. And I look forward to those Wednesdays more than any other day. The activity itself is less important than the intention, which isn't merely to spend time together (remember: quality is greater than quantity), but it's a reminder that our relationship is the priority. Not *a* priority—*the* priority. With this constant, biweekly reminder, Bex's and my relationship continues to deepen in ways that aren't possible with surface-level relationships. With just a few of these deep primary relationships in your life, mixed with the appropriate amount of secondary and peripheral relationships, it's nearly impossible to feel lonely.

Did you know there is now a "Friendship 101" class at the University of Southern California? Can you imagine—a class that teaches you about friendship? Yep. To boot, as of this writing, it has the longest wait list of any course at USC. Why? Because there's a loneliness epidemic sweeping the globe. We've become experts at making "friends" online, but we've lost touch with people. The class at USC is simply trying to correct that disconnect.

Turns out that friendship has evolutionary benefits. "Our ability to form relationships with people who aren't related to us . . . is a critical skill that helped turn us into humans. It's a fundamental part of who we are," Shane Parrish wrote in a recent *Farnam Street* essay.

Great. So, friends are important. But you already knew that, right? What we must determine, then, is how to repair and strengthen our existing friendships. First, we identify the qualities that define deep relationships. In our debut book, *Minimalism: Live a Meaningful Life*, Ryan and I pinpointed the eight elements of great relationships, and if I were to characterize those elements today, I'd redefine them as follows:

Love. A deep affection and bottomless devotion toward another person. When you love someone, you're willing to prioritize that person's interests over your own fleeting desires. Love breeds more love, which pushes aside self-interest in favor of strengthening the relationship.

Trust. The willingness to rely on another person without questioning their motives or requiring evidence. When you're able to establish trust with someone, you become the best version of yourself because trust breeds more trust, which encourages habitual honesty from both parties.

Honesty. Sincerity that is free from deceit or coercion. When you refuse to lie, you're making a commitment to avoid shortcuts and stay on the same path as the other person, even when the terrain is rough. Honesty breeds more honesty, which establishes a solid foundation for any relationship.

Caring. Actively displaying kindness, compassion, and concern for another person. When you care about someone, you're concerned enough to express it through your consistent actions. Caring breeds more caring, which feeds and strengthens the relationship through conduct rather than intentions alone.

Support. A supportive person provides help and encouragement to others. When you are a champion for the relationship, you show that you are reliable, nurturing, and devoted to the other person. Support breeds more support, which fortifies the commitment of both parties in a relationship.

Attention. The ability to be present in, and focused on, the relationship. When you're able to concentrate fully, your undivided attention shows the other person how important they are. Attention breeds attention, which heightens the connection between two people.

Authenticity. The ability to be genuine. When you're authentic, you display your integrity and consistency throughout the relationship. Authenticity breeds more authenticity, which brings legitimacy to the relationship.

Understanding. Sympathetic, deep awareness of another person. When you understand someone, you make an effort to bore past the surface and understand the entire person—their feelings, desires, and deeds—without judgment or protest.

While we've spent a good chunk of this book focusing on the nuances of most of these eight elements—*trust, honesty, attention,* and *authenticity* have been thoroughly mined in previous chapters, and *love, caring,* and *support* are touched upon in this chapter—I'd like to spend some time, in this section, expanding on my understanding of *understanding.*

It is difficult to truly understand others, but understanding is like exercise for your relationships. The more you work out at the gym, the fitter you'll be; likewise, the more you work to understand others, the fitter your relationships will be. The strongest relationships make an effort to avoid misunderstandings because, when blown out of proportion, our confusion and mix-ups lead to larger disagreements and arguments and fights. To avoid this downward spiral, and to strengthen our relationships, we want to work through the four stages of understanding: tolerance, acceptance, respect, and appreciation.

Tolerate. Tolerance is a weak virtue, but it's a solid start. If someone's behavior seems bothersome, it is best to avoid the knee-jerk reactions of fight or flight and, instead, find ways to tolerate their differences. For example, let's say you're an aspiring minimalist but your partner is an enthusiastic collector—a clear dichotomy of preferences. Maybe your partner finds satisfaction in collecting porcelain figurines or vintage guitars, while you believe their treasures are clutter. So you're left scratching your head, wondering how to convert them to your singularly valid viewpoint, which can be mind-numbingly frustrating for both parties. Don't worry, though. You needn't get on the same page right away; you need only recognize that you both have your reasons for being on separate pages. By tolerating someone's quirks and allowing them to live happily within their own worldview, you will at least be on a path toward understanding that person—and that's a big first step, even if you may not understand their obsession with inanimate statuettes or unplayed musical instruments.

Accept. To truly live in concert with others, we must quickly move past tolerance toward acceptance. Once you've made a concerted effort to at least tolerate the other person's quirks, those quirks begin to seem less silly and, in time, more meaningful—not meaningful to you, but meaningful to the person you care about. Once you realize your partner's collection has a *purpose*, it's easier to accept because that desire to collect is a part of who they are as a whole human, and, while you may not like a particular behavior, you still love the entire person, foibles and all.

Respect. Accepting—not just tolerating, but truly accepting—someone's idiosyncrasies is challenging, but not as much as respecting that person *because of* their idiosyncrasies. Think about it. It took you this many years to arrive at your current credo, so it's unreasonable to expect someone else to meet you there overnight, no matter how cogent your counterargument. Okay, so perhaps you'd never hoard figurines or guitars, but there are many beliefs you hold that, at face value, seem ridiculous to someone else. Yet even when other people don't agree with you, even when they don't *understand* your stance, you still want them to respect your preferences, right? So why not extend them the same courtesy? Only then will you move closer to understanding; only then will you begin to realize your stated worldview isn't the solitary axiom by which everyone must live. Sure, it's nice to have a clutter-free home, but it's also nice to share your life with people you respect.

Appreciate. With respect in your rearview, understanding is right around the bend. Continuing our example, let's say your partner experiences great satisfaction from their collection. Why would you want to change that? You care about their well-being, right? Well, if their collection brings contentment to their life, and if you care about that person, then their collection might even bring joy to your life, as well, because joy is contagious—but only after you get past the arguments, past the stages of tolerance, acceptance, and respect, and you honestly appreciate the other person's desires. Many of us navigate different roads toward joy, but even if we travel separate routes, it is important that we appreciate the journey—not only ours, but the journey of everyone we love. When we appreciate others for who they are, not who we want them to be, then, and only then, will we truly understand.

So, the next time you reach a fork in the road, remember this acronym—TARA: tolerate, accept, respect, and appreciate. If you travel this path frequently, your relationships will flourish, and you'll experience a richness that wasn't possible without a deep understanding of the people in your life. This path works not only for significant others, but for friends, coworkers, and anyone else with whom we want to strengthen our connection. Of course, there will be times when values clash, and you won't be able to appreciate the person for who they are. And there will even be rare times when TARA is the inappropriate path: if someone engages in self-destructive behavior—drugs, crime, racism—then you needn't tolerate their conduct. Sometimes it's okay to say goodbye, walk away, and travel a separate path.

Ultimately, *understanding* answers the most germane questions about relationships: What drives the other person? What do they want? What do they need? What excites and encourages them? What are their desires? What are their pains? What do they enjoy? What makes them happy? If you can answer these questions, you'll be better equipped with the understanding you need to meet their needs. And if you're able to meet someone's needs, and they meet yours, you're all but guaranteed to have a vibrant, passionate, thriving relationship.

Thirteen Overrated Virtues

Now that we've surveyed the most pertinent qualities of worthwhile relationships, we must also consider the virtues we've been acculturated to believe are noble but are often overrated.

Loyalty. Yes, it is important to be loyal to loved ones, but loyalty alone is typically misguided and may even degrade your relationships by creating a smokescreen between rationality and reality. Being loyal is fine, but loyalty at the expense of integrity is detrimental to a relationship.

Honor. Yes, we want to honor our parents, neighbors, friends, and family. But to what extent? If your best friend becomes a violent criminal, should you still hold him in great esteem? While an appropriate degree of honor is crucial, barefaced honor can inadvertently tether us to the convictions and conventions that prevent us from living in accordance with our values.

Righteousness. We all want to be "right." But if you constantly assert your correctness, it comes off as self-righteous or gloating, and that's never healthy for a relationship. When in doubt, "I don't know" are the three most freeing words we can utter.

Transparency. You want to be honest and open with others, but you needn't let every thought that enters your brain spill out of your mouth unfiltered. If you aren't careful, you can hurt the ones you love—and hurt your relationships with them in the process.

Pleasure. Pleasure isn't "good" or "bad," but too much pleasure is hedonism. Our relationships aren't supposed to be vectors of perpetual delight. Although our interactions can be pleasurable, pleasure shouldn't be the star by which we navigate our relational vessels. If we do, we're likely to forsake many of the elements that make the relationship worthwhile.

Comfort. A close cousin to pleasure, comfort is tricky. The Stoic philosopher Musonius Rufus argued that someone who tries to avoid all discomfort is less likely to be comfortable than someone who periodically embraces discomfort. Thus, if we seek discomfort, we have the ability to expand our comfort zone.

Lust. We all have impulses, but we often confuse our desires and passion with lust. And when lust takes over, we lose all our senses. Today more than ever, our lust extends well beyond sexual desire: we are consumed by a craving for cars and clothes and camera equipment, and, for some odd reason, a large swath of our puritanical culture has agreed that yearning for stuff is an acceptable alternative to sexual longing. But both desires, when not pursued with intention, lead to obvious deleterious consequences.

Agreeability. Most of us wish to be in harmony with the people we love. It seems the quickest route to this harmony is to agree with others as frequently as possible. Yet this impulse is misguided. If we placate people, it's not only dishonest—it closes the door to individuality. It is possible, however, to disagree with someone tactfully, while keeping their point of view in mind. Ryan and I disagree all the time, but we almost never argue. If you can make that distinction, your relationship will improve, because when you do agree, the other person will know it's genuine and not just an attempt to win their favor.

Empathy. Perhaps the most controversial of the overrated virtues. These days, we hear everyone from preachers to pundits proclaim the power of empathy. But most of these people are actually talking about *compassion*, not empathy. If that's the case, I have no argument: compassion—that is, concern for the misfortunes of others—is useful, and we could use more of it. Empathy, however—that is, the ability to feel the suffering of others—is not a desirable outcome. The Yale researcher and philosopher Paul Bloom makes this point in his book *Against Empathy: The Case for Rational Compassion*: "We often think of our capacity to experience the suffering of others as the ultimate source of goodness. . . . Nothing could be further from the truth." Bloom goes on to say that empathy is "one of the leading motivators of inequality and immorality in society. . . . Far from helping us to improve the lives of others, empathy is a capricious and irrational emotion that appeals to our narrow prejudices. It muddles our judgment and, ironically, often leads to cruelty." According to Bloom, "We are at our best when we are smart enough not to rely on it, but to draw instead upon a more distanced compassion."

Negativity. This one might be confusing at first. How is negativity an overrated *virtue*? Does anyone actually think negativity is a "good" thing? If we were to measure popular opinion, almost everyone would recognize negativity as being "bad." Why, then, do we constantly bicker, complain, and gossip? Because it's a perceived shortcut. If you complain about the same thing as someone else or gossip about another person, it increases your bond with your fellow complainer. There's an old saying that "hurt people hurt people," and that's what's happening whenever we walk around infecting the world with negativity.

Jealousy. The most wasteful emotion, jealousy is rooted in suspicion—suspicion that you're not "good" enough, that you're not doing enough, that the other person isn't as deserving as you. Jealousy is a selfish emotion, one that does not serve the greater good in the slightest. The antidote to jealousy is a little-known virtue called *compersion*—the feeling of joy one has while experiencing another person's joy, such as witnessing a toddler's smile and feeling joy in response. When you experience joy based on the joy of someone else, no space remains for jealousy in the relationship.

Sentimentality. The Greek philosopher Zeno believed that humans were designed to be reasonable, but he also recognized that we are human beings, and human beings are propelled by emotion. Thus, we needn't shun reason or emotion, but we must avoid sentimentality—that is, excessive tenderness, sadness, or nostalgia—

because it crowds out reason in favor of overpowering emotions. When we're feeling overly emotional, it is helpful to gain additional perspective by involving the reasoning of a grounded outside party.

Solemnity. Yes, we want to be taken seriously, and we want to approach relationships with dignity, but we must leave ample room for humor and levity. Otherwise, we'll be burdened, and eventually buried, by our own self-seriousness. Ergo, make room for jokes, even in—especially in—the most trying times.

While some of these so-called virtues are best avoided altogether—jealousy, righteousness, and negativity are especially worth steering away from—most can serve you well when you find the appropriate balance.

On Sacrifice and Compromise

There are two other virtues I used to think were overrated, but I've changed my mind about both: sacrifice and compromise. After a series of toxic relationships with bosses, coworkers, so-called friends, significant others, and even family members, I reasoned that I had sacrificed too much and had made too many compromises, and that's what made those relationships untenable. While that may be partially true, the problem wasn't that I'd sacrificed or compromised for those people, it was that I made foolish sacrifices and compromises throughout each relationship.

Sadly, I sacrificed my values in an effort to make relationships work. As a result, I made silly compromises to appease others: I avoided the truth because I didn't want to hurt people's feelings. I tried to pacify people with material possessions instead of showing them real love. I forsook my own mental, emotional, and physical health to take care of others.

But appeasing others doesn't work. At least not beyond the moment. Think about it. How would you feel if you suddenly discovered that everyone you know was trying to merely conciliate you with kindness? In medicine, doctors refer to this type of treatment as "palliative care," which means to make a disease or its symptoms less severe or unpleasant without removing the cause. In relationships, however, we call it *placating*. These types of sacrifices and compromises are disingenuous at best, relationship-ending at worst.

Yet, occasionally, you must sacrifice, and you must compromise, because the world was not created only to gratify your desires. Your life isn't only about you.

Fundamentally, a certain level of sacrifice—that is, giving up something important or valued for someone else—is necessary for a relationship to work. Relationships take time and energy and attention, three of our most precious resources, which we must be willing to part with in exchange for the relationship itself.

Compromise—that is, to settle a dispute by mutual concession—is also necessary within a working relationship. Because no two humans have identical preferences, you are bound to have to meet in the middle at some point. The key, then, is to avoid sacrificing your values on your way to the meeting point.

Parenting is the perfect illustration of the need for sacrifice and compromise. I see this in my own life. On the surface, parenting is burdensome, tedious, and boring. But thoughtful parents are willing to sacrifice their own busyness, excitement, and interests for the sake of their child. It is this compromise—this meeting in the middle—that improves the well-being of all parties.

Naturally, this lesson extends beyond parenting. Think of the best relationships in your life. When has it made sense to give up something valuable to improve the relationship (sacrifice)? When have you had to settle a dispute by mutual concession (compromise)? If you were able to do both and your values remained unscathed in the process, then there's a solid chance you made a high-quality decision for the relationship.

Letting Go of Toxic Relationships

"They claim that love is blind," said Marta Ortiz, pausing before adding, "There's definitely some truth to that." Ortiz, our packing partyer from Mexico City, is no stranger to toxic relationships. "When I was in my twenties, I did my fair share of exploring, running with some crowds that were a little rough. In the process, though, I thought I found a diamond in there." She was speaking about a romantic relationship that had blossomed. "At first, everything was great. He treated me well, and he was very sweet and handsome."

She didn't know there was a dark side. "He was good at hiding his chemical addictions from me for a while." That is, until they started to manifest in verbal—and eventually physical—abuse. "Blinded by love, I tolerated it for way too long," she confessed at the end of her unpacking experiment.

"Toxic people defy logic," according to *Emotional Intelligence 2.0* coauthor Travis Bradberry. "Some are blissfully unaware of the negative impact that they have on those around them, and others seem to derive satisfaction from creating chaos and pushing other people's buttons. Either way, they create unnecessary complexity, strife, and worst of all stress."

Like Marta Ortiz, we've all held on to a relationship that didn't deserve to be in our lives, and most of us are still involved with people who continually drain us: People who don't add value. People who aren't supportive. People who take and take and take without giving back. People who contribute little and prevent us from growing. People who constantly play the victim.

In time, people who play victim become victimizers. That's when the relationship grows dangerous. Victimizers keep us from feeling fulfilled and from living purpose-driven lives. And, over time, these toxic relationships become part of our identity.

We can slog through life with disempowering toxic relationships, or, like Marta Ortiz, we can choose to move forward without them. When you say it out loud, the choice seems obvious. Yet we repeatedly decide to stick around, to hope things will change, to put off the inevitable until tomorrow. But then tomorrow arrives, and we postpone another day, another month, until, before we know it, several years have passed us by, and the people we surround ourselves with are not the people we would choose if we had the chance to start over today.

Why do we allow this to happen?

There are two main reasons: familiarity and fear.

First, we stick with that which is familiar because change is onerous. A successful relationship requires dedication, compassion, support, and understanding; a mediocre relationship requires only proximity and time.

Second, we don't move on because we're afraid. If you were to make a list of all your current relationships—everyone from all three groups—how many of them would you reselect to be a new relationship in your life today? If you'd pick a person again, that's wonderful (we discussed how to repair and strengthen those relationships earlier in this chapter). But if you would avoid that relationship, then you have to ask yourself why you're clinging to it now. Perhaps you have a good reason, but usually, we cling out of fear. We're afraid to make a change, to hurt another person's feelings, to lose love. But I'd posit that the most loving thing you can do is be honest with others, even if that means loving them from a distance.

Naturally, making a change is difficult. If it were easy, you'd have already made it. But change is a must if you want to make the most of your relationships. Here are a few considerations that will help you navigate relational change:

You can repair a relationship, but
You can't "fix" other people.
You can't alter their nature.
You can't force them to be "better."
You can't change their personality.
You can't assign them new preferences.
You can't coerce them to be more like you.

You might be able to help someone see your point of view, but you can't drag them toward change. No matter how much you want to alter someone, it's a futile exercise. Which leaves us with at least two options for faltering relationships: acceptance or moving on. Both options are a form of letting go.

If you're willing to accept someone for who they are—rather than who you want them to be—then you must be willing to let go of your previous expectations for that person and communicate new standards for the relationship along the way. Sometimes, this can be achieved through a single conversation. Other times, when a relationship has experienced significant enough corrosion, acceptance might take a series of conversations that help redefine and reshape the relationship. In dating parlance, this is referred to as a DTR (defining the relationship) agreement. The best time to define a relationship is at its onset; the second-best time is now. As a relationship progresses, it makes sense to update the terms along the way, taking into consideration both parties' needs, desires, and perspective. My wife and I, for instance, engage in at least one "deep discussion" each month to align our expectations and ensure our standards are closely aligned. And then, once a year, we review our values together to see whether any significant shifts have occurred.* It's sort of like renewing our vows, except way more practical.

These measures might seem formal to some, but they don't have to be. Rebecca and I have fun, lighthearted conversations about difficult subjects, and those discussions never feel ceremonial or dour. Even with my more distant friends—my secondary relationships—I throw myself into semi-regular conversations about standards, expectations, beliefs, and values. These difficult discussions help me better understand my friends' lives, and they give me a chance to marshal vulnerability, which is another way to strengthen a relationship. Ultimately, communication is the only way to make sure we're moving in the same direction together.

Some relationships, however, are not worth the energy, time, or attention we provide them. Some people's behavior is fundamentally toxic. The signs are usually clear—thoroughly toxic people are often:

Manipulative.
Threatening.
Insulting.
Spiteful.
Malicious.
Malevolent.

---

* We use the Values Worksheet on page 321.

Cruel.
Violent.
Bigoted.
Underhanded.

Others are subtly toxic. These people might be more difficult to spot but are equally important to filter out, because a single turd in the punch bowl makes it taste like . . . well, you get the point. Be on the lookout for people who are:

Unreasonable.
Disingenuous.
Thoughtless.
Pessimistic.
Hotheaded.
Narcissistic.
Enervating.

Whether someone is aggressively toxic or just vaguely so, it's crucial to create distance in these relationships so you can make room to let go. In time, you may choose to have a departure conversation with each toxic person, but, often, the best approach is to simply walk away, especially if a difficult discussion would escalate things and make the situation worse. It is possible to forgive without confrontation. Closure is preferable, but, in my experience, closure is overrated because it doesn't magically fix things. As a matter of fact, we often get the closure we thought we wanted, but it doesn't deliver on its promise, and it's not the same thing as moving on. Closure is merely a defined breaking point, but not everything ends with a clean break. Sometimes, the end is brought about by a gradual fade into nothingness. So, you needn't feel obliged to return phone calls or respond to text messages or meet with a toxic person for dinner. You shouldn't be impelled to explain yourself. You are not obligated to maintain a tie with anyone. Friendship, companionship, and love are a privilege, not a right, and if someone has squandered that privilege, you aren't required to stick around. The toxic person is entitled to nothing.

There are times when a relationship remains toxic even after it's over. You may not know why the relationship ended—or perhaps the other person doesn't want to give you the closure for which you yearn—and so the relationship turns toxic after the fact because, even without contact, the other person still lingers in your mind. Unfortunately, not everything ends on *your* terms or on *your* timeline. And there's only one way to evict these people from your emotional headspace: forgiveness. Just as we set down heavy luggage we no longer want to carry, we forgive others so we can move forward without the weight of the past.

DEEP DOWN, HOW YOU SEE YOURSELF IS THE WAY EVERYONE ELSE WILL SEE YOU.

Leaving a toxic relationship is like choosing between graduation and divorce. Often, it's better to leave now on the best possible terms, to move on and be grateful for the good times and the lessons you've learned throughout the relationship (graduation). Or, you can wait around and try to withstand the bickering, maneuvering through a series of arguments until, eventually, inevitably, everything ends up broken beyond repair (divorce). Letting go is more difficult now, but less difficult in the long run.

Letting go of someone does not mean that you don't love that person; it means only that their behavior won't allow you to participate in the relationship anymore. It doesn't make you bad or evil or negligent to walk away. You're making room for a better life. A life of discourse, not dispute. A life of quality, not quarrels. A life of caring, not clashing. When you graduate from a toxic relationship, you're not quitting—you're beginning again.

MINIMALIST RULE FOR LIVING WITH LESS

Willing to Walk Rule

There's a scene in *Heat* in which the main character says, "Don't let yourself get attached to anything you are not willing to walk out on in thirty seconds flat." Whoa, how crass! But what if your preparedness to walk away is actually the ultimate expression of love, because if you could walk away at anytime, then you must be staying for a reason, right? Think about it. How freeing would it be to possess the ability to walk away from *anything* at a moment's notice? You can. We call it the Willing to Walk Rule. This rule highlights the freedom found in nonattachment. If you purchase new material items, don't assign them any meaning, because if they remain meaningless, you can walk away whenever you want. If you take on new ideas or habits, don't tether yourself to them, because when they stop serving you, you can walk away if you aren't attached. This rule even works with relationships: your willingness to walk away from toxic people actually strengthens your bond with others, because nobody thrives in a union birthed from pious placation. Even if you can't walk away in "thirty seconds flat," if you're unattached, you can decamp when these people, places, and things disturb your well-being.

Apologize to Move On

It turns out that sometimes the toxic person in the relationship is *you*. It takes self-awareness and strength to realize this and admit when your decisions have been inappropriate, negligent, or even toxic, poisoning the relationship with your noxious behavior. Other times, the poison is subtle, a mere microdose of toxicity: you've made honest mistakes and errors that stain your relationships. Either way, you are at fault, and you have two options: dig in your heels or apologize.

Apologizing feels like the more difficult option because it involves admitting when we are beyond the pale and then taking actions to make amends. Ego gets in the way of our apologies. So we double down on our positions, discarding rationality in favor of self-righteousness, degrading our bond in the process. When we are cognizant enough to set aside our ego, however, we have a unique opportunity to rebuild with the broken pieces, perhaps making the relationship even stronger.

Coincidentally, I made one of these relational mistakes the week I wrote this. On *The Minimalists Podcast*, I inadvertently disclosed some personal information about a friend of mine, whom we'll call "Mike." The error was not malicious; at the time, I didn't realize the details were private. To me, they seemed perfectly innocuous—until I got an email from Mike stating otherwise. My first inclination was to reject his frustration. "It's not a big deal," I thought. "He's just overreacting." But I was projecting. Just because something isn't a big deal to me doesn't mean it's not upsetting to someone else. If I acted in a way that hurt my friend, it doesn't matter what *I* thought or how *I* felt. What matters is the damage *I* inflicted. There was only one respectable way forward.

I called Mike immediately, and I explained that, while I didn't have any malicious intent, I wished I would have thought about what I was saying before I said it. Then I told him I was sorry, and I made two commitments: to learn from this blunder so that I wouldn't repeat the gaffe, and to do what I could to fix the problem. While I was too late to undo the damage completely, we were able to edit out the error so that future listeners wouldn't stumble upon Mike's private info.

During my early corporate days, a towering man named Jim Harr was one of my favorite mentors. Jim, whose personality was even bigger than the man himself, was full of no-nonsense aphorisms that shaped me as a young adult; his wisdom helped me systematically assess and ask better questions about my own behaviors. Sometimes, however, his inspirational sayings twisted into malapropisms that were actually more profound than the intended aphorism.

> **IF YOU'RE WONDERING WHETHER A RELATIONSHIP IS TOXIC, IT PROBABLY IS.**

Jim uttered my most treasured Harr-ism after I had badly bungled a sale in one of our retail stores. He looked at me earnestly and said, "Hindsight is fifty-fifty." While you and I both know he meant to say that hindsight is twenty-twenty, the resulting locution seemed far wiser. That is: you won't know the outcome until you've taken action. At least that's how I interpreted it. I'm not sure why, but Jim's slip of the tongue has stuck with me over the last two decades.

I suspect there's a universe in which my friend Mike didn't care about the information I disclosed on the podcast, but in this universe, he did care and I hurt his feelings, so the only appropriate way to respond was to apologize and move on.

The Symbiosis of Love

I had a chance to sit down with the iconoclast Erwin Raphael McManus to talk about his thoughts on relationships. At age sixty, McManus beat stage 4 colon cancer and wrote about the lessons of that battle in his book *The Way of the Warrior: An Ancient Path to Inner Peace*. One of the lessons was that, in the grand scheme of things, our relationships are one of the few things that actually matter.

"I used to look for relationships that elevated *me*," McManus said. "But, as I got older, I realized that I was buying into the cultural narcissism that says, 'This relationship is all about me.'" He realized that instead of simply pursuing relationships that elevated *him*, he needed to become the kind of person that helps—not *changes*, but *helps*—others.

LETTING GO IS MORE DIFFICULT NOW, BUT LESS DIFFICULT IN THE LONG RUN.

"We focus on how to get more for us," he continued, "but that's the irony of relationships. If you spend all your time asking the wrong questions—How can *I* find that right person for *me*? How can *I* find what *I* need? How can *I* get what *I* want?—you're missing the entire point of relationships: it's not about *you*; it's about how you can invest in others, how you can be a gift to others." McManus believes that the healthiest and most profound relationships are "the ones in which you care about the other person more than you care about yourself."

On the surface, this may seem like McManus is contradicting much of what I've written in this chapter. But he's not suggesting you undermine your values. No, McManus wants you to know yourself so well that you understand how to elevate others without weakening yourself. "You were not designed to 'do life' alone," he said. "Even if you are the most talented, gifted, intelligent, passionate, creative person on the planet—and even if you have a complete understanding of your intention, your purpose, your reason for living—you are still not designed to do life alone." He went on to say:

> I know what you're thinking:
> "What about my dreams?"
> Whatever your dream is,
> you can't fulfill your dream alone.
> "What about my purpose?"
> Whatever your purpose is,
> you weren't designed to fulfill that purpose alone.
> In fact, if you are pursuing a purpose
> in which you don't need people,
> that is not the purpose of your life.
> If you have a dream
> in which people are simply tools
> to be used to accomplish your outcome,
> that's not a dream at all. It's a nightmare.

We all need people, McManus says, because we all need help. Coincidently, we all possess the need to help others, too. Not to *use* others, nor to be used, but to be *useful* for each other. That's the interplay of relationships. That's the symbiosis of love.

When you're surrounded by disempowering people, you might wish to be alone. But when you are truly alone, you realize you need people. The alternative is solitary confinement, which is the worst kind of incarceration. There's something so bad about isolation that many humans would rather spend time around dangerous murderers and violent criminals than be all alone.

MINIMALIST RULE FOR LIVING WITH LESS

Thirty-Day Minimalism Game

The easiest way to organize your stuff is to get rid of most of it. If a Packing Party is too extreme, consider the 30-Day Minimalism Game, which has eased thousands of people into decluttering their homes, cars, and offices. Decluttering is usually boring, but this game makes it fun by injecting some friendly competition into the mix. Here's how it works. Find a friend, family member, or coworker who's willing to minimize their stuff with you next month. Each person gets rid of one thing on the first day. Two things on the second. Three things on the third. And so on. Anything goes! Collectables, decorations, kitchenware, electronics, furniture, equipment, supplies, bedding, clothes, towels, tools, hats, you name it! Donate, sell, recycle! Every material possession must be out of your house by midnight each day. Whoever keeps it going the longest wins. You both win if you both make it to the end of the month.

Keep track of your progress. Visit minimalists.com/game to download our free Minimalism Game calendar.

Love Is More

We have a language problem. I love my wife, but I also love burritos. I love Ryan, but I also love the new Mat Kearney album. I love my daughter, but I also love the various colors of flowers in my neighborhood.

One love involves bottomless devotion birthed from deep affection. The other, a preference or fondness for something enjoyable. And then there's the distinction between "loving" someone and being "in love" with them. The same root word, two utterly different meanings.

The Inuit dialect spoken in Canada's Nunavik region has at least fifty-three words to describe snow. Imagine if we had even half as many for love. Instead, in our culture, we stretch "love" to apply to people and pick-up trucks, friends and fried chicken, lovers and Louis Vuitton bags. But when you extend anything beyond its natural limits, it loses its strength. This is especially true with love.

What do we mean when we end a phone call with "love ya"? Is it just a nice way to say goodbye? Or is it simply the lazy way to say "I love you"? And when we remove the "I," do we alter the meaning even further, abdicating ourselves of the responsibilities of love by removing ourselves from the sentence?

We all need love. But love isn't all we need. We need to be seen, we need to be heard, we need connection. We need sincerity and grace and kindness. But these characteristics are suppressed without love. Can you even imagine sincerity without love? How about grace? Kindness? Take it a step further: Can you imagine getting everything you ever wanted, fulfilling all your dreams, without love? Not a chance. Like building a two-dimensional house or drinking from an empty cup, a life without love is flat and empty.

If love opens the door to the best parts of life, why, then, do we not seek to be loved more often? Why would we rather be sexy or cool or "liked"? Because it's easier. We can manipulate our surface to increase our status, but when you look at someone who's trying too hard to be trendy or glamorous, what do you find? A person who lacks integrity, a person so uncomfortable with themselves that they hide from love by draping themselves with shiny adornments. That's why love is difficult: it can't be shaped by trinkets or transactions, only fidelity and support and understanding. Sex appeal and likability quickly fade in the face of uncertainty. Love, however, makes room for risk and rejection and even pain. There's also plenty of space for joy and pleasure and tranquility. The only thing, in fact, that won't fit within the confines of love is self-centeredness. Love is too big for the self alone.

If you consult your nearest dictionary, you'll find that love has several meanings—an intense feeling of deep affection, a great interest and pleasure in something, a person or thing that one loves—but my favorite definition is one I never thought much about. The fourth entry in the *New Oxford American Dictionary* defines love as a tennis term: "love: a score of zero." In the context of a tennis match, that means one thing. But, as a broader metaphor, it means *everything*. Real love, when removed from the desires and commodification of the modern world, doesn't keep score. There's no balance sheet, no barometer, no measuring stick for love.

A decade ago, I didn't know my wife, Rebecca. But after we met, and as we cultivated our love, I didn't have to extract love from some other relationship to cast ours. When we give love, we don't run out. If anything, it multiplies. Love is fully renewable, 100 percent sustainable.

People don't simply "fall in love"—love is cultivated. Love can't be found. I know because I searched for love for years after my failed marriage. But the more I looked, the more distant it seemed. Inexplicably, I found love only when I stopped looking for it—when, instead of concentrating on falling in love, I focused simply on being loving.

In a strange way, being loving might be the opposite of falling in love. This makes sense in hindsight since, when I was obsessed with falling in love, the pursuit was egocentric. But when my main concern was loving others, the love swelled because it was no longer exclusively about me.

It may seem paradoxical, but the best way to hold on to love is to let go. Love expands if we don't hold it tightly. So if we want it to stick around, we must loosen our grip.

You don't need permission to be loving. During difficult times, you may want to help, you may want to fix problems, but that's not always possible. You can't help everyone. You can't fix everything. But you can love no matter the situation.

Indeed, amid a disagreement, an argument, or even a total fallout, we can love people. Sometimes that love is nearby; sometimes we must love from afar. Loving someone doesn't mean that you approve of their actions. You can love a cheating spouse, a gossiping coworker, or a lying friend—loving the person, not their behaviors. It is possible to dislike certain parts of someone and still love every piece of them.

While love is heavy and demanding and enigmatic, our biggest challenge isn't love itself—it's how we've conflated excitement, lust, and attraction with love. Nowhere is this more evident than in our relationship to our material possessions. We say we love our televisions, our cars, our cosmetics, but we're confused, blinded by the propaganda that tells us the things in our homes are just as essential as the people in our lives. It's easy to see the absurdity of this manufactured love when we extend it to less enticing items. No one I know "loves" their toilet-paper dispenser, their mailbox, their key ring. Yet we use these things just as much as, if not more than, the things we think we love. When we realize this—that we can use things without loving them, that we can treat our iPhone the way we treat our lip balm, as useful but not worthy of our love—then we are better able to understand real love, a love that is reserved for people, not the things that get in the way. It is possible to love people and use things, because the opposite never works.

Coda: People

Hey there, friend—it's Ryan, here to help one last time. Joshua gave us a lot to think about when it comes to how we're handling our relationships with others, and now I'd like to take some time to see how you're fostering those relationships. The people around us shape who we are and who we become, so I'd like you to fully explore each exercise below to ensure you're giving your best to others, which will inspire them to share their best with you.

QUESTIONS ABOUT PEOPLE

1. What is your Myers-Briggs Type Indicator (MBTI), and what does it tell you about your preferences?
2. How can you use tolerance, acceptance, respect, and appreciation (TARA) to develop a deeper understanding of the people in your life?
3. How can you be unapologetically *you* so that you're able to contribute more to others?
4. Love, trust, honesty, caring, support, attention, authenticity, and understanding: Which of these elements will elevate your relationships the most, and how will you incorporate them into your life?
5. If you were to make a list of all your current relationships—family, friends, coworkers, Facebook "friends," and even the folks you see only once or twice a year—how many

of them would you reselect to be a new relationship in your life today and why?

THE DOS OF PEOPLE

Next, what did you learn about your relationship with people in this chapter? What will stick? What lessons will encourage you to reprioritize and improve your relationships? Here are five immediate actions you can take today:

- **Describe your Us Box.** The first step toward meaningful relationships is to get clear on what you want to give to, and what you want to get out of, your relationships.
  - Identify the ways you enjoy helping others. Write down what you want to contribute.
  - Write down what physical, mental, emotional, and spiritual boundaries you need people to understand and respect.
- **Define your relationships.** Now it's time to pinpoint each personal relationship and how it fits into your life. To do this, follow these steps:
  - First, write down every person you can think of who you give your time, energy, and attention to on a regular or semi-regular basis.
  - Second, beside each name, note their relationship group with a 1 (primary), 2 (secondary), or 3 (peripheral). Don't mark them based on how you *wish* they'd fit into one of these groups; rather, identify the type of relationship according to how you treat them currently.
  - Last, be honest and identify the toxic people on this list by adding an X next to their name.

- **Recast your relationships.** Review the people on your list, and determine whether they are in the appropriate group. This will help you identify people in your life that you are distanced from but want to bring in a little closer. And, conversely, it will help you identify the relationships you want to create more distance within. So, for each person on your list, place a D for distance or a C for closer to denote how you'd like to adjust the relationship. If you're happy with the current dynamic, simply write "OK" next to the person's name.

- **Repair your relationships.** Now that you are clear on where your relationships are compared to where you want them to be, let's consider the work necessary to repair or shift your relationships.

  - First, let's look at the toxic people in your life. Before you push them away, ask yourself whether there is a way to repair this relationship. Ask these people for the boundaries they wish for you to understand and respect, and then outline your boundaries in kind. If you find that they are unwilling to respect your boundaries, then it is appropriate to express how you are going to start to distance yourself from their toxic behaviors.

  - Second, let's look at those whom you want to distance yourself from. These people are not necessarily toxic. They may be an annoying neighbor or coworker, or they may just be someone with whom you no longer have shared mutual interests. If necessary, use nonviolent communication to express that you will be spending less time with this person; explain that you're not saying *no* to them—you're saying *yes* to something else.

  - Lastly, let's look at the people you want to bring closer. The next time you have a chance to talk to people that fall into this category, express to them how you wish to bring them closer into your life. You'll say something like, "Hey, Stacy, I appreciate you, and I'd like us to spend more time together. Are you open to that?" If they say *yes* (it must be consensual), determine ways you might add value to their life.

- **Contribute beyond yourself.** Now for the most rewarding part of any relationship—the act of giving. You'll start by giving others the gift of your attention—by being present when interacting with others. Being present means active listening, showing compassion, expressing love. Each morning for a week, look at your list of people you want to draw closer to and pick one person to elevate. It needn't be a grand gesture—you simply need to show them love and support: text them a goofy picture, write a letter, leave flowers on their porch, mow their grass. There are endless things you can do for the people in your life to create meaningful and lasting relationships.

THE DON'TS OF PEOPLE

Finally, let's discuss what's getting in the way. Here are five things you'll want to avoid, beginning today, if you want to improve your relationship with people:

- Don't placate people simply to protect their feelings.
- Don't be agreeable for the sake of being agreeable, or sacrifice your values just to fit in.
- Don't use "virtues" like loyalty or empathy as an excuse to stay in a pernicious relationship.
- Don't use tactics like passive-aggressive speech to discuss a relationship shift with someone.
- Don't forsake living a worthwhile life in favor of another person's preferences.

EPILOGUE

We are each a collage of contradictions. On the one hand, I am a hypocrite. I'm a minimalist, but I own a house, a couch, and more than one pair of shoes. I sometimes avoid the truth, seeking acknowledgment or praise or convenience instead. I break my own rules for simple living, drooling over glossy magazine ads for Range Rovers and giant billboards for Rolexes. I neglect to meditate, exercise, and eat healthfully from time to time. My actions don't always match my values. I believe in climate change, but I drive a gas-powered vehicle and power my home with electricity from a coal-fired power station. I think exploiting workers is wrong, but I'm typing this sentence on a computer that was assembled by underpaid workers in China, and I'm willing to bet I own more than one article of clothing that was made in a sweatshop. I spend money on things I don't need (jackets are a particular weakness of mine). I occasionally watch television alone, and I use my smartphone too much, both of which stifle my creativity. I love my family, but I'm not a particularly adept parent, and I don't make an effort to see my brother as much as I'd like.

On the other hand, I'm a better person than I was a decade ago. My life is simpler now, more focused and honest and peaceful.

My lust for stuff doesn't run the show. I'm more conscious of my health and well-being, more joyous, less stressed, more apprecia- tive, calmer. And my health, while far from perfect, has improved markedly since the New Great Depression of 2019. I understand my values, as well as the obstacles that get in the way of living a meaningful life. I'm unapologetically and enthusiastically debt- free, and I contribute more to charity than I ever did when I was earning those corporate paychecks. I'm more creative and less dis- tracted, even as the world points its informational fire hose at my head. More considerate and patient than I used to be, I'm a kind friend, a competent business partner, and a loving husband.

It's true, I'm imperfect, and no amount of simplifying will erase all my flaws. I still make mistakes, and minimalism has not proven to be a panacea for all of life's woes. It has, however, improved my life immeasurably. And although I still have problems, they are better problems, problems that make life richer, more nuanced and vivid. As I solve those problems, new ones always emerge. Our struggles end only after our heart has ceased its rhythm.

I have scars, but those scars make up the best parts of me. As I turn forty this year, I aspire to be my fifty-year-old self. Me, but better. I say all this because, in many ways, I am *you*. You might be scarred, but your scars are what make you *you*. Like me, you have flaws and problems and you've made mistakes, but now you're at a crossroads. You are standing at the precipice of your next dread- ful decision. The next lie. The next impulse purchase. The next harmful habit. The next breach of your values. The next dollar wasted. The next technological distraction. The next minute spent consuming instead of creating. The next victim of your judgment. This barrage of negativity is a pattern you've grown used to—a persistent white noise that has been lingering in the background so long that you didn't even realize it was there.

It is important to not live in the past but to learn from it so we don't carry the same mistakes forward. Your past self is merely an ancestor who birthed you, but they are not who you are today. Their faults and indiscretions are no longer yours unless you choose to cling to them. You have the tools to break the pattern. You can create a new beginning. Not a radical, overnight transformation, but a slight pivot in a new direction that will change the trajectory of everything to come. And to get there, you must let go of some of the stuff that's in the way.

ACKNOWLEDGMENTS

I didn't know whether we'd ever write another book about minimalism. After finishing the first draft of our simple-living memoir, *Everything That Remains*, in 2012, Ryan and I thought we'd said everything we needed to say about living with less. Clearly, we were mistaken. After six years and four false starts, Ryan and I came to a realization: the main thing that had changed since we first embraced a minimalist lifestyle was our intimate relationships. With his wife, Mariah, Ryan was in the most fulfilling and joyous relationship of his life. Ditto for me and Bex. Paradoxically, those relationships were, in many ways, our most difficult. Which begged the questions: Why? And would it be possible to write a minimalist-relationship book? And with those questions, more questions emerged.

What if some of our most important relationships aren't with others? Must we first understand ourselves before our relationships can flourish? In what ways are Ryan and I different from our former selves? What necessary changes did we make over the last decade? Did we have to let go of anything—or anyone—to move forward? What stories are so personal that we've never shared them publicly? How might those stories, if told honestly, serve the greater good?

The result was *Love People, Use Things*. This book is dedicated to Rebecca and Mariah, not only because of their love but because without them, it wouldn't exist. (I mean, we probably would've written another book, but not this one.) I wrote the first draft of *Love People, Use Things* during the two most difficult years of my life. When it comes to suffering, there isn't even a close second place. After my *E. coli*–poisoning event in September 2018 and until the manuscript was finished in 2020, I struggled daily. At my lowest points I lost my love for writing—and for life altogether. But Bex was always there to pull me back from the brink. She was there to support my healing and to take care of me when I could barely care for myself. She held my hand through the worst of it, and she continues to inspire me to be the best version of myself as my health continues to improve. And while, thank God, Ryan didn't have to endure the same agony as me, his life certainly hasn't been pain-free; since 2013, as things have broken, Mariah has been there to help Ryan pick up the pieces. Thank you both for existing.

Frankly, I was afraid to write another book because I didn't think I could top *Everything That Remains*, which, I could argue, took thirty-two years to write and, until now, has been my favorite creation. Only time will tell whether this book becomes my new favorite—and, more important, a reader favorite. It was, by far, the most challenging book I've written, but also the most rewarding, which doesn't seem like a coincidence. I wanted to give up at least a dozen times. The first four attempts were stillborn on the page. But I drudged through the drudgery, jettisoning tens of thousands of words along the way. Starting over. Again and again. The book didn't take its current shape until our agent, Marc Gerald, nudged me in the right direction. He and our editors, Ryan

Doherty and Cecily van Buren-Freedman, pushed me beyond my comfort zone, encouraging me not only to write about The Minimalists' personal mishaps, but to interweave those passages with expert insights and interviews and the stories of people who have benefited from simplifying their lives. Thank you, Marc and Ryan and Cecily, for the encouragement.

When my illness hit, I was wiped clean of inspiration, drive, creative impulse. I'm not one to miss deadlines, but I couldn't help it. Many days I was too sick to write, and as I grew more ill, several deadlines passed me by. Fortunately, my friend "Podcast Shawn" Harding was there to drag my tattered remains across the finish line. His hundreds of suggestions, in-depth research, and countless edits made this book immeasurably better. Shawn, thank you for letting me lean on you each time I ran out of strength. And thank you for wearing your many hats well. Not only are you an outstanding podcast producer, tour manager, and director of operations, but, in my eyes, you're the best copy editor on the planet. Ryan and I are lucky to have you on the team.

To everyone else on The Minimalists' team, Ryan and I are grateful for your contributions. Jessica Williams, thank you for communicating our message so beautifully on social media. Jeff Sarris and Dave LaTulippe, thank you for being the Mozarts of design, for raising the aesthetic standards of everything we create. Jordan "Know" Moore, thank you for making two goofy guys from the Midwest look compelling on camera. Matt D'Avella, thank you for reminding the world that most wedding videographers suck (and for being the most talented documentarian alive). To our booking agent, Andrew Russell, thank you for taking a chance on us and for taking our live shows and tours to the next level. To our publicist, Sarah Miniaci, thank you for accepting The Minimalists before anyone else and for setting the media ablaze with our message. To our business manager, Allan Mesia, and our bookkeeper, Angel Dryden, thank you for organizing the zeros and ones so Ryan and I can focus on producing meaningful creations. To Shawn Mihalik, thank you for managing The Minimalists' online writing and budgeting courses; the work you do improves people's lives, including my own.

To Colin Wright, thank you for exposing me to minimalism in 2009. If it weren't for you, I might still be clinging violently to the corporate ladder. I think the David Foster Wallace quote "Everything I've ever let go of has claw marks on it" is one of my favorites because it perfectly describes my life before minimalism: the only way I was willing to let go of anything was if it was pried from my clammy talons. But, of course, that isn't letting go at all, and it was Colin Wright and then Leo Babauta and Courtney Carver and Joshua Becker who showed me that not only could I let go, but that doing so was a kind of superpower. Together, the four of you provided a sort of recipe book for living with less, from which Ryan and I were able to prepare a more meaningful life. Thank you for helping me help myself so that I could eventually help others.

To Dave Ramsey and his team—Elizabeth Cole, Rachel Cruze, Chris Hogan, Anthony ONeal, Ken Coleman, John Delony, Christy Wright, Luke LeFevre, Mckenzie Masters, Connor Wangner, and everyone at Ramsey Solutions—you are an inspiration to us all.

To the cast of doctors and healthcare professionals who helped me bear the weight of my illness—Christopher Kelly, Ryan Greene, Lucy Mailing, Tommy Wood, Adam Lamb, Payton Berookim, Megan Anderson, Elise Guedea, Sunjya Schweig—thank you for carrying me out of the crater in which I was stranded.

To Zana Lawrence, thank you for believing in our message enough to convince your team at Netflix to share it in 190 countries. You're responsible for the proliferation of this movement.

To our partners—Joshua and Sarah Weaver and the team at Bandit; Carl MH Barenbrug, Alberto Negro, and the team at *Minimalism Life*; and Malcolm Fontier and the team at PAKT—thank you for helping The Minimalists work on meaningful projects outside our normal purview.

To everyone mentioned throughout this book, thank you for your insights. There are too many of you to name again, but whether we spoke in person, on the phone, or via email, or whether your work simply inspired some of the passages of this book, I'm grateful for your sagacity.

To my mom, Chloe Millburn, it is my biggest regret that I didn't spend more time with you during your last year on Earth. After an eventful life as a nun, a stewardess, a secretary, a wife, a mother, and a total bombshell of a woman, your death was not for naught: it helped me question everything, especially my life's misguided focus. Ultimately, your life is a reminder to us all: everything is ephemeral. Instead of obsessing over wealth and status and material possessions, it's best to spend our time loving, caring, contributing. I miss your kindness, your hugs, your warm smile. You had the heart of a servant. I remember when you told me I'd "understand life" one day—maybe by the time I turned thirty-five, you said. Well, that's five years in the rearview, and I don't completely understand yet, but I'm getting closer. Thank you for giving me life, for being my mother, and for making regular guest appearances in my dreams. I'm grateful. I love you.

To my brother, Jerome, thank you for being a kind of father figure throughout my childhood. You are only a year older than me, but, for as long as I can remember, you've always been a man. I aspire to possess just 10 percent of your unflinching strength.

To Adam Dressler, thank you for being a loving friend ever since we waited and bussed the same tables at the same restaurant throughout our high-school days. Our conversations over the last decade have been the best podcast episodes I've *never* recorded.

To Karl Weidner, thank you for being a mentor and a friend. For more than half my life—during our corporate days and now—you've taught me a great deal about business and life and real estate and personal perspective. I know I won't ever be able to repay you, so I'll continue to pay it forward.

To Annie Bower, do you remember meeting in that coffee shop back in 2011? That conversation for the *Dayton City Paper* was The Minimalists' first print interview. Who knew that meeting would blossom into a lifelong friendship. Thank you for being you. And thanks for the discussion about closure that made its way into the "Relationship with People" chapter of this book.

To T. K. Coleman, thank you for all the meaningful conversations, both on and off the air. We're able to artfully disagree and change each other's minds without arguing or changing each other's hearts.

To Keri and Colleen and Austen, thank you for showing me what love is. I'm sorry for my errors and inconsiderate decisions, and I would do a million things differently, but I'm thankful for you. Your love guided me through my adult life and into the present day.

To Dayton, Ohio—the city that made Ryan and me men, the main character of our first thirty years—we are proud to be your non-prodigal sons.

There are many people to whom Ryan and I owe a debt of gratitude: Dan Savage, Jennette McCurdy, Adrian McKinty, Kapil Gupta,

Nicole LePera, Anthony de Mello, Annaka Harris, Lewis Howes, Dan Harris, Jamie Kilstein, Jacob Matthew, Chris Newhart, Tim Frazier, Nate Pyfer, Drew Capener, Justin Malik, AJ Leon, Andre Kibb, and countless others. To the people I forgot to mention, I'm sorry. It's not you, it's me.

—JFM

NOTES

7 *The average American household contains more than 300,000 items*: Mary MacVean, "For many people, gathering possessions is just the stuff of life," *Los Angeles Times*, March 21, 2014.

7 *you'd think we'd be beside ourselves with joy. Yet study after study shows the opposite*: Jamie Ducharme, "A lot of Americans are more anxious than they were last year, a new poll says," *Time* magazine, May 8, 2018.

8 *The average American carries approximately three credit cards in their wallet*: Louis DeNicola, "How many credit cards does the average American have?" *Credit Karma*, October 6, 2020.

8 *the average credit-card debt is more than $16,000*: Jessica Dickler, "US households now have over $16,000 in credit-card debt," *CNBC*, December 13, 2016.

8 *Even before the pandemic of 2020, more than 80 percent of us were in debt*: Susan K. Urahn et al., "The complex story of American debt," *The Pew Charitable Trusts*, July 2015.

8 *with the total consumer debt in the United States greater than $14 trillion*: Jeff Cox, "Consumer debt hits new record of $14.3 trillion," *CNBC*, May 5, 2020.

8 *We spend more on shoes, jewelry, and watches than on higher education*: Peter G. Stromberg, Ph.D., "Do Americans consume too much?" *Psychology Today*, July 29, 2012.

8 *Our ever-expanding homes, which have more than doubled in size over*

the last fifty years: Margot Adler, "Behind the ever-expanding American dream house," *NPR*, July 4, 2006.

8 *contain more televisions than people*: Hillary Mayell, "As consumerism spreads, Earth suffers, study says," *National Geographic*, January 12, 2004.

8 *even though 95 percent of it could be reused or recycled*: Eleanor Goldberg, "You're probably going to throw away 81 pounds of clothing this year," *HuffPost*, June 8, 2016.

8 *our communities are peppered with more shopping malls than high schools*: John de Graaf et al., *Affluenza,* September 1, 2005.

8 *93 percent of teens rank shopping as their favorite pastime*: John de Graaf et al., *Affluenza,* September 1, 2005.

8 *we spend $1.2 trillion every year on nonessential goods*: Mark Whitehouse, "Number of the week: Americans buy more stuff they don't need," *The Wall Street Journal*, April 23, 2011.

9 *over 50 percent of us don't have enough money on hand to cover even a month of lost income*: Maurie Backman, "Guess how many Americans struggle to come up with $400," *The Motley Fool*, June 5, 2016.

9 *62 percent of us don't have $1,000 in savings*: Maurie Backman, "62% of Americans have less than $1,000 in savings," *The Motley Fool*, March 28, 2016.

9 *nearly half of us couldn't scrape together $400 during an emergency*: Maurie Backman, "Guess how many Americans struggle to come up with $400," *The Motley Fool*, June 5, 2016.

9 *nearly 25 percent of households earning between $100,000 and $150,000 a year say they'd have a difficult time coming up with an extra $2,000*: Maurie Backman, "Guess how many Americans struggle to come up with $400," *The Motley Fool*, June 5, 2016.

9 *60 percent of households will experience a "financial shock" event within the next twelve months*: Hassan Burke et al., "How do families cope with financial shocks?" *The Pew Charitable Trusts*, October 2015.

9 *the average new home is rapidly approaching 3,000 square feet*: Robert Dietz, "Single-family home size increases at the start of 2018," *Eye on Housing*, May 21, 2018.

9 *more than 52,000 storage facilities across the country*: John Egan, "Guess how many U.S. storage facilities there are versus Subway, McDonald's and Starbucks," *SpareFoot Blog*, May 11, 2015.

9 *we still don't have enough room to park our cars in our garages*: "Almost

1 in 4 Americans say their garage is too cluttered to fit their car," *Cision PR Newswire*, June 9, 2015.

9   *American kids consume 40 percent of the world's toys*: "University of California TV series looks at clutter epidemic in middle-class American homes," *UCTV*, n.d.

10   *the average child owns more than 200 toys, but plays with only 12 of those toys each day*: "Ten-year-olds have £7,000 worth of toys but play with just £330," *The Telegraph*, October 20, 2010.

10   *children who have too many toys are more easily distracted and don't enjoy quality playtime*: *University of Toledo*, n.d.

10   *we would need nearly five Earths to sustain our unchecked consumption*: Malavika Vyawahare, "If everyone lived like Americans, we would need five Earths," *Hindustan Times*, August 2, 2017.

11   *Dayton is the overdose capital of America*: Chris Stewart, "Dayton tops lists of drugged-out cities," *Dayton Daily News*, August 12, 2016.

17   *Less than 5 percent of Americans are diagnosed compulsive hoarders*: Ferris Jabr, "Step inside the real world of compulsive hoarders," *Scientific American*, February 25, 2013.

19   *"the mind has a great propensity to spread itself on external objects, and to conjoin with them any internal impressions."*: David Hume, *A Treatise of Human Nature*, 1740.

39   *According to the American educator Edgar Dale's learning pyramid*: Heidi Milia Anderson, Ph.D., "Dale's cone of experience," *Queen's University Teaching and Learning Modules*, n.d.

42   *to impress people they didn't like*: Will Rogers, "Too many people," *BrainyQuote*, n.d.

53   *Americans are exposed to around 4,000 to 10,000 advertisements each day*: Jon Simpson, "Finding brand success in the digital world," *Forbes*, August 25, 2017.

54   *advertising has topped half a trillion dollars a year*: Jasmine Enberg, "Global digital ad spending 2019," *eMarketer*, March 28, 2019.

54   *Edward Bernays, who is sometimes referred to as the founder of modern advertising and public relations*: "Edward Bernays, 'Father of public relations' and leader in opinion making, dies at 103," *The New York Times*, March 10, 1995.

55   *created a raging $3 billion–per–year blue pill*: David Kushner, "How Viagra went from a medical mistake to a $3-billion-dollar-a-year industry," *Esquire*, August 21, 2018.

55 *it's illegal in every country in the world—except the United States and New Zealand—to advertise drugs to consumers*: "Should prescription drugs be advertised directly to consumers?" *ProCon.org*, October 23, 2018.

55 *Henry Gadsden, then CEO of Merck & Co., told* Fortune *magazine that he'd rather sell drugs to healthy people because they had the most money*: Emma Lake, "Who was Henry Gadsden?" *The Sun*, September 27, 2017.

55 *Viagra seems to be a relatively benign drug*: Akira Tsujimura et al., "The clinical studies of sildenafil for the ageing male," *PubMed.gov*, February 2002.

56 *Listerine was previously used as a floor cleaner*: "Listerine," *Smithsonian Museum of Natural History*, n.d.

56 *Coca-Cola was invented as an alternative to morphine*: Tony Long, "May 8, 1886: Looking for pain relief, and finding Coca-Cola instead," *Wired*, May 8, 2012.

56 *the graham cracker was created to prevent young boys from masturbating*: Natalie O'Neill, "The graham cracker was invented to stop you from masturbating," *New York Post*, September 13, 2016.

58 *When São Paulo introduced its "Clean City Law" in 2007, more than 15,000 billboards were taken down*: Kurt Kohlstedt, "Clean city law: Secrets of São Paulo uncovered by outdoor advertising ban," *99% Invisible*, May 2, 2016.

60 *"The prime directive of the mind is to deceive itself," claims the analytic philosopher Bernardo Kastrup*: Steve Patterson, "Non-rationality and psychedelics," *StevePatterson.com*, September 8, 2019.

60 *the American Dream is more out of reach than ever*: Tami Luhby, "The American Dream is out of reach," *CNN Money*, June 4, 2014.

90 *10 percent of communication between spouses is deceptive*: Bella M. De-Paulo and Deborah A. Kashy, "Everyday lies in close and casual relationships," *MIT.edu*, May 27, 1997.

91 *"people tell lies when their behavior violates other people's expectations for them"*: Karen U. Millar and Abraham Tesser, "Deceptive behavior in social relationships: A consequence of violated expectations," *APA PsycNet*, 1988.

91 *Somewhere around age four, we discover the power of deceit*: Romeo Vitelli, Ph.D., "When does lying begin?" *Psychology Today*, November 11, 2013.

94   *"Shame informs you of an internal state of inadequacy, dishonor, or regret"*: Mary C. Lamia, Ph.D., "Shame: A concealed, contagious, and dangerous emotion," *Psychology Today*, April 4, 2011.

116   *In his popular talk* It Is Always Now, *Harris grapples with mortality and priorities*: Sam Harris, "It is always now," *YouTube*, June 28, 2012.

121   *we hosted a discussion between a vegan athlete . . . a carnivore doctor . . . and an omnivore doctor*: Joshua Fields Millburn and Ryan Nicodemus, "Minimalist Diets," *The Minimalists Podcast*, June 10, 2019.

122   *Accutane, a drug that is now off the market in the United States*: Daniel J. DeNoon, "Acne drug Accutane no longer sold," *WebMD*, July 8, 2009.

123   *a bacterium that kills upwards of 15,000 Americans every year*: "Nearly half a million Americans suffered from Clostridium difficile infections in a single year," *CDC*, February 25, 2015.

123   *There's also extensive evidence that gut dysbiosis is responsible for increased inflammation in the human body*: Asa Hakansson and Goran Molin, "Gut microbiota and inflammation," *National Center for Biotechnology Information*, June 3, 2011.

131   *"The circadian system . . . must be reset on a daily basis"*: Jeanne F. Duffy, MBA, Ph.D., and Charles A. Czeisler, Ph.D., M.D., "Effect of light on human circadian physiology," *Sleep Medicine Clinics*, June 1, 2009.

131   *"how much sunlight we're exposed to . . . affect our sleep schedules"*: Kristen Stewart, "How to fix your sleep schedule," *Everyday Health*, February 6, 2018.

132   *Americans spend 93 percent of their time indoors*: N. E. Klepeis et al., "The National Human Activity Pattern Survey (NHAPS): A resource for assessing exposure to environmental pollutants," *PubMed.gov*, May–June 2001

132   *People who are exposed to sunlight in the morning . . . sleep better . . . feel less depressed*: Mariana G. Figueiro, Ph.D. et al., "The impact of daytime light exposures on sleep and mood in office workers," *Sleep Health Journal*, June 1, 2017.

133   *Simon Marshall . . . refers to the free "medicines" mentioned in this chapter with an acronym, SEEDS, which stands for sleep, exercise, eating, drinking, and stress management*: "The pillars of good health," *SEEDS Journal*, n.d.

138   *a series of fourteen tornadoes devastated my hometown of Dayton*: "The first photos: Daylight revealed widespread damage from 2019 Memorial Day storms," *Dayton Daily News*, n.d.

139   *The photos of the aftermath were post-apocalyptic*: Bonnie Meibers, "Oregon District mass shooting: What you need to know," *Dayton Daily News*, August 10, 2019.

141   *I'm intrigued by the word "kenosis," which is derived from the Greek word that means "to empty out"*: "Kenosis," *Merriam-Webster.com*, n.d.

153   *Although the term itself was coined in 1971, the concept of Hedonic Adaptation has been discussed by philosophers for centuries*: Kimberly E. Kleinman et al., "Positive consequences: The impact of an undergraduate course on positive psychology," *ScientificResearch.com*, November 25, 2014.

159   *A recent survey found that "drunk shopping" is an estimated forty-five-billion-dollar-per-year industry*: Zachary Crockett, "The 2019 drunk shopping census," *The Hustle*, March 24, 2019.

169   *"effective altruism is about answering one simple question: how can we use our resources to help others the most?"*: William MacAskill, "Effective altruism is changing the way we do good," *EffectiveAltruism.org*, n.d.

170   *the west side of Dayton, which is one of the largest food deserts in the United States*: Cornelius Frolik, "Grocery targets Dayton food desert: 'We've got to do something about it,'" *Dayton Daily News*, May 16, 2018.

180   *Millions of Americans are living paycheck to paycheck*: Zack Friedman, "78% of workers live paycheck to paycheck," *Forbes*, January 11, 2019.

180   *72 percent of Americans are financially unhealthy*: Kari Paul, "The 'true state' of Americans' financial lives: Only 3 in 10 are 'financially healthy,'" *MarketWatch.com*, November 16, 2018.

180   *earning nearly $200,000 a year . . . I was also one of the 44 percent whose expenses exceed their income*: Kari Paul, "The 'true state' of Americans' financial lives: Only 3 in 10 are 'financially healthy,'" *MarketWatch.com*, November 16, 2018.

180   *Neal Gabler coined that term in* The Atlantic: Neil Gabler, "The secret shame of middle-class Americans," *The Atlantic*, May 2016.

181   *roughly the same percentage of American adults who have no retirement savings*: "Report on the economic well-being of U.S. households in 2018," *FederalReserve.gov*, May 2019.

182   *home prices have gone up 26 percent, medical expenses have increased 33 percent, and college costs have surged 45 percent*: Christopher Maloney and Adam Tempkin, "America's middle class is addicted to a new kind of credit," *Bloomberg*, October 29, 2019.

188 *repeat filers are responsible for 16 percent of all bankruptcy cases*: "Bankruptcy Statistics," *Debt.org*, n.d.

188 *70 percent of U.S. adults are indebted, including 78 percent of Gen Xers, 74 percent of Baby Boomers, 70 percent of Millennials, and 44 percent of Gen Zers*: Barri Segal, "Poll: Only 7% of U.S. debtors expect to die in debt," *CreditCards.com*, January 8, 2020.

196 *you can save $66,000, on average, by attending an in-state community college your first two years*: Anthony ONeal, *Debt-Free Degree*, October 7, 2019.

198 *60 percent of Americans have less than $25,000 saved for their own retirement*: Nanci Hellmich, "Retirement: A third have less than $1,000 put away," *USA Today*, March 18, 2014.

205 *Over the last thirty years . . . the market has averaged a rate of return of nearly 11 percent*: *Morningstar.com*, n.d.

206 *the differences between our closest primate ancestors—bonobos and chimpanzees*: "Some primates share, others (hint, hint) are stingy," *LiveScience.com*, February 2, 2010.

220 *Six out of ten people read only a headline before commenting on an online article*: Caitlin Dewey, "6 in 10 of you will share this link without reading it, a new, depressing study says," *The Washington Post*, June 16, 2016.

221 *we check our smartphones 150 times a day*: "Smartphone users check mobiles 150 times a day: Study," *The Economic Times*, February 11, 2013.

221 *we tap, swipe, and click on our phones 2,617 times a day*: "Cell phone addiction: The statistics of gadget dependency," *King University Online*, July 27, 2017.

221 *using our gadgets as much as twelve hours a day on average*: Nicole F. Roberts, "How much time Americans spend in front of screens will terrify you," *Forbes*, Jan 24, 2019.

221 *86 percent of smartphone users check their phones while speaking with friends and family*: "Smartphone addiction facts & phone usage statistics: The definitive guide," *Bankmycell.com*, 2020.

221 *87 percent of Millennials say their smartphone never leaves their side*: "Z-file: Executive insights," *Zogby Analytics*, n.d.

221 *as comedian Ronny Chieng recently observed*: Scott Simon, "Ronny Chieng on 'Asian comedian destroys America!'" *NPR*, December 14, 2019.

224   *Americans are working more hours than ever, but we are actually earning less*: Alan Pearcy, "Most employed Americans work more than 40 hours per week," *Ragan's PR Daily*, July 12, 2012.

229   *"When you bought your first smartphone, did you know you would spend more than 1,000 hours a year looking at it?"*: Seth Godin, "Wasting it," *Seth's Blog*, February 23, 2020.

231   *set the phone's display to grayscale*: Shifrah Combiths, "Your smartest friends are using their phone's black-and-white setting, here's why," *Apartment Therapy*, April 8, 2019.

231   *MRI scans have revealed that the gray matter in a phone addict's brain physically changes shape and size*: Joe Pinkstone, "How smartphone addiction changes your brain: Scans reveal how grey matter of tech addicts physically changes shape and size in a similar way to drug users," *Daily Mail*, February 18, 2020.

252   *According to Carl Jung's theory of personality difference . . . people can be characterized by their "preference of general attitude"*: Carl Jung, *Psychological Types*, October 1, 1976.

252   *Myers and . . . Briggs, developed their test for two reasons*: "MBTI Basics," *The Myers & Briggs Foundation*, n.d.

270   *"Friendship 101" class at the University of Southern California*: "Rainn Wilson and Reza Aslan on loneliness, forgiveness, and 'Metaphysical Milkshake,'" *Press Play with Madeleine Brand*, KCRW, September 25, 2019.

270   *a fundamental part of who we are*: Shane Parrish, "The evolutionary benefit of friendship," *Farnam Street*, September 2019.

281   *"Either way, they create unnecessary complexity, strife, and worst of all stress"*: Travis Bradberry, "How successful people handle toxic people," *Forbes*, October 21, 2014.

286   *Leaving a toxic relationship is like choosing between graduation and divorce*: Shout out to Rob Bell for this insight.

293   *The Inuit dialect . . . has at least fifty-three words to describe snow*: David Robson, "There really are 50 Eskimo words for 'snow,'" *The Washington Post*, January 14, 2013.

VALUES WORKSHEET

There are two reasons people don't understand their values: First, we don't stop to question what our values are, and so they are shaped by our culture, the media, and the influence of others. Second, we don't understand that some values are more important than others, and many values are, in fact, not values at all, which means they get in the way of what's truly important. The Minimalists believe the best way to live a meaningful life is to align your short-term actions with your long-term values; that is, to make your future self proud of your present self. That's why we created this worksheet—because when you better understand your values, you will better understand the path to an intentional life. For a thorough explanation of each type of value, refer back to chapter 4: Relationship with Values. And to download a printable version of this worksheet, visit minimalists.com.

Foundational Values
My Unshakable Principles

_____

_____

_____

_____

_____

_____

Structural Values

My Personal Values

_____

_____

_____

_____

_____

Surface Values

My Minor Values That Make Life Better

_____

_____

_____

_____

_____

Imaginary Values

The Obstacles in My Way

_____

_____

_____

_____

_____

_____

PART TWO

Once you've completed this worksheet, review it with your accountability partner or someone you trust. And if that person is willing, review their worksheet with them. You'll soon discover that once you better understand your values—and the values of those closest to you—you'll understand how to better interact with them, which will improve the relationship and help you both grow in exciting, unexpected ways.

BOOK CLUB GUIDE

These questions about *Love People, Use Things* are intended to help your readers' group find new and interesting angles and topics for your meetings.

1. Which of the seven essential relationships do you struggle with the most and why?
2. What were your conceptions of minimalism before reading this book? After reading the book?
3. How did you define *love* before reading this book? How about now?
4. When it comes to your material possessions, what are you afraid to let go of? Why? In what ways will shedding your excess stuff make room for a more meaningful and enjoyable life?
5. In what ways has hiding the truth caused you suffering or hurt your relationships? In what ways will telling the truth going forward help you grow?
6. When have you felt like your best, most alive self? When have you felt dead inside? What factors contributed to these feelings?
7. What is your Object A? Why do you want it? How is it possible to live in accordance with your values if you never acquire that object of your desire?
8. What financial stresses do you currently experience? What life changes will you make to improve your spending habits and your relationship with money?
9. How are distractions getting in the way of creating something meaningful? Name at least three distractions you'd like to eliminate.
10. Thinking about all your current relationships, how many of them would you reselect to be a new relationship in your life today, and why? How many of them would you avoid?

CELADON
BOOKS

Founded in 2017, Celadon Books, a division of
Macmillan Publishers, publishes a highly curated list
of twenty to twenty-five new titles a year. The list of
both fiction and nonfiction is eclectic and focuses
on publishing commercial and literary books and
discovering and nurturing talent.